Destiny Stopped Screaming
The Life and Times of Adrian Borland

Simon Heavisides

Destiny Stopped Screaming
The Life and Times of Adrian Borland

The Label and Licensor SOD (Stichting Opposite Direction / Opposite Direction Foundation) was founded to initiate and produce Walking In The Opposite Direction (2016), the documentary-film directed by Marc Waltman about the life and times of Adrian Borland (1957–1999). After the death of Adrian's father Bob Borland, the Dutch foundation inherited Adrians handwritten lyrics-sheets, paraphernalia plus the entire official and unofficial recordings of Adrian Borland to be sorted and (re)released in collaboration with Sounds Haarlem Likes Vinyl.

Lay out: Stichting Opposite Direction

ISBN: 9789090379357 (hardcover)
ISBN: 9789090380834 (paperback)

Websites:
https://www.adrianborlandthesound.com/
https://www.stichtingoppositedirection.com/
https://www.walkingintheoppositedirection.info/

YouTube Channel:
https://www.youtube.com/channel/UC3dAoBSP5MCWd4hbImGBNlg

Vimeo:
https://vimeo.com/ondemand/adrianborland

Destiny Stopped Screaming
The Life and Times of Adrian Borland

Destiny Stopped Screaming
The Life and Times of Adrian Borland

FOREWORD

'My friend became a silverbird, fire wings of chrome'

This biography takes a gentle but fearless look at the life of an extraordinary individual, whose genius and inner struggles have left a deep impression on the world around him. A name that has become synonymous with raw emotion and musical honesty, Adrian Borland lives on in the memories of those who knew him and through the legacy he left behind.

The telling of Adrian's story goes beyond a chronological sequence of events; it is a journey through the complexities of the human soul. Born with an undeniable talent for music, at an early age Adrian found an outlet for his thoughts and feelings in the rhythms and melodies he created. His ability to pour the deepest emotions into his songs struck a chord with listeners around the world.

The biography reveals the many layers of Adrian's personality - his creative passion, his profound reflections, and his internal demons. Although he was admired for his musical achievements, he struggled in silence with his own inner darkness. His artistic vision was like a double-edged sword: it produced beautiful melodies, but also brought to light the painful rawness of his inner struggle.

The year 1999 marked a heartbreaking turning point in Adrian's story. His passing left a deep void in the world of music and beyond. As we look back on his life, it's important to honor his musical legacy while also opening the conversation about the mental health that was such an important part of his story. His battle reminds us that dark clouds can lurk behind even the most seemingly brilliant stars.

This biography was born out of love and respect for Adrian Borland and his legacy. It pays homage to his art, his humanity, and his search for meaning amidst the tumult of existence. We dive into his ups and downs, his triumphs, and tragedies, with a humble understanding that we can only glimpse the complexities of his experiences.

I would like to express my deepest gratitude to Simon Heavisides, Jean-Paul van Mierlo and all other friends and fans of Adrian and his music. Your memories, stories and perspectives have enriched this work and helped to form a more complete picture of the man Adrian was.

As we journey through the pages of this biography, we leave our hearts and minds open to the lessons his life has to offer. Let's not only reflect on his tragic end, but also on the power of his music, his creativity, and his ability to connect deeply with others. May this tribute serve as a reminder of the fragility of the human soul and as an inspiration to all who discover his story.

Carlo van Putten

INTRODUCTION

I can speak louder than words

From the first moment I was 'into the Sound,' Adrian never left my mind for long, and he has been in my thoughts daily now for 40 years.
Yes, you could say I'm quite obsessed with his voice and his lyrics.

I remember very clearly that when I had access to the internet for the first time in my life the very first search, I typed into Alta Vista was, 'Adrian Borland'.

Since the mid-80s I have been collecting everything where Adrian's name was involved or mentioned, and I tried to see him play live as often as possible when he was in the Netherlands. First with the Sound, then with the Citizens and lastly solo.

By the way, my two personal meetings with him ended in a fiasco.....on the one hand I was just probably just too pushy and on the other Adrian made me feel like he didn't need it either. Incidentally, I was amazed when every year, with my greatest music friend Wim Hooijmans, we went to see Adrian play wherever that may be. We could clearly see that he had gained weight again. At that time, we really had no idea what Adrian's life was like nor what he was suffering from.

Adrian's death touched me deeply, even more so because I always had the feeling that I wanted to help him which looked impossible. His lyrics evoked a kind of cry for help in me which I couldn't satisfy. Immediately after his death, I took the plunge, with a Haarlem journalist Willemien Spook, and decided that we should put together a book based on memories of Adrian, which resulted in the *Book of (Happy) Memories*. Family, friends, and colleagues from the music industry wrote down their stories and experiences.

To be able to 'give back' even more to him, after seeing the film about the life of the late Sixto Rodriguez, *Searching for Sugarman*, I decided that one way or another there should also be a film/documentary tracing the life of my hero. Fortunately, my friend Marc Waltman immediately wanted to direct it and with diehard fan Martijn Prins as cameraman we embarked on an adventure that led to a 2016 world premiere of *Walking in the Opposite Direction* at the IDFA in the Rabozaal in front of an audience of 500 people.

It's now clear the film has done its job and that Adrian Borland's music lives on, but also that during and after the production of the film many kindred spirits/fans of his music met each other. In addition, this led to both Adrian Janes (the Outsiders) and Mike Dudley taking up the drumsticks again. On social media, experiences were shared by fans from all over the world, something that was also done earlier via the Brittle Heaven website, which unfortunately 'died' shortly after the premiere of the film.

When the Opposite Direction Foundation, which was founded in support of the film, inherited the copyright on Adrian's music, this was the starting signal for the re-release all Adrian's solo records and more. To date, 10 records have been released in collaboration with Sounds Haarlem Likes Vinyl, all under the inspiring leadership of Paul Kamp, who unfortunately died much too early in 2022. In addition, several box sets have been released by Cherry Red and Demon to honour Adrian, the Outsiders, and the Sound.

At the time of writing this foreword it has been almost 25 years since Adrian passed away, it was therefore time to have a biography written about him. When I asked Simon Heavisides to pick this up, he needed exactly one day to think things over. After all, in some areas when you dig into Adrian's life, it is also sometimes a 'minefield'.

It has become a book that, just like the film, tries to give an honest picture. So, it is sometimes painful, in which not only the bright side but also the dark side is highlighted, and then placed in a historical perspective.

As Adrian's friend James Walton Ingham confirms, and just like Bob Borland explains in the film, it was sadly inevitable that Adrian would die young and no one should feel guilty for not being able to help him.

The help Adrian always cries out for, as it sounds to me in his music, still hurts when I listen now. I regret to this day that I was not able to tell him how much he meant to me personally (and still does), just like he does for thousands of other soulmates 'All Over the World'.

Thanks to Simon Heavisides for his incredible energy with which he has shaped this book, with thanks also to everyone who wanted to speak to him or who previously shared his/her experiences indirectly through an interview for the film.

Also, my personal thanks to Nicky Brown, Paul Kamp (RIP) and Luka Ingelse and their people at 'Sounds Haarlem' for all their support over the years.

Special thanks to my dear friend Mark Ritsema for all his inspiration, help and support/work for SOD for one decade now.

Jean-Paul van Mierlo
Stichting Opposite Direction

CONTENTS

THANKS TO

Thanks to everyone who has helped and encouraged me along the way, including Marina, Luna, Jean-Paul, Helen James, Garce, Nicky Brown, Adrian Janes, Steve Budd, Julie Burroughs, Mike Dudley, Phil King, James Walton Ingham, Cassell Webb, Craig Leon, Dave Long, Keith Cullen, Spencer Rowell, Nigel Grierson, Patrick de Leede, Mark Ritsema, Carlo van Putten, Mark Burgess and Chris Roberts. All of those interviewed for the *Walking in the Opposite Direction* documentary. The many writers who covered the Sound and Adrian over the years on paper, online and on TV and radio, including John Clarkson at Penny Black Music with their fantastically detailed coverage, Ruben Guastapaglia at Arcane Delights, David Eastaugh at the C86 Show and Richard Wyatt at the *Heads and Hearts* blog.

Destiny Stopped Screaming
The Life and Times of Adrian Borland

PROLOGUE

Most of England is sleeping in the sun... but not everyone.

27th May 1987
Location: London

Soho's Wardour Street on an early weekday evening was a lot quieter
back in 1987 than it would be today. Not that the few after work
stragglers and random tourists are particularly interested in the event
taking place that night within the battered interior of the legendary
Marquee club, the Sound's home from home in the nation's capital.

In fact, even the crowd (decent numbers, but not a sell out) and least of
all the band appreciate the significance of the night to come which will be
the Sound's heroic last stand on a stage in the UK, after a show at the
same venue the night before. Of course, the infamous final collapse,
fittingly in the Netherlands, the country that most deeply embraced
them, will be put off until later in the year. But for these British fans, this
is it.

I wonder if they ('we' actually - I was lucky to be there, risking my
university finals, because well, you understand why, don't you?) would
have enjoyed the night more if they'd had that knowledge? I doubt it,
because with the Sound you didn't need any additional reason to lose
yourself in their beautiful noise.

And yes, it was a reliably incredible gig from Adrian, Colvin, Mike and
Graham, but then they always gave their all, even when the clock was fast
running down on their 'career'. Many years later, in the raw and insightful
sleeve notes of *Will and Testament,* Mike brutally summed up their
existence at this point, "we were dragging ourselves through the long
desert of the world's indifference."

Thunder Up was a cry in the darkness and tonight's opener, "Acceleration

Group", was never more apt, a clarion call and a rousing anthem for when the body feels weak and even the spirit falters. Not that you'd know it tonight as the band storm through a defiant set. When Adrian dedicates *Jeopardy's* "Resistance" to "Neil Kinnock and the red rose of England" it sends a shiver down the spine. And what a typically Adrian thing to say, championing the compassionate underdog and yearning for a Britain that offered something more than the unfiltered cruelty of the Thatcher year. That Kinnock's Labour Party would be routed in the general election taking place two weeks later could, with the benefit of hindsight, seem to put the seal on the doomed nature of this final year of the Sound.

Even the venue itself would close and move to far less atmospheric premises within little over a year, ultimately giving way to a luxury hotel, it's blue plaque another stopping off point on a rock and roll tourist trail.

Of course, we now know that not only was there a devastating internal battle going on within Adrian as a person, but the post Live Aid music world itself was heading through changes that would see him left out in the cold, written off by some as a footnote.

The bittersweet irony would come just after Adrian tragically took his own life in April 1999 as gradually, then very quickly, the world became smaller than he could ever have imagined, and all that beautiful music would find a whole new audience.

But before we get to the movie-style coda there's a life story to tell.

Oh, and in the unlikely event that you're wondering, yes against the odds I passed my finals and one day got to tell Adrian of my irrational obstinacy. But don't worry, this isn't my story, it's his.

The Marquee, 90 Wardour Street, London,
with its stage (with Mike) and notorious dressing room (with Adrian)

Destiny Stopped Screaming
The Life and Times of Adrian Borland

CHAPTER 1

The past is a foreign country; they do things differently there

Adrian Borland was born on 6th December 1957 into a society that may well appear like a "foreign country" to anyone who arrived even ten years later. But if you happen to believe in destiny then you may well say it was pretty much perfect timing.

He wasn't alone, in the preceding year Siouxsie Sioux, Sid Vicious, Marc Almond and Peter Murphy had already joined the ranks of the future punk and post-punk players. Mind you so had two eventual members of Iron Maiden, but let's not let reality get in the way of a tenuous theory.

A few months before Adrian's arrival Prime Minister Harold Macmillan declared that, "Most of our people have never had it so good." As with many famous sound-bites, misinterpretation comes with the territory. However, here was a country that had survived war and, battered as it was, now began to see an economic boom that would in part create a new population of consumers: the youth market.

But in 1957 for most young people boredom ruled the day. Rock'n'roll had arrived and caused a degree of mayhem but ahead lay the waiting period of the early '60s before the full flowering of all that pent up rebellion and creativity that unfurled from the middle of the decade on.

Musically the middle of the road still ruled the airwaves. The year's biggest selling single was "Diana" by Paul Anka, closely followed by Harry Belafonte's version of "Mary's Boy Child", Elvis with "All Shook Up" and Pat Boone's "Love Letters in the Sand", Elvis the sole beacon of rebellion in that bunch.

Historian Dominic Sandbrook may have a deserved reputation as a Thatcher apologist but when (in his book *Never Had it So Good: A History of Britain from Suez to the Beatles*) he talks of '50s Britain as having, "a thick vein of anxiety beneath the surface of society" it's hard

19

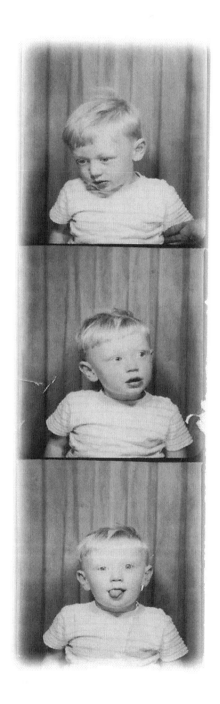

not to think of the unease that Adrian would go on to articulate so well in songs such as "New Dark Age", where he sang, "from the safest places come the bravest words".

Britain has never really escaped that anxiety; it was just pushed under the surface for a while as we enjoyed the 'swinging' sixties, emerging again in full force as punk ripped the mask away to reveal what had been festering beneath.

So yes, Adrian's timing was perfect.

According to Win, Adrian was, "a serious baby, it took ages before he first smiled." In the *Book of (Happy) Memories* (a collection of recollections and tributes published in the wake of Adrian's death) Win makes a striking reference to a lyric from "Solar" a track from Adrian's posthumously released album, *Harmony and Destruction,*

"My mother said I didn't smile until I saw the rays between the leaves".

That yearning for the light and the hope it symbolised would become a theme within his music.

Although his birth was registered in Hampstead, Adrian was actually born in the Kilburn part of West Hampstead. His parents were Win and Bob. Win was from Plympton in Devon. Bob's family had moved around a lot as a result of his dad being in the Royal Air Force and Bob had been born in Egypt. Adrian was comfortably middle class simply by virtue of their very respectable jobs. Win was an English teacher while Bob graduated from Imperial College, the year after Adrian was born, with a degree in physics. He later went on to become Head of Physics at the prestigious National Physical Laboratory in Teddington, West London. These were significant achievements, both parents had worked their way up from relatively humble beginnings showing some of the determination their son would also share.

In terms of the complex and arcane UK class system such occupations were more than respectable, that doesn't mean Win and Bob were especially affluent but their situation was such that Adrian, who was an only child, would have a warm and secure early life. Without pandering to the stereotypical cliches it's important to note his status as an only child, Bob later confirmed it wasn't intentional but rather a mix of monetary constraints and life getting in the way of plans as it often does.

Win with Adrian as a baby

Today Hampstead and the surrounding area is an estate agent's dream, the kind of place where you may see a celebrity or two sipping an overpriced coffee in 'Instagrammable' cafes, although West Hampstead (Kilburn) still retains a little grit. Back in Adrian's early years it was high in rented accommodation but was more like living in an urban village than life would have been a little further into the metropolis.

After Adrian's birth Win and Bob lived in various rented properties in Kilburn and Wandsworth before buying their own home, a neat bungalow in Shepperton.

Their pleasure was short lived after it was announced that the M3 motorway would pass right through their street, Bob was instrumental in successfully fighting the plans but had already decided to move by the time he and the other residents secured a slight change of the motorway's route. The planning fight is indicative of Bob's determined but occasionally inflexible nature.

Clearly London in those years was going through particularly huge changes. The massive damage resulting from the German Blitz and a zeal to build modern homes and infrastructure transformed the city in ways both good and bad.

For Adrian this would mean his family (including his maternal grandmother) moving to 2 Hillview, not far from Raynes Park Station in the wider suburb of Wimbledon. A brand new terraced house in a quiet cul-de-sac and another village-like atmosphere. It was desirable then, even more so today.

Built in 1967, slap bang in the middle of those swinging '60s, the various developments in Adrian's life were very much part of a period of seismic change in the UK. It was a time when the cultural landscape we know today began to take shape.

Just consider this: during the 1960s the UK population saw the end of capital punishment, divorce reform, the right to abortion, and the legalisation of homosexuality. There was a whirlwind of change, much of it happening specifically in 1967.

Away from the human rights that were rightly finally being enshrined in law, popular music was evolving at breakneck speed and was no longer quite so sneered at. After all, money could be made. Meanwhile youth culture was exploding. All of these events contributed to the creation of the path that Adrian would end up following.

Compare and contrast the biggest selling singles of 1967 with those of Adrian's year of birth: perhaps strangely the none more middle of the road Englebert Humperdinck ruled the airwaves with three massive hits, but elsewhere Procol Harum, Sandie Shaw, the Monkees and the Beatles were finally pushing the male crooners out of the way.

Now try to imagine for a moment what it was like for families in the '60s moving into modest modernist homes that were unlike anything they had experienced in their lives, with as standard all the mod cons people could only have dreamt of before.

This was the house where Adrian would grow up, where he would launch his musical career and where he would return to live again and again, licking his wounds and wondering where life would lead him next. It's not hard to picture him back in his small bedroom listening to records late into the night.

Indeed years later Adrian would vividly capture such a scene in *Beautiful Ammunition*'s "Lonely Late Nighter",

"A lonely late nightery
Plays on my stereo
A voice in the darkness sings
Convinces me that I am not alone
And the only sound in here
Is the click of the run-off groove"

But for all his middle-class credentials this was a very modest house by modern standards. Its terraced nature coming complete with the likelihood that you may hear more of the neighbours than strictly desirable and they of you. Who knows how many recording sessions the residents of Hillview were unwillingly privy to.

Downstairs the front room would be ground zero for his early musical life, doubling as a recording studio. Amazingly the house remained in the Borland family's possession for over fifty years, only finally going up for sale in 2018 after Bob Borland's death.

It's bittersweet to imagine its current residents: blissfully unaware of the history of the building or the music that ricocheted around its walls. For fans the address may be familiar from being the 'HQ' of Raw Edge Records, its unassuming appearance belying the emotional significance.

Back in the early '90s I once sat down for a cup of tea there. Adrian's tea making abilities were sketchy so I did the honours before encouraging him to play me an acoustic version of a new song, "Faithful", that would end up recorded for *Brittle Heaven*. It was a strange moment, time stopped for a couple of minutes, the history of the house hanging heavy over us. I remember being surprised that it felt quite forlorn and a little neglected: the feeling of melancholy was palpable.

And then no doubt Adrian cracked a joke and we snapped back to the present, melancholy temporarily dispelled.

Adrian joking around immediately places us back in that late '60s childhood idyll as recalled by some of his friends from back in those fairly innocent days.

Hillview and the surrounding streets were full of newly moved-in families. Lots of kids meeting for the first time and, as was common in those days, out playing around the streets, gardens and open spaces.

Two of Adrian's lifelong friends from that moment on, were interviewed in preparation for the *Walking in the Opposite Direction* documentary (released in 2016 and telling the story of Adrian's life). John Troiano and Robin Bell provide a lovely insight into a late '60s/early '70s childhood, the kind where the doorbell would ring every day and the only important question was, "Is Adrian coming out to play?"

John, "We'd spend a lot of time outside. These were the days before computer games and stuff like that. There were woods behind our houses so we would spend hours out there playing football. Adrian was very imaginative, he always liked motor racing for example. One of the things we'd do in the woods, where there was a hill, we'd go and take go-karts and race them."

John again, "He was an athletic kid, actually, very talented, skinny, quick and competitive. He liked to win and was good at sports."

It quickly becomes clear that as a child Adrian was never some kind of Morrissey-esque recluse looking out at the world from behind bedroom curtains. If there is such a thing then his early childhood was very much in the classic mode of friends, sports and a high energy enthusiasm for life. There's one word that crops up again and again when friends and associates are asked to sum him up succinctly: *enthusiastic,* closely followed by energetic and talented.

In some ways, despite everything, that intense enthusiasm never departed, but simply had to make way for the symptoms of the schizo-affective disorder that, as the years passed, increasingly engulfed him.

But in the eternal summer of youthful life in Wimbledon that was all a long way off.

It's always tempting to look for early signs of creativity in the life of a future artist, with Adrian it's equally pretty easy to find them.

After an afternoon discussing Adrian's impact on he and his friends' lives John Troiano's conclusion that, "I don't think he was ordinary actually" feels significant despite, or maybe in part because of, its understated delivery.

Time and again it's Adrian's drive and creativity that come to the fore, it may leave you thinking of people like that in your own life, if you were lucky enough to have them. I mean this was a boy who didn't wait around for a toy company to design and produce the games he wanted to play, instead he just went ahead and dreamt them up himself.

John, "He would actually invent games. He loved Formula One racing and we used to go to the races at Brands Hatch and Silverstone and basically he would draw out every single Formula One circuit and would devise these rules of how you would race the cars around the circuit. There was a starting line and it would cost you two points on the dice to move out and to overtake. So he had the little blue car and all the other cars like the JP Specials in the black and the gold and the red Ferraris and they were all cut out of little pieces of cardboard. You'd have a whole season of racing".

Perhaps unsurprisingly Adrian's childhood wish was to become a Formula One driver, something that thankfully fell by the wayside as childhood wishes tend to.

But nothing can beat the fact that, as his musical taste developed, Adrian dreamt up his own game that focussed on the ups and downs in the life of a touring band, populating it with members of his favourite acts. In the true spirit of life imitating art and back again, existence for the less successful bands was brutal.

Adrian's notes on his Formula One game

John, "Of course, if you weren't a very successful band, then you had to play these really terrible venues, he was the one who had this idea, these are the sorts of things he did as a 12 year old kid!"

It's important to note how music began to gradually permeate everything, even if it was just naming teams in a cricket game or directing his developing artistic skills towards drawing pictures of Iggy and Bowie.

One thing we learn: life with Adrian around wasn't dull, something that would never change.

Interestingly there was another friend living just down the road, at number 12, by the name of Graham Bailey.

Maybe a year younger than Adrian so not in the same class at school, Hollymount Primary, this didn't stop them becoming inseparable friends. Playing outside at all hours possible, exploring derelict houses, getting into mischief and sharing the details of their latest unattainable crushes on girls at school. Graham spent a lot of time at Adrian's house and no doubt engaged in the kind of low-level naughtiness kids of their age specialise in.

Both were due to go on to Wimbledon Chase Middle School but it was at that point Adrian's dad decided to change his son's educational path and instead to send him to private school. It appears Adrian won a scholarship and was funded by the London Borough of Merton.

It could be that Bob Borland considered Graham and the other local kids might lead Adrian astray and felt private school the best option. Private, or the alternative somewhat confusing term, 'public' school, is the bedrock of the class system in the UK, something which still continues to this day. The contacts and networks set up during those crucial years can serve people very well in their later careers and it's difficult to overestimate the importance it can have on a person's trajectory through life. Fair it isn't but like so much in British society not even the changes of the sixties could shift it. Bizarrely the schools themselves are even registered as 'charities,' for now at least.

Bearing in mind the work Win and Bob had put in to achieve what they had, despite not coming from well-off backgrounds, it's likely they felt this was the best chance of securing a decent future for Adrian, who as we can see was obviously bright and creative.

Of course as far as Graham was concerned thankfully Bob failed to permanently sever their paths as we shall discover a little further down the line.

As it will become increasingly clear, Adrian's parents were supportive to a degree that goes beyond the average. That's not to say his relationship with them was all plain sailing. Naturally, any parental relationship, particularly during adolescence, has its stresses and strains but in this case it was maybe more than that. Adrian at times also struggled with being an only child, while on the other hand benefiting from the attention and material resources available. It was a defining influence in his life, as friend and future Outsider Adrian Janes confirms,

"Two factors were probably most significant in Adrian's early life: firstly the fact that he was an only child, and secondly, as the son of two middle class professionals, his background (though not rich) was sufficiently well-off for his material wishes to be indulged."

In an interview with website Penny Black Music, Outsiders bassist Bob Lawrence described Win and Bob as, "fantastically dedicated parents" but, as may be expected Adrian and Bob's interactions could be tempestuous on occasion, after all these were two strong personalities and that would inevitably lead to conflict at times, in this case maybe resulting in an above average degree of domestic turbulence.

Adrian's cousin Nicky Brown is two years older than him and the pair were close when they were children.

Nicky, "Adrian's relationship with his parents was a difficult one. Bob (like his siblings) was a very strong character and believed he knew best. He and Adrian argued a great deal but they were massively supportive, especially in the beginning."

Julie Aldred was Adrian's girlfriend from 1979 until 1983, and after that the Sound's tour manager. She spent a lot of time at the Borland's home (her own parents weren't totally keen on her dating the singer in a band) and while confirming how helpful Adrian's parents were did see the more difficult elements of the parental relationship.

"Yes, they were very supportive and I know they loved Adrian very much, but Adrian didn't get on very well with his dad. Bob could be very dictatorial."

Adrian Janes paints a vivid picture of childhood and late-teens domestic conflict, that while not entirely unusual still feels more intense than the average, whatever you consider that to be,

"Bob's manner with Adrian was often quite brusque, which sometimes would result in embarrassingly intense arguments for Bob Lawrence and I to witness. It wasn't uncommon for Adrian to be told he was a 'bloody idiot' for some reason or another. I also recall him telling me at school one day that he'd told his dad to 'fuck off' the night before, a feat of daring that impressed me."

Talking to Sound drummer Mike Dudley today reveals a further insight into the father-son relationship based on later encounters with Bob,

"My experience of Adrian's dad was that he did very well for Adrian in that he was engaged in the process and always concerned for his son's health and well-being. But as a person I found him curiously lacking in empathy or emotional response to the world around him. He was an interesting character but not one who appeared to have a lot of emotional depth"

It's not uncommon for someone who may be of above average intelligence to struggle with empathy but obviously that creates challenges for those growing up around them.

Adrian Janes sums up the tension-support dynamic that defined Adrian's early life but then continued as he grew older,

"All three of the family were emotionally intense characters, probably reinforced by Bob and Win's mutual intelligence and high expectations of what Adrian was capable of achieving. But for all that this could sometimes feel like you were stepping into a pressure cooker atmosphere, Adrian always had the family home to come back to if he needed to. Once his mental illness took hold and Bob and Win knew they would have to cope with it for the rest of his life, that remained the case, a practical love that survived even its worst instances."

Adrian's connection with his mum tends to be overshadowed but it was very close, possibly unnaturally so.

Future friend and collaborator Carlo van Putten explains,

"Adrian's relationship with Bob wasn't always easy but I also thought his relationship with his mother Win wasn't healthy, she did everything for him all the time. She even had input to his lyrics, she was an English teacher and would read his lyrics and say 'You can't say this!' It was too much and she was nearly choking him. It ended up that the only thing he could do was write songs, sing and play guitar. But he was such a friendly, lovely guy. I loved him."

Adrian Janes describes what he witnessed as a close friend and band member,

"Win, as both Adrian's mum and also an English teacher, showed tender maternal pride and aesthetic appreciation for what her son did. We would sometimes arrive back at the house late after a gig to find a little plate of supper and some milk left out for him."

Although the signs of future pressure points were firmly in evidence from Adrian's early childhood onwards, importantly there were no visible indications of his later mental health problems. Sometimes chasing down clues and making what appear to be valid assumptions can obscure a simpler reality.

Mental illness ran in the family on Bob Borland's mother's side, although it's fiercely debated, schizoaffective disorder is thought to have a genetic component. This means that individuals who have a close relative (parent or sibling) or family history of schizophrenia, mood disorders, or schizoaffective disorder are at a higher risk when it comes to developing the condition themselves.

However while the future inevitably casts a backward shadow, in many ways this was a very typical suburban childhood, uncomplicated and full of play, in Adrian's case extremely competitive and, crucially, *creative* play.

Listening to his numerous friends talking of these far away days makes you feel like taking a walk through today's leafy Wimbledon streets in the hope they may contain some trace of that sun-dappled past.

Adrian's home itself feels like a character in this story, from its mid '60s origins, full of modernist possibility, to the gradual decline and eventual rebirth.

If you find yourself with a few spare minutes you may like to check your search engine of choice, where, within a few seconds you will be able to take a voyeuristically detailed look at 2 Hillview.

Firstly the undeniable pathos of photos of the house after the Borland's belongings had been removed: the faded '70s decor, 'ghost-marks' where pictures have been removed, all the usual reminders of lives that once filled these rooms with emotions both joyful and painful. It's a moving experience, loaded with poignancy.

And then today's house: a lot of white paint, partition walls removed, bright and airy, new lives in progress, very little trace of the past.

Life rolls remorselessly on, obliterating most if not all that we love. And yet music with a certain almost indefinable quality survives, taking root deep in the hearts of people some of whom weren't even alive at the time of its creation.

How does that happen and at what possible cost to the artist?

2 Hillview, Wimbledon, London

CHAPTER 2

Raw power... I can feel it

And time moves on. The swinging '60s fade to a technicolour memory that will eventually be endlessly recycled and reduced to a familiar series of 'iconic' cliches. British society probably wasn't ready for the cold hard reality of the early seventies, the post-war dream was tarnishing faster than a cheap stainless steel kettle.

You may be thinking, why do I need a history lesson? It's a fair question but perhaps it's better to think of the importance of context. Without it, understanding Adrian's life and music becomes that much harder and a lot less meaningful.

Imagine the children of the '50s who had seen the flowering of possibility that the late '60s dangled in front of them but who then came slap bang up against the grey '70s. Believe me, the classic picture many of us have of the United Kingdom in this era is supported by evidence and experience. It's not something that's been lazily created after the event.

Just think on this: for a two month period in 1973-'74 the Conservative government introduced what has become known as the Three Day Week . As a result of the combined effect of industrial action, and the worsening energy crisis, businesses had to limit their electricity usage to three days a week, TV channels stopped broadcasting by 10.30 pm and ordinary people worked and ate by candlelight, wrapping themselves in blankets to keep warm.

Yes it was pretty grim. Nevertheless, the UK was still one of the richest countries in the world and yet this was still happening.

More was to come with the Winter of Discontent and its mass strike action in multiple industries and services that left bodies unburied and mountains of rubbish decaying in the streets.

Meanwhile Adrian was partially shielded from all this in the possible haven of Tiffin School. Having looked at the possibility of attending another nearby public school, Kingston Grammar (it is possible Adrian spent some time there but didn't feel at home and therefore moved), instead he enrolled at Tiffin School, a boys (there was a separate girls school) grammar founded in 1880.

Today, ironically, the school is noted as a specialist in performing arts. How much it nurtured Adrian's musical abilities back them is unclear but naturally Adrian benefited from the smaller class sizes and better funded resources that the public school sector offered. At a price of course.

What was crucial about this period is that it sees Adrian meeting several figures who would prove pivotal both in terms of his musical development and his future in general.

Not all of those people attended the same school.

14 year old Steve Budd, who would go on to release both Second Layer and the Sound's first records as well as initially managing the Sound, was a pupil at a nearby school, Ewell Castle in Epsom where his best friend was a boy called Clive Bailey (no relation to Graham incidentally) who just happened to be Adrian Borland's next door neighbour. Typical of the complex web of friends and acquaintances that you build as a child.

Steve can clearly remember first encountering Adrian (or 'Bo' as many of his friends then called him), "When we used to have sleepovers, I would go to Clive's house and there'd be this kid sitting in the street with a Burns guitar on his lap. He was a little bit older than me, maybe a year I think, and he was already a very competent guitarist aged 15".

"Christ he can play" was Steve's reaction, as detailed in the *Book of (Happy) Memories*.

Adrian seemed to take his guitar everywhere, he was also jamming with many, many friends during this time, in front rooms, bedrooms, even sheds, learning his craft covering all sorts of current rock on some very nice instruments bought by Win and Bob. Outsiders bassist Bob Lawrence would later make a telling comment about his friend's 'relationship' with his guitars via an interview with Penny Black Music,

"Bo was very complete when he played guitar. I think he was outstanding. He seemed to have complete mastery of the instrument even back then. He would always have it with him – it was an extension of his being in a way – even when not playing it he would use it to add to what he was saying or doing. He could sometimes express frustration better through his guitar rather than, or in addition to, what he was saying. It was always there with him."

Interestingly Adrian shunned Steve Budd's early loves, Hendrix and Santana, and instead was fervently in love with Bowie, Roxy, the Velvet Underground and, slightly less cool, Blue Oyster Cult.

Now step back and again consider the top three bestselling singles of 1973. In first place was Tony Orlando and Dawn with the deathless "Tie a Yellow Ribbon", followed by the Simon Park Orchestra's TV show theme, "Eye Level" and then, fresh from massively popular TV talent show *Opportunity Knocks*, Peters and Lee and the cloying, "Welcome Home."

If evidence was needed of how out of step Adrian was with mass tastes then hopefully that will suffice.

Much more than that though it illustrates the stultifying blandness of mid-seventies UK culture. Something that, depending on your point of view, either reflected the need to escape tough times or simply clashed with harsh reality. Whichever you pick, the seeds were being sown for a serious cultural revolt.

It will come as no surprise to hear that Adrian was one of the many thousands who devoured the UK's weekly music press and used it to find richer seams of potentially life changing inspiration.

Adrian's school notebook

Strange as it may now seem but the country had multiple large format weekly newspapers devoted to music. Often referred to as the 'inkies' because the print would come off on your fingers as you read them, these papers were stocked by every local newsagent (there was at least one of those on every street) and had circulations in the low hundreds of thousands. Anyone who had an interest in music would consult these pages each week, possibly buying more than one of the main papers: *Melody Maker, NME, Sounds* and *Record Mirror*. This was where you got your information in a pre-internet world. No doubt Adrian would excitedly pore over the pages looking for the next musical discovery that would set his heart racing. The impact of these institutions on youth culture at this point in time is hard to overestimate.

Just imagine when later Adrian transitioned from reading about other musicians to reading about himself. Not an always pleasant or comfortable experience as the writers could be utterly brutal and often seemingly totally arbitrary in their delivering of praise or scathing criticism. Oh boy would he learn what that was like.

In addition to the list above there was one more act that Adrian was already deeply passionate about: Iggy and the Stooges, who by this time featured incendiary guitarist James Williamson and had released the blistering slab of proto-punk that was *Raw Power.*

It's highly likely Adrian read of the Stooges in the pages of the *NME* where journalist Nick Kent was a massive fan. Just picture him, in his room upstairs at 2 Hillview, devouring every word, wondering what this music could possibly sound like.

Much later Kent described *Raw Power* as, "the greatest, meanest-eyed, coldest-blooded hard rock tour de force ever summoned up in a recording studio". Mixed by Bowie it was in some ways a challenging listen, the chaotic circumstances of its recording resulting in a mix that could best be described as 'singular' in its approach to recording, err, 'technique'. But then that's all part of its unique power and charm.

Realise that back on release *Raw Power* was a flop commercially not the retrospectively iconic monster of an influence it is now. Also bear in mind this was a world where you had to make an effort to discover and own the records you loved. Not everyone in every street had a copy of this record, far from it. You absolutely couldn't walk into your local record shop and expect to find it in the racks. So Adrian was one of the few that were ahead of the game.

In terms of Adrian's musical inspiration, and what would become the 'sound' of the Sound, in many ways Adrian's acquisition of this album is a kind of ground zero. He would go on to cover *Raw Power* era Stooges songs on at least three occasions: the title track via the soon to come Outsiders, "Death Trip" with the Sound and "Gimme Danger" reinvented for solo shows.

There may be those who don't fully see the Stooges-Sound connection but trust me it's part of their bedrock and burst out in 'raw' electrical energy whenever the Sound hit the stage.

In 1989 Adrian eloquently summarised his Stooges 'thing' in an interview with journalist and Sound fan Chris Roberts of *Melody Maker,*

"Our best gigs were when we pretended we were the Stooges. We'd get completely loaded and fuelled and go "Kill! Kill! Kill!" and we'd go on stage and I'd be part Iggy, part James Williamson and Graham would be Ron Ashton. Actually, they were probably our worst gigs. We'd have a great time, but perhaps our best gigs were the ones where we were concentrating!"

Adrian often spoke of Iggy's influence, something that went well beyond the musical, here he is in an interview with Vara, a Dutch radio station, again in 1989. It's interesting to see just how cognisant he was of the effect music can have on a person and their development,

"I just like Iggy's attitude to things. He likes to shock people, I sort of like that. I've been reading this book, *the Wild One* by some Swedish guy (Per Nilsen) and it's obvious that they were something else, they weren't really rock music, they were more a kind of performance art. With a lot of dubious things going on, with Iggy cutting himself and stuff like that and challenging the audience. I don't think it can be done again. But it's that attitude I like. Even in some of my songs that comes through. Maybe not quite as confrontationally as Iggy Pop. But it must be there somewhere. It's been such a major influence on me. I think it might have something to do with the fact that when you first start listening to music you're about 15 and it makes a big impression on you. If they're good enough, I think these people stay with you, _if_ you pick the right people!"

Ironically the book Adrian referred to actually included a photo of the night Iggy fleetingly 'met' Adrian, but that's a story for another chapter.

But just in case Adrian's love for Iggy remains in doubt, here's Adrian talking to me back in 1991,

"He's my number one. Always will be I guess now, yeah of course he will. There's something about him, I think it's the way he's struggled through and made it."

What comes across so clearly in these quotes is the fact that Adrian had an awareness of the power of music that goes beyond a simple appreciation. In fact his mention of the critical age of 15 tallies with theories that suggest your musical taste is formed during the often turbulent 15th year of existence, if that's the case then yes Adrian did pick the right people.

For him this wasn't just a matter of stylistic musical inspiration, it went much deeper than that. The following years would see bands basing an entire career on ripping off _Raw Power_'s "Shake Appeal", whereas for Adrian he was using these songs and Iggy's attitude as a stepping off point for his own creation. Empty imitations held no interest for him.

Listening to _Raw Power_ today is still an extreme experience. James Williamson's guitar forever loaded with menace and danger, showering sparks of barely contained energy and frustration. I wonder whether within these songs Adrian felt, for the first time, a way he could temporarily escape himself. Something that increased massively when it was his hands moving across the fretboard.

At the centre of it all there's Iggy, achieving a state beyond suffocating external constraints, at least for the duration of a song. It's easy to see how that would appeal to Adrian as he grew to understand the burden he was carrying.

Not only that; soon he also realised that such an escape could be facilitated for an audience as well. A power he would learn to wield with huge skill.

If you're reading this book then it's highly likely you have a deep and possibly complex relationship with music. You may well also be of 'a certain age'. If so, I suspect Adrian's move from childhood pursuits to a long term love affair with music will probably be something that strikes a chord with your own life. It goes beyond simply 'enjoying a good tune' and can be quite obsessive in nature as many of us will maybe admit to. Adrian was able to channel that obsession, or more benignly, enthusiasm, and to develop a skill well beyond his similarly inspired friends and peers.

And that's partly what makes him so interesting.

Meanwhile back in suburban Wimbledon, new friend Steve Budd was already obsessed by music so it didn't take much for he and Adrian to connect over a shared passion, as Steve explains,

"I bought myself a guitar aged 12 and where I lived just up the road there was a kid who also played and we bonded and ended up playing together. He was quite clever and went on to start a PA company and I'd help".

Incredibly this meant Steve would get experience as a roadie at venues like the Greyhound in Fulham and later, more significantly, future punk hallowed ground, the Vortex in Wardour Street, Soho, just down the road from the Marquee club.

Rewinding just a fraction:

Steve, "I was still playing guitar and Adrian would come round and jam in the front room of my parents' house. There was a drummer and we had a three piece band, we'd just jam away".

What becomes clear during this period is just how many neighbours' lives must have been impacted by all these nascent bands taking their first fumbling steps. Most headed towards well deserved obscurity but at this particular time, in the years immediately before punk, just playing like this was vital preparation for the opportunities to come.

Yet another important meeting was due to take place that would place another piece of the jigsaw puzzle of Adrian's early life in position. Naturally when you're a teenager meetings aren't stiff and formal events but often take place in school corridors or perhaps out on the playing field at break time.

The name Adrian Janes will be familiar to anyone who has scoured the credits of their Sound albums. More commonly known as Jan, in many ways he is emblematic of a particular type of person who was caught up unintentionally in the pre-punk slipstream. It wasn't always attention seekers who powered the revolution ahead. Quiet, self-effacing, thoughtful and politically engaged, perhaps a good foil for Adrian's more energetic personality with all the ups and downs that came with it.

Jan, "I first met Adrian at school when we were both about 14, we were in the same class and naturally gravitated to each other through music. Adrian always had more pocket money to spend on albums, he was one of the hipper people."

Adrian's role as a catalyst, in terms of turning people onto music that was effectively 'underground', was no doubt repeated in schools across the country where the more clued-in kids took a lead that others would follow. Looking back it was a truly organic process that took place with minimal 'market' led interference. Many of the artists championed by such taste-makers are now recognised as canonical pioneers of punk, whether they were individually actual 'punk' acts or not. Very few, beyond maybe Blondie, actually sold records in huge quantities at the time.

Jan remembers Adrian's guitar playing beginning on a novelty plastic 'Beatles guitar', a toy designed and manufactured to cash in on the boom surrounding the band and first appearing in shops in 1964. Today one in decent condition will set you back around £300 if you fancy learning guitar like Adrian did.

This shared musical experience quickly moved to Jan taking over on drums at those jam sessions.

To be clear, this wasn't yet their future band the Outsiders, it was a more amorphous garage band type arrangement, or, as Jan describes them, "a lounge band" due to the practice sessions and cassette recording efforts taking place in the front room at 2 Hillview.

Another school friend, Bob Lawrence, had joined by this time and for maybe as long as two years they played under the name Syndrome, as suggested by Bob. We should understand that this was, as Jan describes it, 'a serious hobby' with no real music business designs or aims. The band did a couple of school gigs, as many bands of that time would do, simply because anything beyond that was pretty much impossible.

Obviously this determined practising and recording, simply for enjoyment's sake, laid the foundation upon which their more formal future efforts as the Outsiders would eventually build. (Intriguingly around this time Adrian also briefly played in an unnamed band with future Cardiac, the late Tim Smith).

But during that innocent period, outside the Wimbledon bubble, the pressure that would push punk into the tabloid headlines and out across the country was building.

An insane amount of time and wordage has been expended analysing the creation and effect of what would prove an epoch defining movement. Anyone who needs to go deeper is directed to the 'bible' Jon Savage's *England's Dreaming,* a book which beautifully details the social conditions, key characters and most importantly, the music, that briefly outraged sections of the media and for a short period succeeded in confusing the hell out of a complacent music industry.

For the purpose of Adrian's story punk couldn't have arrived at a better time as it would perhaps unwittingly propel him into a world that he longed, more than anything else, to be a part of.

Let's not forget however that Adrian was still at school. To him this must have felt like the mundane world dragging him away from his calling in life. It's interesting to look back at some of his school reports of the time. This was his art teacher in 1975,

"I suspect that his creative thinking is being devoted to his music - certainly at the moment he is not working hard enough or well enough."

The classic comment made about a bright pupil for whom the school curriculum just doesn't offer the stimulation needed.

Elsewhere his Master's report delivered this classic assessment, loaded with implicit criticism and threat as well an accidental partial foreshadowing of a future classic Sound song title,

"Adrian seems to lead a busy, active life. He mixes well with his contemporaries, and in his way gains their respect. It would however be wise for him to concentrate upon his 'A' levels with more singleness of purpose".

We can't be sure of the precise approach of the teachers at Tiffins, but still it feels sad that even at a fee paying school the focus wasn't on harnessing Adrian's creativity in a positive way but instead on placing pressure to comply with academic demands.

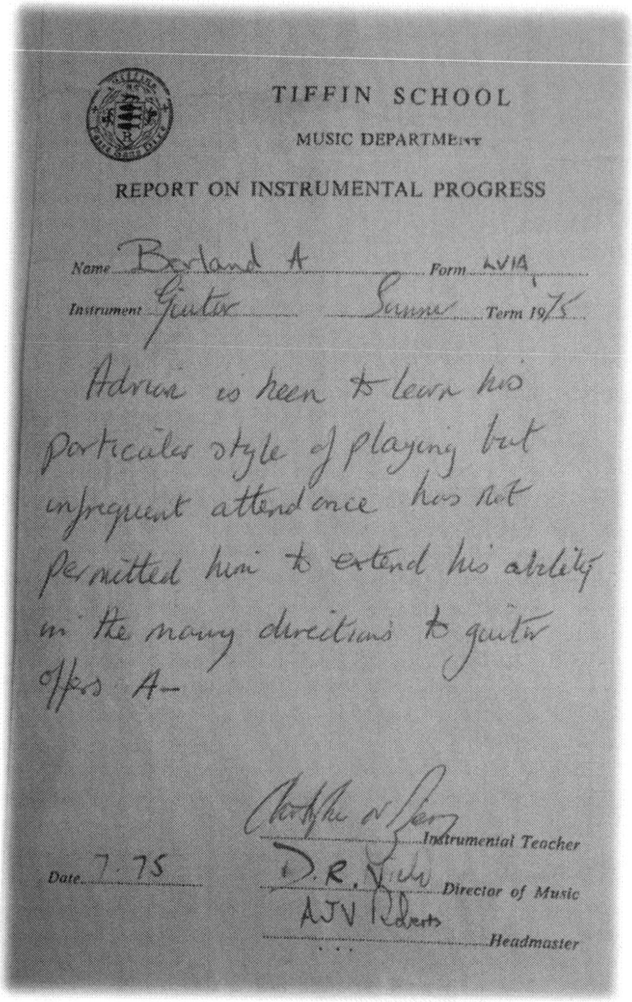

TIFFIN SCHOOL

MUSIC DEPARTMENT

REPORT ON INSTRUMENTAL PROGRESS

Name _Borland A_   Form _LVIA_

Instrument _Guitar_   _Summer_ Term 19_75_

Adrian is keen to learn his particular style of playing but infrequent attendance has not permitted him to extend his ability in the many directions to guitar offers A—

Instrumental Teacher

Date _7.75_

Director of Music

Headmaster

School report re Adrian's guitar playing

Who knows what Win and Bob made of these comments, we do know however that there was some tension between them and Adrian's school. It may be more common today for parents to have direct communication with their children's teachers, but back in the '70s it would generally only happen when things were getting difficult for school and pupil.

There is evidence of Bob Borland writing, in May 1974, to a teacher at Adrian's school to raise concerns about the demands being placed on his son in connection with a specific exam. The response from Tiffins was what we could describe as 'robust'. It's not unusual for children to feel the pressure of exams but I wonder whether this was an early sign of Adrian's underlying fragility? Equally could it be that Bob's involvement at this level was inadvertently increasing that pressure? At this remove it's hard to say, but difficult to ignore.

What we do know is that unlike most people attending public school, then as now, Adrian would not make the move to university. How his parents felt about that we can't know but their fulsome support continued.

For Adrian, the cocktail of circumstances that swirled around him and the wider country was throwing up far more exciting opportunities that would take him where he yearned to go but equally place him under a pressure that would ultimately prove too much to bear.

A young Bob Borland and Adrian's mother Win

CHAPTER 3

Got to be one of the crowd to show you don't conform...

Interview with Adrian 1991:

Me: "Did the Outsiders set out to be a punk band?"

Adrian: "We just wanted to be a band! We wanted to be more like an American band than a British punk band."

The Patti Smith Group played the Hammersmith Odeon in October 1976. Adrian worshipped Patti just slightly less than he worshipped Iggy and so of course was there. In a fascinating July 1985 interview with Richard Wyatt and Ian Lloyd (available on the *Heads and Hearts* blog), Adrian still sounds in awe when he confirms,

"She's a heroine of mine."

Steve Budd today wonders if his mind was playing tricks on him, but no, Adrian Janes confirms what happened that night,

"At some point Adrian just launched himself on stage, he didn't touch her, but the roadie, who was Patti's brother, grabbed him and chucked him off the stage. He didn't get to tell her how much he loved her."

As an event it shows the intensity of Adrian's passion for music and also unwittingly symbolises the changes that punk was bringing about. The established walls between performer and audience were briefly coming down and Adrian would be in the right place to make the full leap from observer to participant.

Sadly though he wouldn't stand on the Hammersmith Odeon stage again.

Adrian, Jan and Bob left school in June 1976. The summer of 1976 has gone down in UK folklore as the hottest summer ever, although that has now been usurped as a result of climate change and 2022's blowtorch summer. But back in '76 there were 22 consecutive days of temperatures over 28 degrees centigrade. Tarmac melted and there was a drought that left people queuing resolutely at water standpipes in the street.

Anyone who was there will remember the cracked and parched ground and may see things through a mix of hazy nostalgia and soft reverie. The UK had recently voted to stay in the EU (then the EEC) and then did something almost as significant, in terms of our commitment to being a part of Europe, when Brotherhood of Man won the Eurovision Song Contest with the execrable "Save Your Kisses for Me". It was inescapable on the airwaves, spent six long weeks at number one and was the bestselling single of the year.

But elsewhere the times were definitely changing.

In September what is generally accepted as the first single by a British punk band, the Damned's "New Rose" was released. Within days Malcolm McLaren's 100 Club Punk Festival took place and in December the beyond infamous Bill Grundy -v- the Sex Pistols *Today Show* fiasco was broadcast live on London regional TV.

At this remove it's hard to talk meaningfully about these events as they've become so encoded within the DNA of punk's endlessly repeated history that they can feel at risk of becoming the equivalent of a faded photocopy, shorn of significance and context.

But significant they were and would all impact Adrian, Jan and Bob's lives. It's funny that Bob had christened their first band Syndrome well before punk's storm finally broke, as it sounds like a pretty perfect second or third division punk band name. As Jan has confirmed in various interviews it was however felt the band needed a new name and it was he who took the literary route and suggested the evergreen existential classic, Albert Camus' *The Outsider*. Credit to Jan for admitting he hadn't actually read it at that point. (Adrian probably hadn't either as he has long been up front about his lack of reading of the acknowledged classics, certainly in his later life he favoured rock biographies).

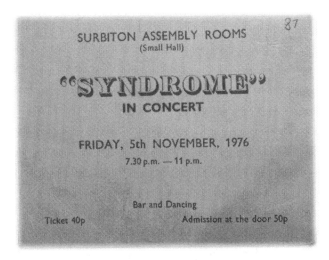

If you came across a dramatisation of the early days of punk that featured someone strolling down a suburban street, much like Hillview, while loud guitars and shouted vocals launched the lyrics of the Outsiders' "Calling on Youth" into the air, you may think it was a little too literal or on the nose. And yet in this case that is quite possibly a description of lived reality.

John Clarkson at Penny Black Music (where Jan is a writer) has done a great job in exploring Adrian's music and in particular the earlier stages of his career. Bob Lawrence was interviewed by John in 2021 and had this to say about those house sessions,

"Bob and Win were just fantastically dedicated parents. They were prepared to do what they could to support their son. We practised in the Borland family home and this was no problem at all. Win would lay on food for us to cook and they would just leave us to it. Bo had a fairly tempestuous relationship with his dad - but in relation to the band they were united. It was such a positive force to support us like he did. I can see now from my perspective as a father that Bob Borland was utilising his skills in the most productive way to help his son. Win as well was positive and supportive towards us – we were helping Bo do what he wanted to do – so we were very OK in her book."

As the band sweltered through their rehearsals in that fabled summer, crammed into the 2 Hillview living room (or occasionally at friend Martin Real's house), a shift occurred in their attitude towards the newly christened band.

As Jan relates in the sleeve notes to the Cherry Red Records five CD Outsiders box set, *Count for Something,* the mere existence of which I'm sure would have been met by Adrian's pure disbelief,

"By the time we had left school in the summer of 1976 our ambitions had grown to the point where, without any real knowledge of the music business, we hoped to 'make it'".

It's very likely Adrian's drive was already at a velocity somewhat faster than Jan and Bob's but when the members of a band unite in a shared aim everything moves up a gear.

Before long they even had a manager of sorts, teacher Geoff Cummant-Woods, and their first real gig, supporting Generation X and Siouxsie and the Banshees at the Roxy on 21st December 1976. Early gigs for all three bands and part of a trilogy of shows that effectively opened the infamous punk venue.

It must have been a baptism of fire for Adrian, Jan and Bob. But within their progress lay the seeds of future problems: three boys from Wimbledon, with public school origins and a manager with a double barrelled surname, setting sail within a movement where working class credentials were crucial. As we've seen neither Adrian, nor his band mates could be described as having been born with 'a silver spoon in their mouths'. So the future backlash would seem sadly unfair, but this perceived lack of 'cool' credentials would exert a drag on Adrian's progress when it came to his perception in the music press. It may all sound hopelessly irrelevant today, but in the UK at this time your career lived or died according to the arbiters of cool.

For now however it was all systems go with a series of gigs supporting genuinely iconic names from the punk period.

The funny thing though? The Outsiders really weren't a punk band as such.

Certainly Adrian was out experiencing the punk world, Bob Borland has described how he can allegedly be seen pogoing furiously in a TV clip of the Sex Pistols playing live.

Sex Pistols & The Clash - London Weekend Show 1976

Adrian in the audience during a Sex Pistols gig

And yes, Adrian did wear what appears to be a dog collar (as in an actual dog not a piece of clothing worn by a vicar) as evidenced on the cover of the *One to Infinity* EP but even then: take note of his hair.

Interviewed by Colin Fancy's *Safe as Milk* fanzine in 1978, Adrian was asked the priceless question, "When did you change into a punk band?" His response was,

"Well that's it, we never really were punk. We never really went all the way. For a start we all had pretty long hair as we'd just left school, I was at a really shitty grammar school, and it sounds like such a stupid thing, but to grow your hair long was an example to everybody that you're not going to be fucked around any longer".

The following exchange may seem silly but shines a light on the difficulties of navigating the cool kid's board game,

Safe as Milk, "What was that about (Tony) Parsons (influential *NME* journalist, ironically now a Tory supporting Brexiteer) having a go at you for having long hair?"

Adrian: "Well in one review I read Julie Burchill (part of a 'tag team' with Parsons, then another prominent *NME* writer who became a right-wing contrarian and who TV station Channel 4 voted 85 in their list of the *100 Worst Britons*) said I rung (sic) her up and told her not to mention we had long hair, but what I actually said was I don't care if we've got long hair, it makes no difference to the music. Ok it doesn't fit in with the image, but we're not trying to."

Safe as Milk, "What about the thing Parsons wrote about you putting bicycle clips round your flares to make them look punky?"

Adrian, "That wasn't true at all."

Safe as Milk, "They made it up?"

Adrian, "Yeah, I don't know why."

It's hard not to feel for Adrian having to deal with the fraught world of do's and don'ts he had stumbled into. And of course for him it really was about the music. However he did have an all too clear awareness of the need for coolness and, inspired by his 'education' provided by the music press and their coverage of his idols, part of him yearned to be as effortlessly iconic as Iggy, Patti and Lou. Something that would always remain frustratingly outside his grasp.

You may say, why should we care? And of course it's the music that counts but, whether we like it or not, these things matter if you want to climb the ladder to a higher level of success playing the type of music Adrian dealt in. Just ask Echo and the Bunnymen, a comparison that dogged Adrian for years. Put simply, if you're Coldplay, coolness is irrelevant but for alternative icons it sells records, tickets and definitely t-shirts.

So the Outsiders were neither cool nor musically punk as we'll discover. An interesting quandary to be in when you are latterly credited as the band that recorded and released the first "self released punk album" - copyright Wikipedia.

The Outsiders had been looking for a record deal, ironically however it was still relatively early in the brief punk era and the time when record companies waved their cheque books at anyone wearing bondage trousers was still a few months away.

Virgin sniffed around and paid for some studio time at Pathway Studio which the band used to record "Hit and Run" and "Calling on Youth". But no contract was forthcoming.

At this point it's fair to ask, were the Outsiders any good?

Adrian has been relatively brutal about their legacy, when I interviewed him in 1991 and asked for his opinion of the Outsiders his response was maybe what you would expect from an artist who valued his legacy but was always thinking about what came next,

"Yeah, that stuff's pretty awful although *One to Infinity* is OK and I think *Close Up is* actually on the verge of being quite a good band."

The truth? They were a band with a lot of promise. Some of that was realised but in the main it was a great environment for Adrian to try stuff out that would come to full fruition with both the Sound and Second Layer and to naturally discard his less appealing teenage musical tendencies. Punk allowed the band a limited profile but one that possibly was higher than it would have been without the heightened attention the era brought with it. The downside of that was the exposure to people such as Parsons and Burchill, but perhaps that was good practice for the future and a reminder that a thick skin was required when you navigate the British music press.

The band had been recording tracks at 2 Hillview since July 1976. Extraordinarily Bob Borland had taught himself the rudiments of recording technique and was engineering the sessions.

The famous TEAC four-track tape recorder

Bob described the course of events to Keiron Tyler at the Arts Desk website,

"It was 1976, I was an ordinary square. I went to an audio shop in Tottenham Court Road and got some good advice from a knowledgeable salesman called Dave on how to set up a relatively inexpensive recording facility".

Back in the '70s and '80s Tottenham Court Road was the place to go for Hi-Fi and electronics and it's lovely to imagine Bob scouring the shops for a bargain and then coming home with his TEAC four-track tape recorder and a mixing desk. How Win felt about the cables snaking their way up the stairs to Bob's study, where he operated the mixer and tape recorder, is sadly not on record.

Jan, "Adrian's dad set himself up at home to be able to record us and taught himself how to engineer music. It was quite something. Every band needs some figure who has some kind of influence or some way to push the band forward, and in our case we had the good fortune to have Bob and Win".

It seems these sessions could get quite heated with Adrian and his dad frequently butting heads. Talking of later sessions in an interview for *Walking in the Opposite Direction,* Graham Bailey recalled,

"I don't think there was a single time when I was round there recording which didn't end up in a shouting match between Adrian and his dad. Adrian would get mouthy and start swearing and his dad would come down and say I'm turning off the recording as your swearing is damaging my equipment!"

Still, this arrangement was key, here you had a genuinely independent band who wanted to take the next step but faced apathy from record labels. They owned the means of production and soon would access a method of distribution. In microcosm this was the movement that would soon sweep the UK and revolutionise the music scene, not that independently released records hadn't existed before but in the past private pressings tended more towards the vanity project than an attempt to bypass the existing system.

Many in this position record two songs and release a single, although even at this stage in 1977 that wasn't routine by any means. Bob did the sums and decided it would make financial sense to simply record and release an album's worth of songs and so, *Calling on Youth* was born.

In the sleeve notes of the 2012 Cherry Red re-release of *Calling on Youth,* Bob said the description 'independent' and 'self-released' meant little to him. He and Win were in effect Raw Edge Records and very much felt they were releasing the album on the bands' behalf just as any label would.

Combining the two tracks recorded with Virgin's funding and a selection of songs written between 1974 and the end of '76 and recorded during '76, probably initially as demos, *Calling on Youth* made its way into the world in May 1977.

Decked out in an appealingly minimalistic cover designed by Adrian the album was savaged by critics.

Appropriately it was future *England's Dreaming* author Jon Savage who did the honours in a June edition of *Sounds.* His review is actually quite balanced and apologetically critical,

"The Outsiders are all 19, and have played a few gigs at new wave venues. The Roxy hated them for their clothes (they didn't conform) which engenders a certain amount of sympathy. This is their first album, privately financed (a loan from their parents) and pressed (1,000 copies). So good for them - but was it worth it? Only just. I wish they'd waited until they'd gained a whole lot more experience because an album is terribly premature. The playing's OK (esp. "Walking Through a Storm").. but the lyrics generally are too full of intensely personal teenage angst and empty of art. Yeah - I've no doubt Adrian Borland feels what he sings/writes, but the result is a mess of cliches adding up to embarrassment. You know: Poetry. The sound is very monotonous, with even the acoustic songs failing to provide a change of mood, amateurish and ultimately self-indulgent. The garage-band sound without the redeeming raunchy sneers and swing. I'm sorry to be so damning, but, enterprise aside, this really isn't good. A home demo maybe but otherwise... Still, I suppose it's something to show people, and maybe they'll get more gigs... it's a start."

And oh yes it was Julie Burchill who did the honours over at the *NME*, who knows what Adrian felt when he finally found a place on its smudged inky pages, only to receive this roasting,

"Boy, these bozos sure blew the opportunity of the year! "Albert Camus and the Outsiders" - great name, eh? The Outsiders are three Wimbledon grammar schoolboys named Adrian, Adrian and Bob who've been together now for just one year, supporting The Jam and The Vibrators at the Roxy. The title track's archetypal running-scared riffs are chased by lyrics of quite astonishing naievete (sic) "On the Edge," your usual "live fast, die young" spiel, is amusing if you've ever seen The Outsiders - a more plump, well fed bunch of boys you've never seen, and apple-cheeked Ade has a complexion that would turn a Devon milkmaid green with envy. "Hit and Run" is your token misogynist muck; "Hit and run! Sure way to have some fun!" Honest, I could take it from a cute thug type, but I went to school with chicks who were more bad-ass than these boys. Hey, look! The next track's called "I'm Screwed Up". Great! But it's boring - nay, tedium incarnate. And all those moaning guitars, like on your big brother's "Heavy Metal" records - you know, the type of guitar that sounds like it's trying to get off but is getting castrated instead.

"Start Over" is a limp bit of acoustic torture. However I was stunned by a song called "Break Free". Abysmal lyrics "I saw you as a princess, now I know you as a slut" but a beautifully simple arrangement of chords, drums and guitars coagulating into a smooth blue aquatic soul tune, evocative of early sixties Stax. It broke my heart to see such a beauty not waving but drowning amongst such a morass. And so on until the

Outsiders fling themselves over the edge of their frantic finale, "Terminal Case". "I'm a rock and roll terminal case!" they screech. How silly. They don't even take drugs. Let me just quit the hostilities long enough to say that The Outsiders play as competently as any 19 year olds whose parents were rich enough to buy them electric toys last Christmas. The album is produced as nicely as would be any album put out on a label set up especially by the rich Daddies. But I'm just so BORED with these well-bred little students toying with our music like it's the latest coffee-table conversation piece. I'm so sick of rich bitches hooking their claws into our cause. I'm so tired of people who need to think about breathing."

Wow. Of course Julie had already created a persona that required a degree of obnoxiousness to be on constant display unless people thought she had somehow gone soft, but still it's a painful read. Setting aside the ridiculous talk of "our music" and the tedious obsession with the band's allegedly 'rich' parents, sadly there are some salient points within the vitriol.

Calling on Youth is a young band's debut album and it therefore comes with all the naivete and awkward growing pains you would expect. It's not a lost classic but, taken in context, it is a fascinating insight into the rapid progress of Adrian's songwriting.

Crashing in with the title track, it's hard not to be swept up in its Stooges via MC5 rama-lama fuzz storm. Yes it's naive but still totally right especially for the time, actually maybe for any time.

It's over too quickly to feel any doubts and then "Break Free" totally wrong-foots the punk-primed listener. Surprisingly sophisticated it's not hard to imagine some purchasers wondering if they'd bought the wrong record, particularly as the bluesy guitar solo stretches out. And yet there's a big 'but' coming. Yes Burchill was, it pains me to say, correct. As it becomes clear this is a standard girl leaves boy messed-up song, Adrian drops the word "slut" into the mix and our hopes for an interesting deviation are crushed. Yes it's standard explicit misogyny that was unacceptable then and unthinkable now.

So let's move on. "On the Edge" clears the air with an effective but derivative slice of very American sounding proto-punk. Just think how far Adrian would develop its themes of alienation only a short way down the line.

Most Outsiders songs were written as collaborations between Adrian and Jan, with Jan contributing most of the lyrics. But he can feel relieved he didn't write the lyric for "Hit and Run," another that trades in more common or garden misogyny, some nice riffing though so that's a plus.

"Start Over" is another track to confuse the would-be punks. Jan gives us a reflective slice of angst that is exactly what you would expect from an intelligent, thoughtful teen, set to an acoustic plod that sparks up a bit before fading out.

"Weird" marks a nice reaction to the bewildered and aggressive response punk as a movement was receiving. It's resolutely more like Mott the Hoople than punk and that's fine.

The self-explanatory "I'm Screwed Up" sounds for a few seconds as if it's going to turn into the Stones "Get Off of My Cloud" before continuing in Stooges-lite style with a song of very literal self-loathing.

And then we encounter the five minutes of "Walking through a Storm". It's lovely to picture the band recording this at 2 Hillview, the low-key acoustics something Adrian would do to hugely greater effect many years later.

Jan describes "Terminal Case" as, "a love song to rock'n'roll'. Sparky James Williamson style guitar locates this firmly in pre-'75 territory, but still it has a pleasing angst-filled energy.

So the Outsiders had landed their first slab of vinyl. Almost certainly never considering it would end up fetching high collectors prices in the years to come. Maybe Tim Peacock's assessment in the liner-notes of the 2012 reissue sum it up best, "not bad for a record mostly laid down by three 19 year olds in a front room".

Last word to Adrian as told to Jan in 1996,

"It was just the start, maybe *Close Up* would have been a better debut but that was part of punk, stuff got released that maybe wouldn't normally have been."

What happened next though was exactly what you'd hope, increasing skill, confidence and impressively rapid development.

The gigs continued and November's *One to Infinity* EP clearly reflects the positive effect of their move out of the living room. Hopefully they all managed to dodge the gob successfully, Bob's habit of wearing his actual fishing gear probably assisted.

In amongst the inevitably mundane gigs came an extraordinary event. Accounts differ slightly but during a brief period when the band were managed by Jock McDonald, later of the infamous punk band the Bollock Brothers, Adrian got to share the stage of the Roxy with his ultimate hero.

Adrian, "We used to do "Raw Power" live and for a joke I put Iggy and David Bowie on the guest list. Bowie didn't turn up. But Iggy actually did. I met him beforehand, but I was like 19 and I couldn't think of anything to say to him. I was just dumbstruck. I mean this was my hero! So there I was, I tried to start a conversation about the Stooges but it didn't work. I said, 'I think James Williamson is the greatest living electric guitarist'. He was drinking a whisky and he just said, 'Yeah! ' The time came for us to play and we started up "Raw Power" and he jumps down the stairs and does the second verse with us, and there's all these cameras going off left right and centre. It blew me away! Of course it blew me away! I was 19, I was just gone!"

Knowing what we know about Adrian it's not difficult to see how his mind was well and truly blown, fantasy becoming reality in the less than salubrious interior of what is now thought of as an iconic punk stomping ground.

In his interview with Penny Black Music Bob Lawrence recalled Jock McDonald being involved,

Bob, "Our manager then, Jock Mcdonald, pulled it out of the hat, and somehow managed to organise it without us knowing."

Iggy Pop on stage with the Outsiders at the Roxy, 29-09-1977

That September night (29th September 1977), when the band had been third on the bill to Sham 69, was immortalised via Per Nilsen's Iggy biography, *The Wild One*. Adrian is out of shot leaving a bemused Jan to share the camera lens with a raging Iggy Pop.

Maybe a little of Iggy's fairy dust rubbed off on the Outsiders or perhaps that's wishful thinking. Nevertheless the critical response to the band appeared to mellow a little with the redoubtable Mick Mercer speaking astutely in an *NME* live review of, "the promise of greater things to come".

One to Infinity is accordingly a huge step forward and really the point when the future Adrian Borland became recognisable, swapping awkward generic angst for something far more interesting.

This turns out to be the Outsiders most, and really only, 'punk' record, once again recorded at 2 Hillview you can only marvel at Bob's engineering skills.

The title track is a stirring ball of furious punk energy, lyrics moving up several levels from the debut album.

Next, "Uniform's" expression of disappointment in the rapidly calcifying punk movement is indicative of just how quickly promise turns to predictability and tedious 'uniformity'. Incidentally the live version featured on the Cherry Red box includes a tellingly cheeky dedication from Adrian to Sham 69.

Third track "Consequences" is an efficient Saints-like one minute forty-nine seconds that serves to clear the palate for the highlight of the EP.

With its backward tape effects, churning guitars and hypnotic bass-pulse, "Freeway" (we're still lyrically in the USA) announces Adrian's arrival in the post-punk world. Maybe this was his version of Kraftwerk's ode to the motorway, "Autobahn", whatever the intention, as it daringly leaves us with 30 seconds of spacey effects that predate what would become Second Layer's modus operandi, there's a distinct feeling of promise being realised.

This is what separated Adrian from most of the eager pretenders vying for attention in the whirlwind of 1977: a talent that grew and flourished with exposure to the light.

However the critical response was depressingly predictable.

Vivien Goldman in *Sounds* described the EP as, "nihilistic, dispiriting dross" while at the *NME* Tony Parsons was still fighting the punk fashion wars, "tuneless, gormless, gutless. The Outsiders are obese midgets who wear bicycle clips on their flairs because they think it looks punky."

No matter, *One to Infinity* was a firm step in the right direction and what came next would take us that bit closer to greatness.

CHAPTER 4

Sitting in the cafe, by the record machine...

Adrian: "I think *Close Up* is actually on the verge of being quite a good band, it's pretty Sound-like isn't it?"

At some point the years began to lose their distinct nature. Can you be sure you could culturally define, say, 2023 against 2021, or 2015 versus 2016?

Back in the late '70s and early '80s each passing year had a texture and quality that left an indelible mark on the music that fell within the apparently arbitrary borders of date and time. Yes of course there was blurring of the lines, the bands still hammering away at creating low-grade, generic punk survived well into 1978, but elsewhere the better music was morphing into something far more interesting. In such a landscape it's not hard to see where Adrian saw his future.

As the established record companies scrambled to keep up with new music that they often didn't understand or appreciate, let alone like, the music scene was changing by the month not year.

1977 had seen records hitting the UK top ten that no A&R man could even have conceived of 12 months prior. In the Silver Jubilee encrusted June, The Sex Pistols lodged the incendiary "God Save the Queen" in the top three of the singles chart and many classics from all the main players followed them onto *Top of the Pops* the UKs flagship TV chart show. And yet at the top things went on as they had for years, with the years' best selling single proving to be Paul McCartney and Wings inescapable "Mull of Kintyre".

As 1978 began grinding into gear, even though its top seller would turn out to be "Brown Girl in the Ring" by Boney M, the real story was to be found elsewhere. It was a case of innovate or die: punk would soon be pronounced dead in the water and many artists were already painfully aware of its limitations. It was now the post-punk bands that were Adrian's natural peers, not that the term post-punk was really in usage in the UK at the point, punk and new wave being an extended catch-all.

The roll call of post-punk brilliance that began in 1978 included, but wasn't limited to: Wire, Magazine, Gang of Four, Siouxsie and the Banshees, Public Image, Devo and many other hugely different and influential bands.

As Jan explains, "We thought punk was really exciting, for young people it was a massive release, but it settled down into a new conformity. For us, and the more ambitious bands like the Banshees, Public Image and the Clash, you really didn't want to be restricted to this 'three chord trick'. So people went beyond punk and people invented the term 'new wave' to cover what was happening."

Adrian must have looked at the crammed pages of *NME* and *Melody Maker* and felt both inspired and acutely conscious of the urgent need to move forward.

Around him in the wider world, economic pain, unemployment and nuclear paranoia were keeping people awake at night and rightfully so. Waiting in the wings for her chance to rise to power, Margaret Thatcher was already stoking fears of immigration early in 1978, describing the danger of the UK being, "swamped by people with a different culture".

As cultural stimuli all of this fear and unease would become the foundation of much of the most vital music of the following few years and certainly fed into the next stage of the Outsiders' musical development as illustrated by their second album, *Close Up*.

Stepping out of the front room at 2 Hillview the band decided to record at a professional studio and chose the relatively well-known Spaceward Studios, which at that point was located in a basement in Victoria Street, Cambridge.

The songs selected for *Close Up* (aside from "Conspiracy of War" which went back to 1976) were written between late 1977 and early 1978 and marked a clear lyrical and musical move forward when compared to the band's earlier repertoire.

However the cracks were already starting to show. In mid-1978, before recording began, Bob Lawrence dropped the bombshell all bands dread. He'd not unreasonably begun to feel that things were moving too slowly and had decided to go to university that autumn, staying on to record the album first.

Committing to a band is a strange and fragile thing, in many ways it requires people to place their life on hold based on a remote dream where some sort of success is attained. It's a huge stretch and can put a lot of pressure on people, especially in a country where unemployment was such a growing concern. For Adrian it may have already been the case that he was approaching the point of no return; work, in any conventional sense, as an alternative to pursuing a life in music, was becoming unthinkable. Beyond that was the growing dawning that he was just not remotely suited to such a 'regular' life and maybe never would be.

In a hilariously monosyllabic section of the previously mentioned *Safe As Milk* fanzine interview, Adrian's work status is probed,

Colin, "Don't you work?"
Adrian, "No"
Colin, "Do you get more money out of it than they (Jan and Bob) do?"
Adrian, "No"
Colin, "Do you get any money?"
Adrian: "No, well some, not very much though, not enough to live on."

Adrian goes on to confirm he's 'signing on' which meant he was on unemployment benefit or the 'dole' as it was known. In 1978 it was still possible for people to access such benefits without the labyrinthine performative cruelty that was later introduced into the system by successive Conservative governments. It's no exaggeration to say that without the dole Britain's independent music scene would have been decimated.

While this served Adrian's massively strong desire to pursue his musical muse it would also expose him to the strange, often listless and formless life of a musician at the lower end of the table of financial success. Such an existence may not be a problem for some, but for him it held inherent dangers. While Jan has confirmed that there were no obvious signs of Adrian's future mental health issues during the period of the Outsiders' existence, the experience brought a taste of what the future would hold more of: lots of waiting, between gigs, before recording and after that before releasing the product of those labours. It's not difficult to see the lyrics of at least one future Sound song as a pained and rueful reflection on the isolation Adrian would experience,

"These are the longest days
I've ever known,
Groan out of my bed,
Look at my watch, way too soon,
Too much daylight leads to
A night life and the fear
Of another day that's going
To last four or five years."

The Sound, "Longest Days"

As we shall see, there's much about the life of a working musician that doesn't exactly lend itself to the maintenance of good mental health.

But right now the important thing is that the Outsiders have recorded what will be the last release on Raw Edge Records and, although they don't realise it yet, the final Outsiders record.

Close Up slams out of the gate with what should have been a single, in fact it was planned as one as early as March 1978, but for some reason that never happened.

"Vital Hours" is a fantastically strong barnstormer that definitely draws from the swagger of the Saints again. Adrian's delivery has moved up a gear and the whole thing tears along at high speed, who knows whether it would have made an impact as a single, it's certainly possible as it's genuinely catchy. Once again there's a very entertaining exchange in *Safe as Milk* specifically about "Vital Hours,"

Colin, "Who did you want to spend some 'vital hours' with?"
Adrian, "Well at the time, anybody!"
Colin, "So there's no feeling in it?

Adrian, "NO FEELING IN IT?! Well of course there is! If you're shut in a bedroom and you think of what you could be doing. Of course there's feeling in it! Desperation!"

Even at 44 years' remove you can feel the pent-up angst and don't you just love the sheer cheek of the interviewer? A great snapshot of the wonder of fanzine culture, not afraid to put an artist on the spot.

As track two begins we have a strongly recognisable glimpse of the Adrian Borland to come. "Observations" starts with a strummed chord and then Adrian's voice enters the picture, its tone sounding far more controlled and subtle as befits a song of detached 'observation'. It's quite a moment and is reinforced by the almost 'Sound-like' guitar work and the subject matter of suburban monotony. Interestingly we're back on a 'freeway' although now it's definitely a British motorway. Adrian is leaving his influences behind as we listen, it's a significant step.

"Fixed Up" takes us back to punkier territory but is still a pretty effective blast of energy that makes its point and gets out of the way for "Touch and Go" with its churning rhythm and slashing guitar, delivering a nice slice of nervy tension. Again Adrian's playing demonstrates how fast he was developing at this point. Nice bass from Bob as well.

Back in the *Safe as Milk* interview an allegation of racism is levelled at "White Debt".

Fairly clearly a misunderstanding, as the song consists of an attack on the cruelty and greed of empire that ends up let down by a clunky lyric. In the early Outsiders/Sound era the biggest musical risks came when attempting too literal political or social comment, but then it's a tough area to stray into, hard to articulate and easy to lampoon.

Side one's closer is on much safer ground, "Count for Something" deals in justified existentialist angst raising questions that remain eternal, musically it's an efficient rocker, no more, no less.

"Out of Place" on the other hand bears definite traces of the 'sound' to come, subtract a little of the guitar raunch and it's not difficult to see it sneaking into the early Sound repertoire.

"Keep the Pain Inside" sees Adrian's singing edging away from proto-punk aggression into something more nuanced and familiar. Jan has mentioned trying for something like the Stooges "Dirt" with this one which you can kind of hear, nice double tracked vocal effect about two thirds of the way in, but perhaps not enough going on to justify a duration heading towards the five minute mark.

Some very Sound-like guitar and bass makes "Face to Face" more interesting musically, but the lyric isn't quite fleshed out beyond its title conceit.

More suburban angst drives the pretty enjoyable "Semi-Detached Life", Bob Lawrence is great on this one driving it along effectively and setting us up for album closer, "Conspiracy of War". Jan's lyric again foreshadows what the Sound would do far better with "Missiles" but is too heavy handed to survive the passing of time. Striving for the epic, the track ends up falling just outside the limit of the band's abilities.

The word 'promising' undoubtedly applies to *Close Up*, in places we are tantalisingly close to a future where Adrian would move up the leagues to a point where he had no need of feeling subservient to his influences. As a record it absolutely demonstrates the role of the band for Adrian: namely a place he could try things out, finding out what worked and what didn't, then either discarding or developing those ideas. What this means for us is that when the Sound finally appear from the wreckage the awkwardness is gone and we're thrust straight into the presence of greatness.

At the time the critical response was predictably mixed. John Hamblett's *NME* review reminds us how even-handed some critics tried to be in those days, describing the album as, "patchy but promising" he rightly had concerns about the songs that dealt in 'social criticism' but concluded by correctly assessing the Outsiders as, "a band with a future".

Correct in that they would have a future, but just not as the Outsiders.

Ironically our friends at *Safe as Milk* really didn't like it, dismissing the songs as, "sub Stooges yawns sung in a half-baked yankee accent." Ouch.

But back to that interview, seek it out because it's hard not to read Adrian's playful and humorous responses without smiling, his earnestness and desire to make music that mattered shine through. In your head you can hear his voice, anxious to please, ready for the future.

When he says, "we're taking a very different direction now" it's crystal clear he was already moving on.

Despite being recorded in summer '78 *Close Up* didn't make its way into the world until March 1979.

By that time the Outsiders were already a different band. The sleeve, with its endearingly homemade lettering, features a fisheye lens shot of the trio, but it's not the band that recorded the record. A certain Graham Bailey is standing at stage left, with the rear of the cover greeting him, "Hello to Graham Green, new bass guitarist as on sleeve".

Allegedly not named after the author but, according to Jan, rather his on-stage clothing colour of choice at one point (briefly each band member chose a colour). Graham, by then working at the BBC, had remained close to Adrian despite being separated by attending different schools. He'd been at several Outsiders gigs, including Iggy at the Roxy and even provided a source of transport for the non-driving Adrian and Jan.

More interestingly he and Adrian had already been messing around writing and recording songs at 2 Hillview. Clearly that house was a veritable hotbed of music in the late '70s. The Outsiders came first and Second Layer (or as originally intended, 2nd Layer), well, second, as per the name. As we shall see, the role of Second Layer and the way it provided Adrian with a far more electronically focussed creative outlet, beyond straight ahead song-based post-punk, shouldn't be underestimated but probably has been over the years.

The paths of the two acts inevitably criss-cross, so it's no surprise at all to find that Graham replaced Bob in the Outsiders, appearing on stage with them for the first time on November 18th 1978 at the London School of Economics. Graham was already playing bass and so smoothly integrating himself into the band was not difficult.

Interestingly also joining the band onstage towards the end of the gig that night was none other than Bi (more correctly Benita Biltoo at that point) Marshall.

Bi was then studying psychology at university as she explained to John Clarkson at Penny Black Music in an extensive and illuminating interview,

Bi, "I was in the first year of doing a psychology degree, and a friend of Adrian's was on my course. We happened to be talking about music, and when I told him the bands that I liked – Kraftwerk, The Stooges, early Roxy Music - he said, "My God, I have a friend who has exactly the same tastes as you. He's the only other person I know with such bizarre tastes, I must introduce you both," and that friend was, of course, Adrian."

Next thing she knew, Bi was sitting in on an Outsiders rehearsal following Graham's arrival (Bi and Graham were in a relationship at the time).

It's a wonderful thing when you feel something great taking shape whether by accident or design.

When interviewed for the *Walking in the Opposite Direction* documentary, Bi paints a vivid picture of the sheer randomness of events,

"I was just sitting there and Adrian said, 'Do you play anything?' yes piano, 'Well that's a bit big, can you play anything else?' Yes, clarinet, to which he replied, 'OK bring it along to the next rehearsal...' "

"I was a bit concerned, basically they're a punk band, what on earth do they want a clarinet for?"

Bi was primarily a keyboard player but at least initially found herself adding improvised clarinet and sax to a few numbers at live gigs without being a formal member of the band.

This was classic Adrian, the breadth of his musical knowledge and appreciation meant that seemingly unusual juxtapositions like this were welcomed rather than avoided. Just consider: within a relatively short space of time Adrian had helmed a touring band with multiple record releases, while simultaneously exploring industrial electronics via a side project and was now the driving force behind a musical evolution that would bring both elements together, placing him in a position to take advantage of the next wave of musical changes to come in 1979 and beyond.

In amongst all this activity was a fun diversion: the Crazies, featuring Adrian, Graham, Bi and Jan. Bi detailed the background to the recording that belated appeared on vinyl in 2021,

"It was some songs recorded with (the late) Pete Williams, who became Lord Sulaco (of Adrian's later side project, the Honolulu Mountain Daffodils). He was a friend of Adrian's and was one of the Crooked Billet crowd. We used to call them the Crooked Billet crowd because they all used to meet at the Crooked Billet pub in Wimbledon, and Pete was part of that group.

Pete was working full-time and had a bigger budget than any of the rest of us, and one night down the pub he said to us, "Well, if I write the lyrics will you guys write the music to go with my lyrics?" The thing with Pete was that he always coming up with these schemes that never really amounted to very much. We said, yes, that we would and didn't think about it any further. Then a couple of months later he said, "Oh, by the way I've finished my set of lyrics and have booked a studio." We looked at the lyrics, and they were quite, well, odd!"

Bi has said it was the most fun she had recording with Adrian and the evidence certainly suggests it was an enjoyable experience, you can hear the Outsiders/Sound crossover in action but your mileage may vary depending on your reaction to Pete's vocals.

No doubt it provided extra impetus for the final metamorphosis of the Outsiders into the Sound.

This very brief and fluid period of the band would have gone undocumented but in 2021 Cherry Red Records released the exhaustive *Count for Something* five CD box covering pretty much every nook and cranny of the Outsiders' existence. There on disc four is something to make any Sound fan's pulse quicken. After the November LSE gig and before the end of the year, the band convened for a rehearsal at 2 Hillview. It was very shortly after this that Jan reluctantly decided to announce his departure from the band disheartened by the response to *Close Up* and planning, like Bob Lawrence, to go to university the following autumn.

But before all that we are able to witness the Outsiders in full-on transition mode. Sadly Bi wasn't there but Graham was and so we get to hear his familiar insistent bass tones as soon as unreleased track "Settled Dust' comes to life. It's a thrilling experience and feels like being allowed to sit in and witness a new beginning. "Settled Dust" itself rides that tense clipped guitar style that Adrian would deploy to great effect in the next few years, but really the signs are all over this session.

Three songs would endure as far as the Sound's posthumous *Propaganda* 'album' and in the case of, "Night vs Day" all the way to *Jeopardy*.

Although Adrian, Graham and Jan didn't realise it yet, in spirit, the Sound had been born.

CHAPTER 5

It's a physical world and I wanna feel…

And we're there.

1979 dawned and change really was far more than just in the air. The dramatic shifts in music of the previous three years were finally making waves in the mainstream as a trickle became a flood. This years' bestsellers can't hide that shift. Nudging Art Garfunkel for biggest selling single of the year came Blondie with "Heart of Glass" while Tubeway Army scored a massive number one in the shape of the monumental "Are 'Friends' Electric?"

Numan's impact is probably underestimated. His success took many by surprise, certainly within the music press who never forgave him for it. Overnight he demonstrated how an essentially indie artist could translate a singular musical vision that utilised electronics and punk to create something entirely new. But more importantly you could make it sell.

Elsewhere, not yet in the charts but nevertheless having a deep and long-lasting influence on 'alternative' music: the arrival of Joy Division. A band whose impact would touch Adrian personally and a name that critics would occasionally throw at the Sound with accusations that they were somehow copycats.

Socially and politically the curtain was coming down on a decade that had failed to deliver on the promise of the late sixties, while a new even more brutal reality was waiting in the wings. The country would reject left-wing politics and within months vote to begin what would become the Thatcher-era of extreme capitalism with, for some, all the pain that came with it and for others the often obscene gain.

Incidentally Adrian's politics were probably highly influenced by the events of the next couple of years. I once asked him about this and his response was interesting but probably not surprising,

Me, "Do you like England anymore?"

Adrian, "Yeah, I like England. I don't like Thatcher's vision of it, I hate the Tories!"

Me, "Yeah, it goes unsaid."

Adrian, "Does It?! Can you tell from my lyrics? Yes I'm left-wing, not extreme, I vote Labour. I think that what they're doing is largely right. Anyway, I like what England could be, not what England is, although I still love the place."

The country he loved was undergoing a process of change that would leave it a colder and harder place to exist in, something that would directly impact Adrian and couldn't help but influence his music.

It was in this shifting landscape that the Sound were finally to take their first steps.

But right now they needed a new drummer. Jan was still around and would assist the new recruit as needed but without the right person the band, still called the Outsiders, couldn't move on.

Luckily manager Geoff Cummant-Wood had a friend who might just fit the bill, Mike Dudley, at 28 quite a bit older than his future band mates.

Mike described the process to John Clarkson of Penny Black Music,

"I'd been playing in a little band locally at the time, in Kingston in Surrey where I used to live, and a friend of mine who was managing the Outsiders was looking for a replacement drummer. He asked me to go along and watch them with a view to joining, so I went up to somewhere in Clapham. The 101 Club I think it was called. To be honest, I didn't really like them very much. I thought they were a bit of a racket, but a couple of friends that I'd gone along with convinced me to give it a go."

In an interview with Robin Murray at Clash Music, Mike hints at the difference in approach his joining would bring,

"I suspect that Adrian had known from early on that, although he was as enthusiastic about the first wave of punk as we all were, it wasn't going to last. He soon wanted to move on and explore more creative depth and this is why his manager, Geoffrey Cummant-Wood, approached me as being a different type of drummer when Jan wanted to leave the Outsiders. I tried to encourage a more exploratory approach to making music with the band, although I do remember one very early rehearsal round at my place where Jan was trying to teach me how to play along to The Stooges' "TV Eye" – 'Just hit the kit four to the bar, Mike....' "

Jan tells a similar story in the sleeve-notes of *Count for Something,* and says Mike was, "unaware of our main influences and visibly taken aback by the radical simplicity of the drumming on our version of "TV Eye." "

Mike was living in a squat at the time and the band actually set up in a room there for the 'audition' that was more a case of drummer trying out the band rather than the other way round. David Eastgh interviewed Mike about this period in some depth via the *C86 Show* podcast and gives a fascinating insight into the changeover underway, including hilariously his total unawareness of the existence of Iggy Pop.

I'm sure that amused Adrian no end.

In John Clarkson's Penny Black Music interview, Bi touches on the age gap and possible difference in aspirations between Mike and rest of the band,

"We didn't share the same musical tastes as Mike Dudley. He was eight years older than us. When you are in your early twenties and somebody is that kind of age older than you, it can make a huge difference. He was living in a squat, while we were all still living at home. He was in a way much more grown-up and wasn't from London. He had totally different ambitions as well as totally different tastes in music. I think he thought a lot of the stuff we were doing was too 'way out'. I can believe that was what he said."

But Mike had already been transfixed by punk so maybe he wasn't so far off the rest of the band's wavelength. There's a fascinating section of David Easterhaugh's interview where Mike vividly describes hearing the Sex Pistols, "God Save the Queen" on the John Peel show and it being a turning point in finally knowing what he wanted from his life. Mike has recounted the 'bolt from the blue' type experience to me and it neatly sums up the energising effect punk could have for people who weren't, by any description, actual punks.

Whatever the differences in experience, age and taste, Mike was in.

This was very early in 1979, and with Bi's involvement deepening, the first Sound line-up was effectively in place under the guise of what would be the final incarnation of the Outsiders.

In another excellent interview with David Eastaugh, Graham Bailey confirms that at this point the band felt like, "a really tight gang" whose only mission was to make music and if they made a living from it then that would be enough. (Although there are repeated suggestions Mike Dudley had greater aims success-wise, and really, why shouldn't he have?)

More generally such modest aims were very much typical of the indie scene in its glory days.

We can now look back and assume the band was on a broadly untroubled trajectory to at least some level of success, but the passage of time has a habit of smoothing out some of the bumps along the way and certainly erases the doubts that people lived with at the time.

Interviewed for *Walking in the Opposite Direction* Bob Borland outlined his parental concerns for Adrian during this period,

"I was slightly concerned that Adrian was in danger of not having a proper career. I recall just before the Sound were named that he was contemplating doing a business management course."

(Interestingly later in the *Book of (Happy) Memories* Win Borland confirmed he had applied and been accepted at a college).

This may well have been wishful thinking on Bob's part as it's hard to imagine Adrian submitting to the organised tedium of a business management course. Back in 1992 I asked him whether he'd ever had a job,

"No, music is my job. I did once (around 1979 - '80) work for a photographer packing wedding albums. I used to wonder what would become of all those people."

In a later interview he also expressed the desire to see what he could do to "unsettle" the people he saw in those wedding photos...

The thought of Adrian wistfully packing those albums away underlines the picture of him looking at conventional life as if through a window, wondering how it all worked.

Talking recently to Adrian's then girlfriend, Julie, it seems he used to get his work done pretty quickly and then spent much of the rest of his time writing notes and stories for her. This was also typical of Adrian as Julie confirms, "He was very, very sweet, really lovely, totally different to the sometimes manic person you'd see on stage."

Instead he continued with what could be described as a 'shadow life' while everyone else was out at work he was totally band and music focussed, justifiably, but later as the career momentum died down then the real challenge began and the risk of isolation hovered ever present. When the thing you love provides the impetus behind your life, and at least in part helps to block out the noise in your head, then when that drive begins to ebb away life can become problematic and potentially tenuous.

In terms of romantic relationships, over the years Adrian had only a small number that went beyond the opening stages. As we shall see this was in part a case of loving the intensity of the initial period of a relationship and struggling with what came next, but by the early '90s he was confessing, "I'd love a serious relationship, that's what I'm searching for."

But at this time in Adrian's life such cares were still a way off. Instead he must have begun to feel the thrill of having the personnel in place who could help bring his rapidly evolving music to life, in a way potent enough for the right people to finally take notice.

In early 1979 the Outsiders recorded twelve songs that were used as a demo tape by manager Geoff Cummant-Wood who sent them out to venues to get gigs. The tape was never intended as an album but was eventually released in 1999 (very shortly after Adrian's death) by Renascent under the title, *Propaganda* and credited to the Sound.

In fact the sleeve-notes contradict the above and say the 'album' was recorded AFTER the name change. Never mind, things can get hazy when a band is naturally evolving into something else. Adrian completed a detailed note for the release which was remixed by him and previous Sound producer Wally Brill. It's a great piece of writing and further supports the idea that Adrian had a fluent understanding of the broader sweep of the music scene he was part of. It's funny to think he could surely have had a decent career as a music journalist, but of course that wouldn't have satisfied him.

He does clarify that some of the songs were recorded by the Outsiders and others after the name change, explaining that, "The Sound are caught here at a blurred moment of metamorphosis emerging from the Outsiders."

Adrian is suitably self-deprecating about the "Surrey meets Detroit" vocals, the youthful angst and Roxy-style clarinet bursts. What's particularly interesting is his mention of Joy Division, reminding listeners that the band hadn't heard them yet, stating, "Ian Curtis had yet to affect my vocals or outlook as he obviously did post *Unknown Pleasures*".

He sums it up astutely by saying, "a parallel life was had by all it seems." Clearly Adrian had a great sense of how music was changing and realised his place within that. Sadly that means he would also be acutely aware of the unfairness inherent in the parceling out of praise and credit, as critical consensus takes form and solidifies over the years, sometimes relegating the Sound to the role of followers something that was absolutely not the case, as the evidence here shows.

Mike Dudley has expressed his liking for the recording and correctly says that, "It sounds like a completely different band, there's much more melody and structure. It had obviously taken a few steps forward into something more interesting."

Listening to the songs now, it's hard to disagree.

"No Salvation" goes as far as to mention a 'new dark age' and is driven by a very fluid bassline from Graham, some nice *"yeahs"* in the background suggest the band was deep in the groove. Lyrically? Nuclear paranoia and creeping unease and, as Adrian notes, a "faithless adolescence.'

Even groovier, "Deep Breath" convinces in a way the Outsiders generally tried but failed to do. It speaks volumes of the band's speed of development that this song would soon be outclassed by newer material.

As a phrase the "Cost of Living" has inexorably taken on an ever more sinister tone, a price you must pay as the alternative, while free, is no alternative. As a song, it ups the game on the Outsiders by delivering social commentary in less prosaic (lyric from Jan), more eloquent terms, while rocking out very enjoyably.

Lovely creeping dynamics are conjured on "Quarter Past Two," Adrian delivering what he describes as "Blue Oyster Cult guitar figures" the recording places you in the centre of that living room watching everyone's eyes lock.

And then a familiar friend arrives: an even more stripped back and ashen version of *Jeopardy's* "Night Versus Day". Great bass, fun sax and memorable lyrics from Jan guiding us into similar territory the Cure inhabited on 1980's *Seventeen Seconds*, a key album by another band of suburban outcasts. The "huddled homes" that "shine like sequins and sapphires" and the queasy second verse where reality slips and the line between "savage and civilisation" blurs, are gems whether in this version or the very slightly slicker later take. Sublime.

Strangely the song had been cited as referencing Adrian's illness by using the theme of the tension between darkness and light. Of course the lyric was composed by Jan, so possibly a good reminder not to be overzealous in joining the dots too neatly.

Future single, "Physical World" is purely (slide) guitar, bass and drums and was presumably unintentionally self-referential when it asks, "Can you hear the sound?"

Oh, and how great is "Static"? Atmospheric, unsettling and really worthy of a place on *Jeopardy,* it's strangely timeless and possibly the undiscovered jewel of the album. Bet it was great live.

Clearly Adrian was under no illusions about the depressingly dirty business which he was diving headfirst into. Listen to his and Graham's guitar/bass interaction, groovy yet again for two suburban kids. Not the worst lyric ever despite what some have said, it's far too sardonic and dripping with scorn and sadly truth, for that. Would have made a fun B-side.

Adrian continues to exorcise his James Williamson fixation on "Propaganda" itself, something he's happy to own up to in the Renascent sleeve-notes. A fairly slight but enjoyable song that wouldn't make the grade when new material arrived.

It's hard to top Adrian's description of "Words Fail Me" as, "Stax on speed" and interestingly to note a rare acknowledgement of soul music influence on the Sound. When Adrian sings, "trying to speak from the heart" you realise how hard it is sometimes to tell his and Jan's lyrical perspectives apart. 'Post-punk power' in excelsis.

Apparently, according to Adrian, "jammed up in dank Waterloo rehearsal rooms" (maybe Alaska Studio?), "One More Escape" was built on a Graham Bailey bass line and moves along very nicely. It probably should have been retained for further work, as Adrian suggests when expressing the view that it needed a producer to, "realise this one fully."

The Bunnymen famously mocked "Missiles" but it's hard to escape the sheer logic of its very simple question, "Who the hell makes those missiles, when they know what they can do?" Why would someone not ask that of someone? It's a socio-psychological rabbit hole down which we could easily go, but a valid plea for an explanation and a shatteringly raw version of a future live Sound juggernaut.

And that's *Propaganda:* the album that wasn't actually an album but still works very well as one all these years later, fading out on a lonely sliver of echoing feedback and static hiss.

What it does reinforce is the impact Graham, Mike and Bi had in terms of bringing Adrian's songs to life, no doubt pushing him to further heights with his songwriting.

In an unpublished mid '90s interview with Jan, Adrian commented on this process,

"It was a pretty natural progression from the Outsiders to the Sound really, one of the main things was that I took over more lyrical control. That was important to me. Focussing the music and the lyrics together, it was always a slightly strange situation doing the music for tracks you'd not written! There were things at the end of the Outsiders that were close to the Sound, it was a natural evolution really."

Adrian's own description of the 'process' is beautifully honest,

"With the Outsiders I was so hooked into that Stooges noise thing, then I woke up one day and thought, the best thing to learn from Iggy is to be yourself, take their attitude, but be yourself. A year when you're 19 is such a long-time. You're so attentive to everything around you. I can never take away from the Outsiders letting me get closer to what I wanted to do. Without that the Sound would never have been able to get on stage at the Amsterdam Paradiso and knock 400 people flat!"

The band were now rehearsing two or three times a week fitting in around each other's work and study commitments, Bi recalls weekday sessions ending at 10:30 pm so she could get the last train back to Camberwell where she was living.

All were ready for something more but first a name change was needed in order to fully shed that old skin.

Around this time Adrian decided to call old friend and jamming partner Steve Budd, saying he'd decided to revamp the Outsiders and he wanted Steve to see and hear the results.

Steve, "They were rehearsing in Mike Dudley's house and then they went and did a gig at a place called the Kaleidoscope (today a nationwide Christian charity), a drug rehab kind of hang out in Kingston".

The band were really in flux and Steve recalls at that stage unnamed. Things get predictably murky but it seems the final Outsiders gig took place on the 29th April 1979 at the Old Swan in Kensington.

Steve, "They didn't have a name and I remember having a discussion with Adrian about it. 'the Sound' as a name is pretty naff and I can't recall if it was Adrian who came up with it."

Names are so crucial, the Sound is obviously not a moniker made for the internet age and yet I've always felt it had a direct simplicity that worked perfectly for the band's music and stance.

Today Mike confirms no one loved the name but it was something that everyone, sitting round the table in the pub that night, could at least accept. Not an unusual situation when it comes to band names and their origins. As the years have slid past he's become more or less happy with it. Who actually suggested it? It looks as though it was down to Mike himself or possibly Steve Budd, time has rendered memories indistinct.

Certainly Steve was ready to guide Adrian towards the recording studio.

Steve, "I was there at the first gig and I thought, oh, this is good! I'd saved up some money from going out on tour as a roadie with a few bands. Not a lot of money, maybe a few hundred quid. I fancied trying to put out a couple of records and spoke to Adrian. He had this drum machine and had bought a Wasp synthesiser and said he'd just come up with this stuff with Graham, we're gonna try this little side project and I want to go in and record it properly, how about we do something? He also said, 'How about you come and play guitar on it?' I said, 'OK, great!'"

And so Second Layer, perhaps unexpectedly, overtook the Sound in the queue for a debut record. As a result we are about to visit a fairly important location in Adrian's story, Elephant Studio and, more importantly, to encounter a significant character in the Adrian Borland story: engineer and producer Nick Robbins.

Steve, "I hired Elephant Studio and we recorded and mixed all three tracks in a day. I came away with the quarter inch tape after paying fifty quid. I looked in the back of *Melody Maker* or *NME* (probably *MM* as it was the main place for advertisers linked to the mechanics of the music business) where there were small ads for pressing records. There was a factory somewhere out in East London who could do the mastering and the pressing. I went there, delivered the tape and ordered 500 copies."

This was typical for the times, enthusiasts finding their way around the process of making and releasing a record, a journey Bob Borland had been on before him. Steve had actually forgotten the labels and sleeves but luckily the pressing plant reminded him.

Steve, "We ended up with 500 pre-folded sleeves and I got my mate Kevin, who did the rest of the sleeves for the label, and we screen-printed them. I remember being so excited that we had 500 records, but had no idea what to do with them. Then I remembered Rough Trade (trailblazing record shop in London's Ladbroke Grove) who would buy independent records. I went in with a box of singles and walked up to the counter and was sent down to speak to Geoff Travis (legendary Rough Trade boss)"

Figures like Geoff, although at the margins of Adrian's story, still have significant influence over events. It was after all Travis who gave Bob Borland advice when he set up Raw Edge Records. In the days before 'how to books' or the internet, knowledge such as his was like gold dust, Geoff had made the mistakes and learned the hard way and was happy to help others find their way. That day after listening to the three Second Layer tracks he agreed on the spot to buy all 500 copies, paying cash straight away. Imagine the sheer thrill of having that happen with your maiden release? The result was that Steve immediately ordered 500 more.

Geoff had a network of shops that would take copies of a good record on the basis that, in the climate of the day, it would sell. DIY in action to the nth degree.

John Peel plays and good sales followed and for a split second it seemed the stage was set, not for the Sound but Second Layer.

CHAPTER 6

"Somewhere between the Clash and Kraftwerk: that's where you'll find me..."

Second Layer occupies a strange unresolved place in Adrian's labyrinthine catalogue. It's probably safe to say an under-exposed zone that, as we shall see, was a project he felt didn't reach its full potential. Still, its significance shouldn't be underestimated.

Not that one creative outlet was more important than the other, Adrian's brain didn't seem to work in that way. When he devoted his time to something, whatever it was, he gave his all. It was rather a case that ultimately the Sound went on to take precedence simply because the momentum built in that direction and the music was clearly capable of connecting with a wider audience which isn't always something you can say of Second Layer.

And, after all, there are only a certain number of hours in the day.

But right now Steve Budd's Tortch-r Records had their first release: Second Layer's *Flesh as Property* EP, catalogue number: TOR 001.

The positive critical response must have been a novel experience for Adrian. In the *NME*, Andy Gill described the EP as, "Easily the best of the current bunch of home-grown electronic garage-band product."

'Electronic garage-band' was probably a genre that should have gone further as it was a pretty good description of Second Layer's modus operandi.

Record Mirror's review was beautifully prescient, Mark Nicholls giving an 8/10 and taking the view the EP was, "What I think will be relevant in the eighties."

Melody Maker's Ian Birch was equally keen, "More than a hint of the

Human League in the vocals. The songs actually jostle now and again with some muscle and inventiveness."

They were all pretty much right. Listening to "Courts or Wars" now is a thrilling ride. Drum machine pushed to the point of collapse with Adrian's overdriven guitar and Graham's brutally plucked bass. It's more of a sonic collage than a song, but still it's actually really memorable. So much so that the House of Love may well have come across it and used the track as a jumping off point for their future indie classic, "Christine." Something that can't have missed Adrian's attention.

Adrian loved Suicide, the musical incarnation of Alan Vega and Martin Rev's more than unsettling urban visions, and the bleak and brief "Metal Sheet" bears this out, a sonically efficient piece of musique concrete.

Although uncredited on the sleeve Bi Marshall contributed a very distinctive component of "Metal Sheet," as she explained to John Clarkson at Penny Black Music,

"With 'Metal Sheet' I said to Adrian, 'You should have a beeping noise like a heart monitor on a life support machine,' and he said, 'That's a good idea. How would we do that?' He had a go on his Wasp synth and it sounded absolutely dreadful. It's really difficult to play the cardboard keys due to the electro-static sensors. You had to be really precise, hitting it right in the middle of each note as otherwise it wouldn't sound at all, and so he said, 'When we go into the studio, you'd better come and do it because you're the only one who can!' "

Finally, "Germany" with its wandering bass, and a vibe similar to something like Iggy's "Mass Production," Adrian's guitar taking distant inspiration from something more 'heavy metallic'. Lyrically we're back on the autobahn.

It feels like some kind of vindication to hear these songs today and think, yes Adrian and Graham were comfortably at the head of the pack when they made this music. Second Layer was emphatically NOT Adrian and Graham being dilettantes and dabbling with proto-industrial styles. Yes this is technically a little harder to grasp than the Sound but it's not willfully inaccessible.

It's the epitome of what Adrian told Jan back in 1996,

"I've always been true to what I wanted to do (musically) and that doesn't mean you have to be Einstürzende Neubauten! It doesn't have to be avant garde."

This is crucial when it comes to understanding Adrian and his music and, beyond that, his approach as a person. Honesty in intent and execution was at the centre of what he wanted to do and he paid a price for that commercially, however he wasn't willfully obscurist so pretty much all the music he made is accessible on some level.

Adrian later correctly pointed out that Second Layer shared some of their sound with Joy Division, but this was music written and conceived before either he or Graham had heard a note of Curtis and company.

Adrian, "The guitar sound and the way that Graham played bass in 1977 was already 'Hookish' but (Peter) Hook became the prominent figure so Graham apparently was copying him, well bollocks! You should listen to Graham playing bass with Second Layer, he always played like that!"

These were acts working simultaneously and without knowledge of each other in a pre-internet world. Products of the strong currents spreading across music, combined with a complex, very specific, mix of the social and political conditions of the time. Make no mistake Adrian loved Joy Division and felt a kinship with Ian Curtis that ran deep. But the wider point here is about the 'texture' of music in the late '70s. The simplistic view taken by some critics of who was first seems in hindsight to be based more on their own knowledge and awareness at the time, rather than an actual reflection of the development of individual acts.

Julie Aldred (at the time Adrian's girlfriend and later the Sound's tour manager) has a partial recollection of, together with Adrian, attending a Joy Division gig at the legendary Nashville Rooms in Kensington. That would date the gig as taking place on 22nd September 1979, which makes sense as by then both Second Layer and the Sound's musical approach was pretty much defined. By all eye-witness accounts the show was as intense as you'd imagine. Clearly a date-night for Adrian was most likely to involve music.

Bi Marshall succinctly summed up part of the drive behind Second Layer when she said,

"Adrian's musical tastes were so diverse, I think that Second Layer satisfied another part of him. As well as allowing him some creative freedom and satisfying that need to be more adventurous."

Sadly Second Layer were destined to be incorrectly viewed as a footnote. But then the passage of time is a great leveller and we can now better appreciate their role in Adrian's story.

Flesh as Property reached the world in December 1979 just as the seventies sputtered to a halt. A pivotal year was about to begin, an event laden stretch of 12 months that saw punk become ancient history, if it wasn't already. A diverse trail of classic debut albums from many legendary names making music in the general orbit of post-punk would follow. From the Bunnymen to Killing Joke, U2 and the Comsat Angels, the list is long and would include a record called *Jeopardy* from a band named the Sound.

As the years pass 1980 feels more and more significant in musical terms. The suicide in May of Ian Curtis cast a long shadow even in a music world where the main source of info was still the weekly music press.

There was a growing range of bands articulating the paranoia of the age in more articulate and interesting ways with electronics no longer a novelty but often a necessity. Meanwhile the new romantic subculture, that was growing in reaction to the apparent dead-end of punk, would burst into the mainstream.

Surveying the best sellers we can see the inroads made by acts who were in some way bringing the influence of punk and post-punk to bear, the Police had ascended to the role of biggest band in the country and topped the list with "Don't Stand So Close to Me" while, Bowie, Blondie, the Jam and Dexys were all firmly lodged in the end of year top twenty.

Socially and politically the country was reeling as a result of Margaret Thatcher's scorched earth economic policies. Recession bit deep, unemployment and inflation rose and riots in Bristol were a taste of more unrest to come as the '80s unfolded.

Adrian and Steve ended the year 'flush' with the success of Second Layer and quickly hatched the idea of another EP, but this time it would be the Sound making their debut,

At the very end of '79 back into Elephant they went, recording three tracks as quickly as the Second Layer songs. The studio was located, appropriately enough, in Elephant and Castle south London, at the time a fairly gritty area, and was on the upper floor of a Victorian warehouse where it occupied a couple of rooms.

As Graham Bailey recalled in his interview for *Walking in the Opposite Direction,*

"Elephant Studios was great, I think we chose it because it was cheap, we may have got a package deal with the Second Layer stuff. It was exciting, Nick Robbins is amazing to work with. One of my memories of Elephant back then was they had a leak in the ceiling in the control room and had polythene stretched across, collecting the water which they had to empty when it filled up. It was a small, friendly studio and that made all the difference."

It was a major contrast to working with Bob Borland as Nick was happy to do weird and wonderful stuff like record a distorted snare drum on "Physical World", whereas Adrian's dad would threaten to turn the equipment off when things started going 'into the red'.

Nick recalls that first encounter with a band he would come to know well,

"I was working in a small eight track demo studio and they were booked in just like any other band. I hadn't heard of them before. When they arrived, they set up in the normal way that a band would do and I put the microphones up. We had a little talk about what we were going to do. I didn't remember thinking there was anything unusual. You know, they were just a young band. But we started to record and it became very clear, very quickly - the band had a particular talent with Adrian, because he knew exactly what he wanted to do. He was very good at directing people and he was very, very determined."

Adrian's enthusiasm and drive again making an impression on people around the band, what's of note is that whilst opinionated and determined Adrian was nevertheless someone that people didn't grow to dread working with, unlike many who show similar traits. This would serve him well throughout his career including when he tried his hand at production work.

Released early in 1979, the *Physical World* EP was catalogue number TOR 003.

Strangely enough TOR 002 was an EP by a new band from Kingston called Cardiac Arrest, (later to become the Cardiacs) formed by the late Tim Smith who had already shared a stage with Adrian when his first band Gazunder had supported the Outsiders. Perhaps more interestingly Cardiac Arrest happened to feature a young Colvin Mayers on keyboards.

Critically, *Physical World* followed the precedent set by Second Layer. None other than the often unfairly maligned Paul Morley greeted the EP at *NME,* his description of the Sound as making, "monochrome, barbed metal music" must have had Adrian feeling he was on the right track. Although the mention of Joy Division would not be the last, still his conclusion, "One of the most promising new groups I've heard lately" would have sealed the deal. It was all a long way from what Adrian had become used to with the Outsiders.

Cardiac Arrest with a young Colvin Mayers and Tim Smith (both right)

Housed in a sleeve designed again by Kevin Grey, the three tracks painted a dramatic picture of the embryonic Sound.

Sharp clipped chords echo back, bass kicks in and drums explode and we hear "Coldbeat", the Sound on vinyl for the first time. It's hard not to feel a shiver down the spine before getting carried away on the release of all that pent up energy. This is the Sound as dance band, functioning much as Joy Division's "Transmission" did at virtually exactly the same time. Artists working in parallel expressing the dread of the time but shaking it off in defiance. As Adrian breathlessly sings, "the fear is never empty," but the beat takes us somewhere else and we survive another day.

They would go on to have greater songs but it's a pretty effective opening shot.

As is "Physical World" itself; serrated-edge guitar cuts through the air and Graham digs deep on bass as Adrian reverses his desire not to feel and now wants to embrace it all. Even at this early stage lyrically Adrian was working with the extremes of feeling, the up and the down, that exist in us all. In "Physical World," he's done with talking and instead throws himself into a brutal world knowing the danger but doing it anyway. The passage of time has loaded the imagery of a fragile body taking its, "chances with the chrome" while cars crash, with additional meaning taking into account Adrian's future failed suicide attempt in the path of an oncoming vehicle.

The mood alters with "Unwritten Law," an early more stripped down version, Adrian's vocals treated with effects. Immediately we're shown evidence that the Sound's range has expanded and now includes pieces where the band can duck and weave, ratcheting up the tension. The later *Jeopardy* take is a little (relatively speaking) sleeker and benefits greatly from Bi's subtle synth shading, but both versions are valid in their own way.

If they'd never released another record *Physical World* would still be a much sought after rarity, a band setting out their stall and playing as if they may be using up their only chance to make a mark. As it is, an original copy will now set you back at least £150 and there's even a facsimile re-release if those prices are too rarified for you.

Perhaps it's no surprise that at this point the Sound became the priority. Steve Budd has an interesting take on why this happened,

"I think he (Adrian) thought he couldn't play Second Layer live. Dudley was a fantastic drummer and when he became part of the band, and you had Bi, who was meant to be just sax, there was kind of this X Ray Spex vibe to it. It sounded so good it was just obvious. The Sound had songs while Second Layer were more influenced by Suicide, not that they didn't have songs, but the Sound was something you could do really well live. There was momentum around them."

Steve's involvement was about to become deeper and more extensive,

"They had Geoff Cummant-Wood managing them but he had no

contacts, he could drive a van and was a nice bloke but Adrian said, 'Could you get involved in helping run this thing?' So I said, 'What do I need to do?' Find an agent, book some shows, find a tour manager, so I was effectively being the label as well and it was at that point that I said let's record an album. I felt that's what we should do. I had around £500-600 and spoke to Nick Robbins and said, 'Can we record an album?'"

Without overstating anyone's importance, the careers of many bands move to a next level of some sort due in part to the abilities, or lack of, on the part of a manager. It's a harsh reality that most musicians are not made with the thick skins and gift of the gab required to gain the cooperation and help of other key people from A&R to bookers and beyond, at all levels of the difficult to navigate music business.

Nick Robbins with Adrian at Rockfield Studios

Don't forget, Adrian had already realised the challenge this presented and sang of the relevant roles in the inimitable *Propaganda* track,

"Music Business,"

"We make the record and the records get sold, the art is in the selling"

He clearly knew where his expertise lay, but also maybe anticipated some of the problems ahead when he sang,

"But treat us like trash and we'll burn up our anger in style."

The Sound and managers: not an always easy story. Reflecting on the issue of management in 1996 Adrian described the Sound as, "the least 'managed' band ever" while understanding the advantage of being in control but conceding it undoubtedly cost them in terms of success and also left them dealing with additional stress when least needed.

It's intriguing to hear Mike Dudley's recollection that at some point later down the line Adrian had a conversation with U2's manager Paul McGuinness. Adrian developed a well documented fixation with U2, and Bono in particular, partly good natured but sometimes verging on borderline obsessional. This veered from believing the band had stolen song ideas to something approaching a love-hate relationship where he expressed an unrequited desire to meet Bono.

But Adrian was a practical person and clearly saw the benefit of having 'heavyweight' management. Mike was certainly right when he commented on the effect such a manager could have had on the band's career saying it would have been like,

"Sitting on top of a rocket, basically."

So Adrian's conversation with Steve Budd was probably a very astute and sensible move, involving a third party who had already proven his worth and who had been known to him since they jammed together as teenagers.

On the other hand you have Graham, who in his interview for *Walking in the Opposite Direction* said of Steve Budd, "I didn't really like him very much. I mean he was nice enough but he was into this weird character building stuff like Exegesis (infamous 'therapy cult'), but he could get things done and was formative in getting us the Korova deal."

But that's the nature of things when it comes to relationships in and around a band, sometimes people don't get on for reasons that come directly from their individual strengths. So naturally a sharp-elbowed manager may not be to everyone's taste. But whatever the feelings, when you want to move forward you need some help.

Fascinatingly at around the same time Steve recalls going out for a meal with Adrian and some interesting companions,

"It was in 1980 after a Moonlight Club gig, Paul McGuiness, U2's manager, took us out for dinner. We ate at the Portobello Hotel, which at the time was a very posh rock'n'roll haunt. I think Adam Clayton was at the dinner too and maybe the Edge."

Although the meeting was social rather than business it's intriguing to wonder what was discussed between the two young bands and their respective managers, and how much this may have fed into Adrian's ongoing Bono/U2 obsession.

In any event it was at least partially at Steve's suggestion that the band soon moved to the stage of planning and recording an album.

Another package deal was arranged with Elephant Studio and work on what would become *Jeopardy* began.

Adrian recalled the process in his 1996 interview with Jan,

"We didn't embellish it much, we recorded a lot of it live, "Missiles" was almost entirely live, we just recorded the vocals on top, a method we carried on using later.

We did it in about three songs a day then we'd have a week off. So basically it took about four months. We'd maybe have something we'd played live and then try to do a new version of it. So it was a combination of things from the live set and brand new songs. We'd get bored so we'd always come in with something new like say "Hour of Need" or "Desire" to spice things up a bit."

Adrian, and the band itself, were moving fast at this point like new bands do when the creativity is bursting to get out and be put down on tape,

"We started recording *Jeopardy* in October '79, so say a song like "Heartland" was recorded very quickly after it was written, maybe two weeks, it became a live stalwart shortly after that."

So we learn a song that became a Sound classic was essentially brand new when its recorded version was created, something that may surprise some people.

As will Adrian's comment that he retrospectively saw a Joy Division echo in "I Can't Escape Myself,"

"Lyrically it was maybe overtly influenced by Joy Division. Musically we did get the sound we wanted on that, we were looking for this kind of 'clanky' Can-like sound. It had a deliberately useless snare drum sound, with Graham and I telling Dudley to turn off his snare so it sounds deliberately crappy! It sounds better like that."

Nick Robbins, who engineered but didn't 'produce' as such, confirms what Adrian says about recording live,

"I was effectively recording their live performance. They came in with all the parts, which they knew from rehearsing. The vocal would be overdubbed and perhaps another guitar part. But they were quick and relatively simple recordings. They were very organised and Adrian had in his head what he was after but still wanted the band's participation, he wasn't dictatorial in any way."

Nick's memories of Adrian tally with what we already know of him,

"He learned very, very quickly. You only had to show Adrian something once and he would remember that. So he could use a technique again very easily. He had an exceptional imagination actually. He could think how things would sound before he heard them. So he was great to work with from that point of view. It was very exciting."

It's worth remembering though that no one, with perhaps the exception of Adrian himself, could anticipate the record's relative importance,

Nick, "I've got to be truthful and say, no, we didn't. Not really. It's easy in retrospect to say that, to see why it would have become important when you see what else happened afterwards. But at the time, no, we didn't."

So with an album 'in the can' what was next for Adrian and the Sound?

Sadly first an event would occur that would cast a shadow over the year for many people, the ripples spreading out beyond the immediate tragedy for family, close friends and bandmates. On 18th May 1980 Joy Division's vocalist Ian Curtis committed suicide by hanging at his home in Macclesfield. Factory boss Tony Wilson has said that Curtis spent the hours prior to his death listening to Iggy's *The Idiot*.

When interviewed for *Walking in the Opposite Direction* Julie Aldred spoke movingly of the affect Ian's death had on Adrian,

"We heard that Ian had committed suicide, and Adrian was really, really upset about that, deeply upset. I think he felt a huge sort of kinship with him and he loved the music, but also particularly the lyrics.

Julie describes a disturbing event the following night,

"I remember we actually went to a party, possibly the night after we found out. Adrian almost couldn't do anything. He wasn't speaking to anyone really, he was just in this world of his own. Then at the party, I don't know why, but they played the theme song to *MASH*, (the single of the TV show theme was number one in the UK that May) "Suicide is Painless." We left and I took him home because he just couldn't cope with it."

More tellingly Julie wondered,

"It wouldn't surprise me if it was almost that he realised it (suicide) was always an option, not a good option, but an option."

But for now Adrian was able to tread the tightrope between pouring everything into his music while not suffering the toll maintaining that intensity took later in life. The sheer momentum the group had built up provided the distraction, if you can call it that, maybe more the fuel for his boundless enthusiasm. The downsides were yet to surface.

Meanwhile The Sound were playing clubs and pubs in and around London, venues like the 101 Club in Clapham, the Fulham Greyhound and the Moonlight Club, while Steve Budd was busy doing the things managers are supposed to do: getting a record deal.

Steve, "We did a gig at the Moonlight Club and I got a call from Greg Penny who was the A&R guy at Korova Records, he was an American producer who Rob Dickins (MD of Warner Brothers in the UK) had hired. Rob and Greg came and saw the band play a storming gig, and on the way out said, "I want to sign them!"

Korova was Warner Brothers' 'boutique' imprint and had been founded the previous year. So far there was one other band on the label: Echo and the Bunnymen.

Steve and Geoff Cummant-Wood, who was still involved, went to see Greg and Rob at Korova. They were keen to do a deal.

Steve, "They wanted to buy the album we'd recorded and to 'tart it up' and release it. So they bought it, for maybe £10,000, the majority of that went back to the band and in effect I became their manager. We had an agent, Mick Griffith at Asgard, who was a dedicated and passionate supporter of the band. We were then pretty much straight into touring with the Bunnymen."

Bi recalled the exact date of the signing in her interview with Penny Black Music: 21st July 1980.

Bi, "At the time we were quite reluctant to sign with a big label. If I remember correctly, both EMI and Korova were interested simultaneously in signing us. We decided to sign to Korova because, even though they were part of Warner Brothers, they were supposed to

be a new subsidiary that was going to concentrate on independent bands."

Adrian's recollection of events was slightly different,

"Steve Budd sent a tape of about 8 bands that he'd got involved with to WEA and they picked out "Heartland" as being the best song and then we just sort of got the deal. From there we got onto Korova which was run by Rob Dickens who was the head of WEA. It was sort of his personal label, with the Bunnymen.

As to whether it was a good deal or not, a few years' later Adrian confirmed,

"It was a terrible deal! Money-wise it was pathetic, but we didn't really care about that. We never really have cared enough about that stuff; on the other hand we have survived."

On signing the band were all given copies of the Bunnymen's classic debut *Crocodiles*. Not exactly an expensive recording, but a world away from the demo album the band had themselves made.

And then money started to get in the way; Greg Penny was told Korova's budget for the financial year was essentially already used up.

So what would become *Jeopardy* would need to be released as it was, making it allegedly the cheapest major-label album since the Beatles' first, costing less than £1000 pounds.

Still, almost immediately, things stepped up a gear.

In amongst all this activity the second Second Layer EP, *State of Emergency,* slipped out with less fanfare or attention than it should have. Its title track was an urgent, almost dub-like slice of vital machine music with Adrian screaming himself hoarse. But the thing is; Second Layer weren't playing live and the Sound emphatically were.

For them live dates took up a large portion of the rest of the year, including the band's infamous tour with the aforementioned Bunnymen and, bizarrely, gigs with the UK Subs.

The Bunnymen tour was a mixed blessing. Playing much larger venues must have been great but not everything was rosy,

Bi,"I got on fine with the Bunnymen personally, but there was a lot of antagonism there because they had been forced to take us on tour and could have had someone buy onto the tour for about eight grand, which at the time was a lot of money. Korova, however, decided that because there was no budget to promote us, the easiest thing would be to put the two Korova bands on the same tour. The Bunnymen were forced to accept us, and some of the guys didn't hit it off."

It was on this tour that certain Bunny-persons mocked Adrian via their own version of "Missiles," with the refrain, 'Who the hell ate those rissoles,' inserted. Scouse humour can be brutal, but Ian McCulloch topped even that with his nickname for Adrian; 'the singing pig.' A cruel reference that others have returned to over the years.

All of this added up to a less than optimal experience from the perspective of some members of the Sound.

In an interview with the Arcane Delights website in 2021, Graham said he believed the shows were meant to be a 'joint headline' arrangement, although that seems unlikely in retrospect as the Bunnymen were by then already far more well known than their junior labelmates.

According to Graham (in the interview for *Walking in the Opposite Direction),* Pete de Freitas and Les Pattinson were friendly and open, Will Sergeant less so and Ian McCulloch as aloof as you might expect.

As is common, there were a fair few practical jokes played during that tour, some funnier than others. It's probably easy to understand how the cream pies in the face wind-up that the Sound were victims of was probably less amusing than intended.

In the same interview Graham expressed some regret the Korova deal itself,

Graham, "It's hard to look back in hindsight but I think signing to Korova wasn't the smartest move. They were OK to work with. But the bulk of their promotion budget went to the Bunnymen. I understand why."

Whether Joy Division or Echo and the Bunnymen it was to be Adrian and the Sound's burden to be irrelevantly compared and contrasted. But that's what critics tend to do, faced with describing a new artist you reach for the easy close at hand comparisons.

New supporter Steve Sutherland reviewed the band at the Moonlight Club in a September issue of *Melody Maker*,

"The story goes that before signing wimp-rock trio America, Warner Brothers first checked with Neil Young to offset accusations of plagiarism. It would be churlish in the extreme to suggest that Korova went through the same procedure with the Sound, but comparisons with successful labelmates Echo and the Bunnymen are inevitable."

It's a prescient review that highlights what would become a recurring issue for the Sound: a band that could blow anyone off the stage but

who were somehow still in the shadow of other acts and were neither charismatic nor mouthy enough to cut through the noise.

Still, Sutherland's final words must have been music to Adrian's ears,

"They're my dark horses for THE sound of 1980."

It was time for that debut album to finally be released.

CHAPTER 7

You've got to hit that peak, before you crash back down...

1980 was hurtling to its end, and for Adrian there must inevitably have been a sense of arriving at the threshold of something he had never dared believe would happen.

From all those front room and garden shed jamming sessions to the half-empty gob-soaked gigs at the Roxy he was now releasing his, and the Sound's, major label debut single.

The front cover of "Heyday," designed by Kevin Grey, feels altogether apposite: a figure resembling Adrian (or is that just me?) pushes upon the doors from a confined dark space opening onto a huge warehouse or auditorium beyond.

The future beckons.

"Heyday" acts as a clarion call to the disposed. Blistering guitar, no longer so in thrall to the Detroit gods, Mike smashing hell out of his kit, Graham's lithe bassline snaking under it all and Bi's interjection of synth at just the right points. Lyrically it feels like a recognition that the young will be betrayed again and again, perhaps Adrian was looking at the wreckage of punk and wondering, what happened?

"You were trying to find your feet, can't believe they'd cut you down..."

B-side "Brute Force" honoured a Sound tradition of issuing tracks that were as good as, or only a fraction of a notch below, their album siblings. Some Sound B-sides were simply album tracks that got bumped because Adrian and the band had come up with new songs in the gap between writing and recording an album.

Hearing the track today is a salutary lesson in the timeless subject matter of many of Adrian's songs. The clear simplicity of the lyrics ensures that.

"It hides behind their orders, strikes out when you answer back."

Apply those words to a country of your choice, here in the UK a person can now be arrested for walking too slowly down a street as a form of protest. I'm sure that would have fascinated and horrified Adrian in equal measure.

Released in the second week of September critical reaction was reassuringly favourable, *Melody Maker* succinct but positive,

"Razor blade guitar and pumping bass push this post-punk song along with an adrenalin kick. Worth checking out."

Record Mirror were equally happy with what they heard,

"Having been told by various sources that this is a band to look out for, you immediately become hypercritical. But this passes the test with flying colours - it's a catchy song, but catchy without being light and throwaway. The excellent drumming deserves a mention too."

But new fan Dave McCullough, over at *Sounds*, was the most vocal in his praise,

"One of the most exciting and most astonishingly adept big label debut singles I've heard since the Jam's 'In the City'".

This level of praise would continue once *Jeopardy* was released in November.

Let's remember what else was happening musically in late 1980. The zeitgeist was located in London down at the Blitz Club not far from where the Roxy had once been. Like the Roxy it would be a brief moment in time but the Blitz and the 'new romantic' scene it fostered would help create a new music movement in which surface became as important as content. Not good news for a band like the Sound who seemed to deliberately cultivate an anonymous image.

Ironically their photo included on the inner sleeve of *Jeopardy* would be taken by a photographer who would go on to huge success later in the '80s,

Bi, "There was no budget for the artwork for *Jeopardy* either. The sleeve is a Russian film poster that Greg (Penny) managed to buy for £50 because it had just come off copyright. He thought that the woman with her face blanked out on it looked like me with my big glasses, and so that it was sort of appropriate. Spencer Rowell, a photographer friend of mine, took the photographs for the sleeve. He was an apprentice photographer who I had befriended in my local pub in Camberwell, and used to photograph food for cook-books. He was quite happy to do it for free other than the cost of the film. He saw it as something else for his portfolio. In fact Spencer went on to take that famous Athean photograph of the man holding a baby. His girlfriend was a make-up artist, and she came along to the photo shoot and did our make-up for free."

The session took place in Hanway Street just off Tottenham Court Road. Looking at the photo today, Adrian staring intensely into the lens, it's easy to imagine the whirlwind the band were caught up in during the final few months of 1980.

Spencer, who at the time was part of the selfsame new romantic culture taking hold in a very different world to that of the Sound, recalls today how the band played a couple of songs at a party he held in his studio in the East End, blowing everyone away in the progress and also remembers seeing the band at one of their Moonlight Club gigs around that time,

"When you were in the room with Adrian, you really got the impression he was using his art to express something from much deeper below the surface, he was brilliant."

(Interestingly there was an earlier proposed cover and track-listing for *Jeopardy,* the song "Falling Boy" being included and becoming the title track and inspiration for the, less impressive and very literal, cover).

Jeopardy's opening song "I Can't Escape Myself" has become one of Adrian's most well-known songs, with the Nouvelle Vague cover version helping that happen. It has also become the subject of speculation in terms of links with Adrian's mental illness. Bob Borland memorably spoke of this in *Walking in the Opposite Direction.*

However we must also bear in mind that Adrian valued ambiguity in his songs, he said as much on several occasions including when talking to me in 1991 about another song on the album, "Unwritten Law",

"I shouldn't really say anything, a song like that is ambiguous, that's how it should be."

For him every song was personal but it's been said that the art of great, lasting songwriting is knowing just how much detail to leave out. There's significant skill involved in making a song both sufficiently universal but at the same time personal enough to potentially mean something to each individual.

As Graham has said, "It's as if he's speaking directly to you, even I would think sometimes, is that song about me?"

So we shouldn't over-interpret Adrian's songs in an attempt to fit them into the narrative of his life. The sentiments expressed in "I Can't Escape Myself' certainly could apply to an internal battle Adrian himself was engaged in, but equally it's part of human experience for many people to find themselves seemingly dragged down to earth by their own behaviour and learnt ways of reacting to events. The song hits home precisely due to Adrian's skill as a songwriter and the bands' vivid and harrowing interpretation, exploding in all the right places and at exactly the right moments. Scarcely believable but possibly the most potent version of this signature Sound song may be the BBC session recording, made for the Mike Read show in October 1980. Faster, more intense, Bi's synth panning across the stereo field like a portent of oncoming violence, it's jaw-dropping. If anyone doubts the Sound's potency, direct them here.

Jeopardy then gives us another Sound classic in the form of "Heartland." A brand new song when recorded, this heroic adrenalin fuelled plea for hope and belief in something better became a keystone of the band's sets and of Adrian's songwriting history. Adrian the bloodied but unbowed fighter refusing to give up.

Side one takes a breath and dives into the dark with "Hour of Need." A beautifully judged band composition that springs from a recurring theme in Adrian's music: the agony of time passing slowly and quietly, its sparse non-production works perfectly.

Bi's sax on "Words Fail Me" is gloriously unexpected, but as thrilling as the song is, she may have a point when suggesting *Propaganda's* "Static" would have made for a good swap in the running order.

By the time we close side one with "Missiles" few can have doubted the raw brilliance of the Sound's debut album. Later Adrian would talk of moving away from agit-prop sloganeering but at this moment "Missiles" was a totally rational response to the nuclear paranoia that was part of living in the year 1980. As a psychological query, "Who the hell makes those missiles when they know what they can do?" feels entirely reasonable and that fact overcomes any attempt to mock the simplicity and directness Adrian was employing to get his message across. Of course it became an absolute monster when played live in its many versions over the years.

Beginning with single, "Heyday" before delivering the questioning title track, side two doesn't miss a beat. Offering a queasy, lurching acceptance of emotional danger Adrian's call and response guitar and feedback solo are minimal genius.

"Night Versus Day" makes the jump from *Propaganda,* along the way trading the sax for a more effective ghostly synth part while Adrian delivers a helping of lovely sustained feedback, something a producer may have baulked at including in those days.

And then "Resistance." Graham tears through the song with a great barely contained bass part swerving across the road but staying in control. More evidence to counter any allegations of fatalistic acquiescence in the face of existential torment.

Another song with multiple interpretations, "Unwritten Law" receives an upgrade from its previously released version. Adrian confessed to me in 1991 that, "I couldn't tell you what it's about!" But when pressed confirmed it was more about suicide than revenge or justice,

"We stab at our faith to keep it alive", that's a good line, but what does it mean? Perhaps it means we criticise ourselves to keep ourselves going, yeah that's a good start!."

"Desire" may for some have been a step too far towards the superficially morose and minimal at the time, but listening now provides an elegantly dynamic close to an emotionally demanding record.

Mission accomplished.

The critics? They loved it.

In *Melody Maker* a totally won-over Steve Sutherland was rightly in love.

"*Jeopardy* is one of those records that makes me want to throw all the windows open, crank it up to full volume and blast it out to the world. It clears my head of boredom, strips away the gloom and single-handedly restores my belief in the power of pop to make people stop, think and question."

He trashed "Desire" but hey we can't all be perfect, going on to conclude that,

"*Jeopardy* has got more spirit, more soul and more downright honesty about it than any other record I've heard this year. I'm sorry if this is all too over the top but take it from me. Investigate now and discover the true sound of the Heartland."

Hidden within the review though was an assessment that sowed the seeds of future problems. While mentioning the Bunnymen, Sutherland praised the band's ignorance when it came to "'the red herrings' of style and presentation", red herrings they may be but sadly factors deemed crucial by many in the months to come.

Both *NME and Sounds* gave a maximum five stars.

Dave McCullough at *Sounds* mentions the Bunnymen/Teardrop/Joy Division 'thing' again, but judges that the Sound are, "on to a winner."

Still he also worries about the Sound's lack of awareness of 'style' while saying Adrian's "passion goes unquestioned." There is then a remark that feels personal in a way that probably would be unacceptable today. Talking of the band's visual incongruity he says, "Borland looks like a ten year old Benny Hill." A description that couldn't be further away from Adrian's heroes and their iconic images.

He finally assesses the Sound as, "a strangely strange band."

Paul Morley did the honours at *NME* in a review that praised the Sound for their simplicity but again concluded on an ominously prescient note,

"The Sound will be forced to hang on and hang on through an ignoble anonymity, waiting for something to happen which never will and then they'll fall apart. Cheated by a media that is perverting the whole course of pop history."

We must be careful ascribing wisdom to music critics, we are all bundles of flesh, bone, blood and endless contradiction after all, however these words feel painful when read back today. They seem to come from a love of the music but an understanding and genuine concern that the band were possibly not set up to succeed in the musical climate of the early '80s, or maybe any era.

Maybe the Sound, and Adrian in particular, had signed up for a fight they could never hope to win?

Looking back the warning signs were there from the start hidden within justified praise.

A few years later, in 1984, the Sound were rebounding from their time in the wilderness and were interviewed by *Jamming,* a fanzine that had briefly become a fully-fledged magazine,

Incredibly Adrian was asked the following question,

"Maybe you're just too chubby to be popular?"

Undoubtedly both crass and cruel but Adrian responded with a self-awareness that hangs heavy with pathos and is tragically disarming when seen in print today,

"Too chubby to be popular - exactly I'd look awful in a video. I wish I was thinner, of course I do, I wish I looked like Iggy or Bowie, because I could still be honest with myself. But if it's really come down to that, to what you look like, then I don't even want to know, I might as well give up."

The interviewer in fact cries out for the Sound to be heard, clearly he or she loves Adrian's music and almost despairs at the brick wall they've hit asking Adrian if he'd rather be an honourable failure?

Adrian's answer is once again very revealing of the integrity that lay at the heart of his approach to life and music, a distinction that for him was meaningless.

"Well, I'm not trying to be successful, that's when things get hollow, when you're calculated and contrived."

Not only does he cleverly reference Bowie in his answer but confirms everything we know of him, for Adrian it was always the real deal or nothing.

He goes on to say,

"There's something in our music that's not meant to be liked by everyone, I know there are certain things I want to say that those people really wouldn't want to hear."

The interview closes with a question and answer that are both heavy with future significance,

"Is it important for you to be successful or is the struggle, the striving, more vital?"

Adrian, "The struggle is important in everyone's life, because to give up is surrender. I do see why people give up and I wouldn't say they're wrong, maybe they can't see the point anymore. I haven't reached that stage yet."

When we understand what Adrian felt about himself and his path ahead it helps to trace the progress of the next few years of the Sound's existence and the obstacles that would be thrown in their way.

Perhaps after all the professional assessments of *Jeopardy* and the portents of future difficulty it's better to simply return to the sweet and succinct view put forward by Dead Can Dance's Brendan Perry. In 2013 he sent a tweet describing *Jeopardy* as a,

"Existentialist post-punk jewel."

Whatever would happen that will never change.

Adrian and the band were in a period when the attention of the music press was on them. Bands dreamt of such an opportunity to be interviewed and splashed across those smudged pages.

Bi Marshall was asked by Penny Black Music whether she was involved in these interviews, her response hints heavily at turbulence ahead,

"Yes, (however) Adrian's paranoia had started to kick in quite early, and he didn't like the fact that there was too much attention put on the only female member of the band, so he actually asked me not to speak at interviews."

Certainly the full page interview in the 22nd November 1980 issue of the *Melody Maker* didn't include a quote from Bi, or Mike for that matter. Par for the course Steve Sutherland describes Graham as "thin" and Adrian as "plump" and mentions Joy Division and the Bunnymen. While the style of music journalism at the time had its various faults, it was nevertheless often thoughtful and constructive, what's very interesting is the way writers expressed concern at pitfalls that could befall the acts they were championing. It all feels like a very different world when contrasted with todays' approach.

Sutherland zeros in on something that was very important for many bands at the time, honesty and integrity. Again a very long way from a world where the environment for artists means a desperation to be liked removes much of the mystery, and the best thing that can happen is to be added to the right Spotify playlist or have your music licensed to a popular Netflix show.

"Their attitude is straightforward, they don't hide behind a disguise. Which brings us to the subject of honesty. The Sound are, if such a thing exists, an honest band. Adrian characteristically spots the pitfalls,

'Anybody who actually comes out as being honest, that might be, or probably is, a pose. Maybe we're degrading honesty right here and now. I don't think we are. Some other people might do but they're the ones who are screwed up, not us.' "

There's something beautiful about listening to Adrian and the sheer idealism he never really lost. He may never have been a true 'punk', but here was a person who grew up through the positivity of the late '60s, was immersed within the tumult of punk and came out of all that with a crystal clear clarity of purpose in terms of what he wanted to achieve and the way he wanted to do it.

This was clearly not a 'pose' and the Sound's audience quickly recognised that. The music came first but the genuine, compassionate and thoughtful approach Adrian brought to what he did deepened people's connection with the band. The result was that many of these listeners stayed the distance regardless of the level of 'success' the Sound achieved.

Right now though the band were enjoying that relatively brief period when the spotlight was on them, something that feels good, as Graham confirmed during an interview for *Walking in the Opposite Direction*,

"It was very elating to suddenly see yourself plastered over the pages of the music papers, "Hey look, mum, dad, you know that proper job I never had, we'll I'm all over the papers!"

But amongst the natural feeling of elation that comes with recognition, the issue of money reared its ugly head, not catastrophically but nevertheless enough for a sliver of bad feeling to creep in.

Both Graham and Bi, when interviewed for *Walking in the Opposite Direction*, have said they were surprised to find the songs on *Jeopardy*, in the main, credited solely to Adrian. There are joint credits on several songs but clearly this caused dissatisfaction as people felt it didn't reflect the way songs were written.

Bi, "When you feel you're in a band with friends, I think the betrayal is felt so much deeper and it just didn't reflect the way that we worked. Not only did it not reflect the way we worked, it wasn't what we'd agreed."

According to Bi, Adrian tried to smooth things over by offering to make up people's share of royalties. Whatever the exact position, or the truth of the claims to joint songwriting credits, the result was problematic.

It's a little too ironic to mention that Echo and the Bunnymen apparently anticipated a similar problem and as a result always went for a four-way credit on all songs.

The atmosphere as 1980 drew to a close must have been somewhat clouded and although there's no suggestion it was a result of the bad feeling over songwriting credit, the first casualty was Bi.

Accounts vary, as is usually the case in such affairs, but it appears Bi was fired shortly after the Bunnymen tour. Certainly she was gone by early 1981.

Even in this part of the story Echo and the Bunnymen play a small role: during the tour Bi had been ill with a nasty bacterial throat infection but had nevertheless continued performing. The Bunnymen camp had made an effort to look after her and so she'd spent a degree of time with their 'gang', something which Adrian was aware of and which could have been interpreted as 'disloyalty,' taken against the background of uneasy feelings around the shows, with also suggestions of the onstage sound being sabotaged.

During the tour the band had been sleeping on people's floor, hotels having been deemed out of budget, not an ideal situation for someone with a temperature of 102 degrees. Subsequently it emerged that allegedly there had been a £2000 budget for accommodation and expenses. Bi's reaction to finding this out was obviously not positive.

Whatever the rights and wrongs there was clearly a mix of factors in motion that ultimately lead to Adrian suggesting a band vote as to whether Bi stay or leave.

By all accounts Graham abstained for obvious reasons but the decision was made that Bi should go and apparently Mike Dudley was dispatched to deliver the news.

Bi, "When they decided that I should be fired, I tried to have a discussion with Adrian about the reasons but all he said was, you were too friendly with the Bunnymen and that was disloyal to the Sound. At the time I thought, yeah, you're not going to tell me the real reason, but maybe that was the real reason."

It appears the discussions were fractious,

Bi, "Adrian was always exploding, he was like an unexploded bomb almost from the very beginning. He had a very fiery temperament and would often just explode. We'd just wait and eventually he'd calm down and whatever it was that had been annoying him just sort of seemed to evaporate."

When I spoke to Adrian on this subject back in 1991, he acknowledged the brutality of the decision but felt it was correct,

"She could only play the things I gave her to do; she wouldn't develop her own style. She had to go really."

Me, "Ruthless!"

Adrian, "No it wasn't, it was heartless! She wanted us to become more like Ultravox or something!"

And that's where the notion that Bi had become a New Romantic came from...

After all these years there's a lack of specifics and still some sadness surrounding Bi's departure. She'd been an important part of the band and had brought something unique and dynamic to their sound. But, just as she went on to a fulfilling career as a professional artist, the Sound would continue to their next stage of evolution gaining a member who was, in different ways, just as important if not more so.

Had Adrian Borland and the Sound already "crashed back down"? No, not yet, there were artistic highs to scale and a second album to write and record. Oh, and a lot of gigs.

CHAPTER 8

A voice says you can't stop...

Adrian began the new year with his head full of opportunities, problems and assorted issues that would need to be dealt with.

The four-piece Sound was now down to three and that gap needed to be filled as there were gigs to play. The band had garnered praise and so expectations were high from press, record company and more listeners than Adrian could have ever dared imagine.

When interviewed by Jan in 1996, one of the first questions was "How has it all turned out compared with what you expected at 18?"

Adrian pauses, chuckles and says,

"I wasn't that optimistic about it actually, so it probably turned out better than I thought it would! You never know what's going to happen do you? So you just think, make a couple of singles then forget it and get a normal job. I'm proud I've had the opportunity to express myself."

It's a disarmingly candid admission that comes across as both humble and realistic. Most people who dipped their toes in the musical maelstrom of the punk period didn't even manage one single. That doesn't mean Adrian didn't have a decent sized ego of course. It's hard to have any kind of performing existence without at least a semblance of one but when you hear the tone of his voice you can appreciate this was a man who, despite the kind of flaws we all have, didn't artificially put himself above others.

Facing the start of 1981 was nevertheless a challenging but exciting place for Adrian. Around him life moved at breakneck pace, people he'd been at school with would now have finished university, begun steady jobs, maybe even married and had kids. He had stepped away from that road and was committed to music as a way of life. Turning back would have been difficult if not impossible for him. That business studies course he was allegedly once considering must have seemed a lifetime ago.

The UK was poised to endure a year of inner-city riots, spiraling unemployment and a polarising Thatcher government. It's hard to fully appreciate now but when the Specials hit the number one spot with the incredible "Ghost Town" it was more realistic social commentary than 'pop' song, speaking to the half of the country that was suffering intense pain under a Conservative government that seemed oblivious or simply uncaring.

Don't underestimate the effect this had on Adrian. He was never one of those artists who somehow remain insulated from the world around them, instead he felt a rising anger at what he saw that he never lost.

The year's music finally saw those bestselling singles seriously infiltrated by the products of punk and post-punk, incredibly the Human League ended up having the years' bestselling single with "Don't You Want Me" surrounded by tracks from Soft Cell, Adam and the Ants and Ultravox. OK, Shakin Stevens and Bucks Fizz were also in there but the UK would always love the ersatz and the warm comfort of nostalgia.

Meanwhile over the ocean an event occurred that would set the visual tone for the decade and beyond: MTV hit the screens.

WEA were no doubt looking at Korova and seeing their boutique 'indie' label as having potential alt-pop stars in waiting. Those future stars were however, Echo and the Bunnymen. Luckily labelmates the Sound had cost them very little money and so to date, in business terms, were a satisfactory investment. *Jeopardy* wasn't a chart record but it was cheap, sold encouragingly and the promotional push had been far from deluxe. All that was required now was for the next step to be sufficiently far up the sales scale to ensure that the album chart was reached.

The Sound   ASGARD

But first the Sound needed to fill the gap in their ranks.

Mike Dudley was still living in a squat, not an uncommon state of affairs for musicians in the late '70s and early '80s. Through the extended 'network' of people around him Mike became aware of Colvin Mayers, at that point calling himself 'Max' (Max inherited the name during his Cardiac Arrest tenure, where the whole band had a variety of identities. He had several aliases, including; Duncan Doilet, Max Cat and Button Poppet.) The one problem was that he was currently playing keyboards in another band, that band was Cardiac Arrest, as they were then known, labelmates of the Sound on Steve Budd's fledgling indie label.

Mike, "They were a very quirky South London band who we'd done a few gigs with and who we sometimes socialised with. We nicked him from them!"

It seems the act of theft thankfully didn't burn any bridges, in fact Tim

Smith of the Cardiacs (as they became) contributed to *Shock of Daylight* and produced Adrian's solo album *5:00AM*.

It's not a question of comparing one band member against another and finding one wanting, but more a case of valuing what the particular person brings to the band at that stage of their development. Max was the perfect recruit based on such criteria, as Mike explains,

"He was a clever guy and a multi-instrumentalist, he sometimes played guitar on our records as well and had lots of previous experience. He gave us a much more panoramic feel and 'rounded' the sound out quite a lot, it was definitely a different keyboard sound. He was a great

influence in the songwriting department and was super on stage too."

Within a band a person's particular character can be as important as their musical abilities. In Max's case no one has a bad word to say about him beyond his legendary unreliability.

Graham, "We hit it off right away and went on to work together for a lighting company after the Sound split. You couldn't ask for a better friend really, he was just so sweet natured."

Mike, "He was a lovely guy, a bit wayward in his habits, but really generous to a fault. I can't say that I was really close to him as a friend, but as a colleague he was a very calming influence on the band. Sometimes Adrian would go into one of his rants about whatever was bothering him that week and Colvin would be a calming influence on the situation."

Julie Aldred, by then off studying at university but still dating Adrian, formed a similar view of Max as being a lovely person and a stabilising influence on the Sound and Adrian in particular.

It's rare to get such a unity of comment and experience regarding a person's contribution to any band but in the tragic absence of Max to tell his tale, (he died of an AIDS related illness in 1991) it seems suitably fitting.

Anyone who witnessed the Sound live will testify to Max's quietly focussed but crucial contribution, above all else he pulled off a trick that few keyboard players of the era managed: he integrated synths into the band's music by weaving them into the fabric of the songs. His contributions never smothered the music.

Max wasn't the only vital person coming on board early in 1981.

Mick Griffiths (who sadly died from cancer in 2021) was already a respected live agent, working for the Asgard agency. In the *Book of*

(Happy) Memories he described his induction into the Sound's circle,

Mick Griffiths (left)

"I was the Sound's agent almost from the start - January 1981. They'd sent me a copy of *Jeopardy* and I was so excited about it that I rang their manager, Steve Budd, and told him that I HAD to work with them - that he didn't really have any choice in the matter, and that with me organising their gigs they would be huge in no time. Steve was obviously impressed - who wouldn't be in the face of such raw enthusiasm and optimism? He said he would get back to me. Six months later I thought I would ring him again, just to see if he'd had a chance to consider my offer: "Hi Steve - it's me, Mick - we spoke recently about the Sound. I was wondering if you've had a chance to consider my offer......" "Mick who?" Oh well. I bumped into Steve shortly after at a gig at the Venue in London (now a burger restaurant), bought him loads of beers, and a deal was done. Three pints: 1 - Raw enthusiasm and optimism: 0."

Don't underestimate the importance of a good booking agent. For the Sound it was crucial, bear in mind a lot of the limited income that kept them afloat came from gigs. Without it they would have struggled to survive. As we shall find out, Mick's path would intersect with Adrian's in the years after the Sound ceased to exist.

The heartfelt comments that were posted after Mick's death speak volumes of his reputation for honesty and his commitment to working with people he liked and respected.

Adrian's year was intensifying in terms of activity. Recorded on 11th October 1980, following the Dead Kennedy's first London gig at the Music Machine (now Koko) the *Witch Trials* EP would have horrified Korova.

Featuring an intriguing line-up of the DK's Jello Biafra, ex-Mott the Hoople keyboard player Morgan Fisher and 'minimal synth punk' Christian Lunch, the four pieces were recorded at Morgan's Notting Hill flat allegedly under the influence of a few drinks.

No doubt Adrian had been keen to see the Dead Kennedys in action and would have enjoyed the opportunity for a brief collaboration.

Adrian, "The *Witch Trials* EP was the thing I did with Jello Biafra. When Jello came over to London he was hanging around with me and Graham. It was him reciting lyrics over a drum machine. I played some good, inventive guitar on that EP, but it all got credited to East Bay Ray (the Dead Kennedys' guitarist), which really annoyed me at the time. It's been re-released now. Jello's great, he knows so much."

The EP sneaked out that year with little promotion and even less information, future reissues included full credits.

More accurately described as 'soundscapes' rather than songs, with Jello's very distinctive voice speaking over the top, the EP was entirely improvised and was clearly an enjoyable night's work. From the cover on in, it's a creepy, uncomfortable but atmospheric listen. Anyone expecting differently would be naive in the extreme but you know what? It's not THAT far from Adrian and Graham's Second Layer world.

Taken together with the Second Layer album that would appear following the release of *From the Lion's Mouth,* these records trace a parallel creative journey for Adrian far from the comparatively lush major label record he would be best known for that year.

All more evidence stacking up to prove the sheer range of Adrian's musical world and his ability to shift from stylistic zone to zone.

For the Sound, Max was now fully integrated within their ranks and gigs were ever more plentiful. In March the band took a trip to a country that would soon take a significant role in their future history: Holland. One of the benefits of having an agent with drive and ambition for his bands, Mick,

"They did my first ever tour outside the UK - March 5 - 8 in Holland. I came over to Amsterdam where it pissed down with rain, the band stayed on a cold houseboat, and Adrian spent quite a lot of the day in the red-light district. I saw them loads of times in Amsterdam after that, and the only thing that really changed was the standard of accommodation. But the gigs! WHAT a band. I see bands for a living, and I've seen most things before, but I'll be a happy man if I can find another band who can play like that."

And here we have a reminder, without hyperbole: the Sound were an astonishing live act. Not just on a 'good' night but pretty much any night they trod a stage.

If you meet someone who was lucky enough to witness them, it's likely they will have their own story to tell. When I spoke recently to Garce of Sad Lovers and Giants for a feature in *Blitzed* magazine, unprompted he brought up the subject of Adrian and the Sound and the effect seeing them had on him at an important stage in his musical career,

"I saw the Sound in '82 when we supported them at the Venue (in Victoria, subsequently finding a life as a restaurant, it was later demolished), they were the best band I'd ever seen at that point. That gig was so very good, it showed me that with the sort of music we have you could still put on a live show at that level, it was the light and shade of the performance."

Think of how many bands you've seen who succeed in both thrilling and moving you, plenty of artists are enjoyable live but don't manage to 'push your buttons' in that way.

Graham made some interesting comments on the mysterious art of playing live in his interview for *Walking in the Opposite Direction,* as well as identifying the switch that occurred after that first Dutch trip,

"And then we went to Holland and things changed."

Drawn on the 'Dutch question' Graham seemed mystified,

"How it happened that we became so popular in Holland? I just have no idea."

It's something we will inevitably return to.

Graham, "It's pure adrenaline when you go on stage. I kind of know why musicians end up on drugs, because when you come off stage, you have to come down off that real high. The more people you play to the more powerful it is. It just lifts you to another place. I mean, you become at one with the audience or they become one with you."

Incredibly there's some grainy footage on Youtube from that first Paradiso gig, there you will see the Sound in all their raw glory. As Adrian has pointed out, all those sometimes soul destroying 'toilet circuit' gigs with the Outsiders prepared him for hitting stages like the Paradiso's fully equipped to take the audience in the palm of his hand and draw them into the music.

This was no act for Adrian, it felt like life and death, maintaining that intensity comes with a price.

Speaking to Jan he explained that, "Putting extreme emotion in a song means you have to carry it off on stage."

Expressing scepticism regarding the trend for reunion gigs Adrian makes a very telling observation about what was important for him,

"It's spirit, not just notes on a page."

And that's one of the reasons we're still listening to his music and talking about him today. There's a cliche that applies: he was the real deal, and some people could feel that.

144

It's a common problem for bands, they have a lifetime to write the songs for their first album and a matter of weeks to come up with enough for their second. But not so much for the Sound. There were a decent number of songs floating about, some from Bi's time in the band, so this was more a case of picking the best and taking full advantage of a comparatively decent major label budget for what would become, *From the Lions Mouth*.

As Steve Budd confirms, "Adrian had written some really great songs, a real step up, I think he was partially inspired by looking at the Bunnymen and their set-up."

For this crucial record Korova suggested the Sound work with Hugh Jones. Today Hugh is rightly known as a skilled producer who has worked with numerous bands often with a post-punk tinge to their music. Back in 1981 he had already been involved in pivotal albums from Teardrop Explodes, Simple Minds and, yes, our old friends, Echo and the Bunnymen.

Hugh had worked on the Bunnymen's classic *Heaven Up Here* at Rockfield Studios, in Monmouthshire in Wales. Rockfield is a legendary studio that incredibly still exists today. It's a rarity now, in that it's a residential facility, in fact apparently the world's first when it opened in the early '60s.

Hearing the Bunnymen link yet again feels problematic and yet there's no doubt that the two records were both classics of their type. Seeing Hugh's name in the credits is, it's safe to say, usually a very good sign.

In their interviews for *Walking in the Opposite Direction*, both Graham and Mike Dudley were asked whether they enjoyed working with Hugh,

Graham, "No."

Although he did go on to clarify, "He was a lovely bloke and is obviously talented as a producer but I didn't like the way he worked at all. We went from being 'hands-on' to everyone but Adrian being kicked out of the studio. We were stuck in this farmhouse and the whole experience was something I didn't enjoy."

Mike, "He was good to work with. He was good at picking out our best assets and focusing on them. The first album was recorded with Nick Robbins, but it was us that were really in control. Nick was really just doing the engineering. I wouldn't say that Hugh was calling the shots on *From the Lions Mouth*, but he was definitely directing things though and getting us to focus on certain strengths and to play to those."

It's fair to say that Graham is clear: he and Mike agree on little these days. However it's equally not hard to understand his views, here was a 'city boy' dumped in the middle of nowhere and subject to unwanted direction. To make it worse Graham was used to 'quick and dirty,' anything goes, recording sessions that up until that point were engineered but not strictly produced. Indeed, he'd that year recorded the debut Second Layer album in one day exactly like that.

For Graham *From the Lions Mouth* ended up, in terms of recording process and end result, boring and too commercial.

It's an interior view of what is often viewed by the rest of us as the Sound's quintessential album.

For Steve Budd, "It was a great, great album."

Adrian knew the stakes were high, but if he was in any doubt his girlfriend Julie Aldred was there to put him right, as he recalled to Jan in 1996,

"I remember Julie saying, 'This is a really important record, you mustn't fuck it up.' It did feel like that to me, there was something about that album, it felt important in a bizarre way. I can't really put my finger on it."

Listening to Adrian laughing at the potentially perceived grandiosity of what he's just said is a reminder of his innate down to earth nature and desire to quickly deflate any notions of self-importance.

Adrian, "It was the first time we'd worked with a producer and it's ended up many people's favourite. It did the best 'business' as they say. It sold around 100,000 copies worldwide."

Don't overlook the detail: the album was a co-production between the band and Hugh Jones. It could be that the credit would more accurately be Hugh Jones/Adrian Borland. What's beyond doubt is that Adrian had a clear perspective on what was achieved with *From the Lions Mouth,*

"I think it's a very coherent record, there's nothing on there that shouldn't be. I've got issues with other records I've made where I think, "Why's that on there? That shouldn't be there". It never felt like that with *Lions Mouth.* Even the order, that final order, wasn't my original idea, but I do think Rob Dickins and Hugh Jones were right about the sequencing."

Adrian had pictured "Judgment" as the album's closer but Rob and Hugh lobbied for "New Dark Age."

Today it's hard to imagine a track listing where anything but the staggering "New Dark Age" takes us to the end, not that "Judgment" is a weak song: there really were no weak songs on *Lions Mouth*.

Adrian, " "New Dark Age" is more climactic, it's more of a 'cliff hanger.' It's also like a 'question mark.' "

Korova heralded the album in September with the release of "Sense of Purpose" as a single. Any thoughts of *Lions Mouth* as some kind of major label compromise are dispelled swiftly. "Sense of Purpose" (subtitled "What are we Going to Do" presumably in an attempt to utilise a memorable part of the chorus) rolls in on a grinding bass line from Graham, Adrian's guitar charged with urgency and anxiety, Max carefully heightening the tension and Mike, unshowy but unswervingly propelling the song forward.

No sell-out and precious little sign of compromise, and no it wasn't a hit. But unlike many contemporary songs that were, it still burns with its own special brilliance today.

Lions Mouth arrived in record shops that November in a luscious gatefold sleeve that today feels ridiculously fitting. Should we read anything into the choice of image? Maybe not, but it's hard to avoid it.

Daniel in the Lion's Den, painted by Briton Rivière in 1872, depicts Daniel, head bowed, facing a pride of lions while standing, hands tied, on a stone floor strewn with bones. It's hard to imagine a stronger or more loaded image. But now consider Rivière's 'sequel,' *Daniel's Answer to the King,* painted twenty years later. Here, moments after, Daniel stands with the same pride of lions. However now Daniel has his back to them, with his face towards a window and the light. A contemporary interpretation by American religious author Mary Baker Eddy almost stops you in your tracks. To her, Daniel had turned his back on the, "lower or bestial elements of the mortal mind." Although clearly a religious interpretation, the sense of a person trying to escape a threat deep in their own mind or nature and turning toward the light, relying on some kind of faith to, against the odds, "hold their hope together" is too powerful to ignore.

After that, album opener and signature Sound song "Winning," feels even more significant.

One of the Sound's most well-known songs, "Winning" is a moment of crystalline despair that's bent to Adrian's will and turned into a message of pure defiance. There are no easy answers here and the final message is a warning as much as a shout of weary, just glimpsed, victory. You may prefer it in one of the various live versions out there as of course this song became a cathartic colossus when played on a stage in front of an audience, however you hear it the experience will stay with you. Yes you can relate the lyric to Adrian's life, but at the same time it's bitterly universal.

"Contact the Fact" always felt to me like a single in waiting but when I listen now I realise just how unlikely that would have been. A lyric that admits fallibility and questions, well everything really, "Contact the Fact" is a plea for communication and honesty. Adrian appears to accept that the song's protagonist will at times appear 'crazy' in their intensity but knows that's all part of *real* feeling. So yeah, probably not something for *Top of the Pops*, but still a shimmering creation of stark beauty, Max again knowing how much to contribute and when to disappear.

And yes his subtle piano works a treat down in the mix of the glorious "Skeletons." Once more Adrian confronts the danger of living an empty life, just to survive day to day. It may get you by but how much is lost?

Side one ends with the much debated "Judgement." More an open questioning of faith than a declaration of atheistic conviction. The mix is careful to allow space for Mike's kettle drums, what sounds like an acoustic guitar, elegiac synths and then a tense rush and... back down to silence. The final bass rumble from Graham is deep and resonant. It's an unusual and moving song that very few artists could have pulled off.

Side one: mission accomplished, will there be an all too common side two slump?

In short? No.

And it starts like this: Martial drumbeat, warm measured bass, vapour light synth and a controlled vocal from Adrian belying the emotional wilderness he probes for the troubled length of the majestic "Fatal Flaw."

Adrian was right, there's a strange atmosphere threaded through these songs, maybe even more so on side two.

I've always seen "Fatal Flaw" and "Possession" as working in tandem, perfectly placed next to each other in that all important track sequence. "Possession" appears to be a direct address to the dark side present in all of us. Adrian uses a curious, almost call and response vocal, one side of him telling the other to, "Get a hold of myself."

Remember, at this point Adrian hadn't shown visible signs of his illness, certainly not in a form his closest friends could recognise. It is of course possible he was aware of something that was 'wrong' within him, but equally he would be one of many to examine the struggle within many a human psyche. In that 1996 interview with Jan, Adrian specifically acknowledges this,

"I was trying to get away from self-righteousness and to delve deeper and question my own motives and maybe my own bad side."

Few did this kind of nuanced ambiguity as well as Adrian, there's little false drama or hysteria in these songs.

But sometimes you really need to let rip. "The Fire" does just that, Graham's bass is irresistible and Adrian's guitar switches from searing to desperate to a kind of post-punk syncopation that allows for some kind of dance floor action, if you're in a mood for exorcising something. My favourite few seconds? That delicious moment where Graham's bass stays with the rise to a crescendo and then shifts gears down into the final flat-out coda. Not sure how he managed to repeat that night after night.

"The Fire" became another part of Adrian's love/hate tussle with U2. Not only did U2 release a song called "Fire" at around the same time as Lions Mouth was released, (the Sound wrote their "Fire" in 1980) but he also felt Bono and the band may have 'stolen' the chorus for one of their songs. Did they? Who knows. One thing is sure though: back in 1980 U2 were dragging themselves around the same pub/club/'toilet' venue circuit at precisely the same time as the Sound, so were highly likely to be fully aware of their contemporaries ploughing a not dramatically different furrow.

Comparisons? Well U2's "Fire" is certainly a decent song, with some very tasteful fretwork atmospherics from the Edge. But, to labour an obvious metaphor, it's rather like a pleasant to watch, well controlled bonfire. "The Fire" on the other hand, is the aural equivalent of a transfixing inferno.

Then we arrive at the final one-two punch.

The quietly devastating "Silent Air" quickly became a Sound classic. As a measure of how far Adrian's songwriting had come it's value is massive, while as a deeply moving piece of music it still has the power to silence. Have a look at those lyrics. There's a haiku-like simplicity, no excess and

no words wasted. The arrangement epitomises the becalmed mood that has descended. That guitar solo, and its sweet aftermath, contains possibly the most beautiful moments encountered within *From the Lions Mouth.* For its duration, for some reason, I always pictured blossom petals gently falling to the ground.

It's not hard to fit a reaction to the death of Ian Curtis into any interpretation of the lyric. But again, Adrian's ability takes us into our own worlds and leaves "Silent Air" to take on whatever meaning it needs to, as and when we require it.

Adrian was interviewed by Allan Jones in the 24th October 1981 issue of *Melody Maker,*

Adrian, "Ian Curtis really believed there was no way out, I listen to *Closer* and that's the impression I get. He probably went through the same confusion as a lot of other people... he just came to more depressing conclusions. For him, obviously, there was no hope."

It's easy to see why Rob Dickins suggested "New Dark Age," as the grimly apocalyptic closer. It's a fantastic edifice of tension and release. The lumbering menace of the verses giving way to a sweeping run for freedom in the chorus. But I'm not sure the characters in "New Dark Age " ever make it. The brutal guitar solo suggests oblivion and the final message seems to be; it's coming whatever you do, just get ready. Adrian is the prophet, stirring the populace, but he would no doubt have hated that description as he certainly didn't seek such a role. But still, the political thread that ran through his songs was more visible than usual here.

Back in the mid '80s I wrote a fan letter to the Sound, not something I did normally, but hey I was an idealistic late-teen and was, and still am, moved by these incredible songs.

A few weeks later an envelope hit the mat with a poster, photo and handwritten letter from Max. I'd mentioned "New Dark Age" in my fan letter and have always remembered Max's self-deprecating response,

"It's difficult for me to explain why Adrian wrote "New Dark Age" but he has a way of putting a lot of peoples' thoughts and feelings into his songs. If only a few more people knew that we might be famous. Ha!"

In 1996, Adrian himself perfectly summed-up the unique quality of *From the Lions Mouth,*

"It's one of those records that just has an atmosphere from beginning to end, it's rock music but it has an underlying atmosphere that's very hard to define. I can listen to that album even now and in a way it's sort of a classic of its kind."

From the Lions Mouth just missed the charts in the UK but did apparently make the top ten in Greece and New Zealand while naturally selling well in Holland.

As a statement it was meant to be a more lavish (relatively speaking), sleeker record than its predecessor *Jeopardy.* It's role in Adrian's discography is not as a foundation stone but rather the impressive structure that demonstrates just what he and the band could do, dull and too commercial it certainly isn't.

The critical response must have been massively gratifying for the whole band but in particular for Adrian, for a rare moment they had the press united on their side.

In *Melody Maker* Steve Sutherland wrote a thoughtful, incisive piece that can be found online and is well worth reading in full. Concluding that the album could be the "end of the line" for him and 'rock' records, "it's that good." "You can ill afford to ignore them again." However within the review are concerns; noting Adrian had realised the need to sell records, Sutherland is concerned at the risk of the Sound appearing as the "party poopers" amongst the colourful sounds of the new pop that was rapidly taking over from the fast fading new romantics.

At *Record Mirror* Mike Nicholls gave the album four stars, his review is another well argued case for the Sound's importance in a world of vacuity. He has a point when he claims *Lions Mouth* could almost be a concept album. But the alarm bells are rung when Mike recognises the band's "unfashionable disposition."

The *NME*'s Andy Gill also did the album justice with a review the likes of which you really wouldn't see in today's largely neutralised and anodyne critical environment where press releases are routinely regurgitated phrase by phrase. He didn't like "The Fire" (too close to U2, I bet Adrian laughed at that) but loved "Silent Air" wisely noting the Joy Division link and the Sound's comparable power and emotional depth.

When he concludes that, "They still care, the foolish boys, in a way others have forgotten how to" it feels all too close to the bone.

Smash Hits weren't so keen though: too much like Joy Division apparently, but you can't have it all I guess.

From the Lions Mouth now feels like an eternal, 'what could have been' record, not in terms of creative achievements, but rather in the sense of WEA failing to put their massive weight behind it. This was the album that ought to have moved the Sound to the level where they could comfortably tour the UK in the way they were able to in Holland. They were never destined for top ten singles but had all the qualities needed for just the right level of cult following, potentially sustaining them for years to come. This should have been their moment.

It didn't happen: *From the Lions Mouth* hit a peak of 164 in the UK album chart and promptly vanished.

The answers as to why are in plain sight within the reviews and press response. The Sound were rightly or wrongly seen as, not exactly dour, but serious, with an emotional honesty and lack of image that were hugely at odds with the prevailing trends in 1981 and beyond. Nevertheless, their close contemporaries the Comsat Angels had

managed to lodge their recent, even darker, *Sleep No More* in the top 60 of the UK album chart. Of course that major label career didn't end well either.

The picture of the Sound as somehow 'uncool' in their fervent sincerity and lack of sellable image stuck. If they'd been less middle class and come from the north or somewhere grittier in London would it have helped up their cool quotient? Probably, sadly.

Even worse, the occasional mentions of Adrian's appearance didn't help. It feels tragically irrelevant today but as we have already seen, mentions of his weight clearly hit home to Adrian.

Julie Aldred confirms this,

"He was always conscious of his appearance, he was always trying to lose weight and I would try to help him with that. It's true the band had no image. They really did try though. But that's where a band like the Bunnymen were head and shoulders above them in that respect, but not musically."

Trivial? Certainly, but these are the realities that conspire to seal your fate when a record company is working out how to allocate precious resources.

We can feel anger at the injustice but the die was cast and the Sound's fate had already been decided even if no one quite knew it yet.

However the artistic achievement that *From the Lions Mouth* constitutes is now clearer than ever. It's a record whose depths and lasting resonance remind us of a sometimes uncomfortable reality.

We tend to need our artists to be extra sensitive to what it means to be alive, something Adrian undoubtedly was. If we were all like that everyone would likely be running around screaming at the simultaneous beauty and futility of life. Instead we have our favourite artists to do that for us, ideally metaphorically. Only on occasion it spills over from the metaphorical to the literal and can derail the unlucky person's life.

Was music Adrian's therapy? Yes in some ways and inevitably no in others. No, because maintaining that level of open-hearted intensity is too much for anyone.

In that 1981 interview with Allan Jones of *Melody Maker*, the whole question of success is acknowledged and dissected. Adrian is well aware of the pressure on him and the band,

"If after maybe three years, nothing happens and we fade away, there will still be people sitting behind their desks in record company offices still refusing to acknowledge that if it wasn't for these bands who are willing to risk everything...

I just want our records to sell. I don't want to be famous after we've packed it in. This is the moment that counts. We want to be listened to now, not tomorrow!"

Allan Jones uses a 'device' revolving around watching a girl in the bar where the interview takes place as she puts her money in a 'record machine.' His final paragraph is, with the passing of time, even more poignant,

"Across the bar, a girl tips another coin into the jukebox. I wondered if she'd ever hear the Sound?"

Tourbooks by Asgard

CHAPTER 9

I spent too long looking in from the outside...

A lot happened to Adrian in 1981, it's almost easy to forget the Sound graced the stage of the Glastonbury Festival.

Back in '81 it was a long way from becoming the media approved social phenomena that it is now complete with glamping and designer Wellington boots.

Adrian was faced with what the *Melody Maker* described as, "the tangled apathy of an audience whose attention seems constantly to be wandering down some cosmic pathway to premature oblivion."

It was a great review for the Sound,

"On a day destined to become an increasingly depressing parade of mediocrity, the Sound were the only band who successfully imposed themselves upon your reporter's severely rattled imagination."

A familiar place for Adrian and the band to be, fighting the good fight against the tedious and the mundane. Adrian would have been pleased to share the bill with New Order, but there was a slightly strange event that day.

A couple of days earlier on 13th June, a man by the name of Marcus Sarjeant had caused some outrage after interrupting the Trooping the Colour ceremony by standing in the path of the Queens' horse and firing six blank shots from a starting pistol. Sarjeant, who was 17 years old, was subsequently sentenced to five years in prison. In a sickly foreshadowing of the Tiktok age, his stated aim had been to become, "the most famous teenager in the world."

A minor historical event in hindsight, but quite relevant in its link to a more modern yearning for celebrity. At the time it caused a lot of outrage in the strongly pro-royal press and allegedly also out across the country. So when Adrian dedicated the as yet unreleased, "New Dark Age" to Sarjeant, asking, "Why the fuck did you use blanks?" it probably shocked even the somnambulant hippies in attendance. Adrian explained himself: "The audience was just sitting there, staring into space, I just wanted to say something that would wake them up!"

Melody Maker felt the behaviour was "ill-judged", certainly today it would no doubt have caused something of a stir if picked up by social media and the papers. Luckily back then it passed by generally unnoticed but is indicative of a certain strand of Adrian's character that was headstrong, forthright and impulsive. Almost a 'damn the consequences' approach that appeared again in the events that would see the Sound's record deal come to an abrupt end the following year.

Another part of Adrian's packed 1981 that would turn out to have implications for his WEA contract, was the November release of Second Layer's (or more correctly, 2nd Layer's) debut album on Cherry Red titled *World of Rubber."*

It appeared that after beating the Sound to vinyl, Adrian and Graham's other love had understandably been pushed to one side by the onward rush of the Sound.

What to make of *World of Rubber* today? Well maybe the key adjective when considering Second Layer's only album is 'trashy.' Adrian uses that word when talking enthusiastically about the 'band's' ethos. These are not carefully crafted, 'traditional' songs and nor were they intended as such. Instead there's a thrilling, homemade immediacy at work here, a sense of anything goes. But crucially Adrian was never interested in just creating noise for noise's sake so there's always enough structure amid the atmosphere to ensure this is a record that you won't play once and file away like so many 'interesting' (mainly for the artist) side projects.

Take opener, "Definition of Honour" with its primitive drum machine (in the Cherry Red reissue sleeve-notes Graham recalls following the instructions to build his own 'rhythm generator'), Suicide-like synth buzz and Adrian's very recognisable, always on edge, guitar. It's a hypnotic, but crucially, always exciting soundscape.

Adrian loved the music of Martin Rev and Alan Vega well before most had even heard of them. I'm sure he appreciated their edge of destruction sound that relied on synths pushed way beyond the instruction manual limits. Suicide are undoubtedly the stepping off point for Second Layer, being artists who sang about freedom, even if only in dreams, and embraced it in their approach to music as well.

Lots of the 'techniques' applied here would probably have horrified many engineers or producers at the time, whereas Nick Robbins was, as ever, happy to oblige. The result is distortion and overloaded circuits galore, but the funny thing is; this is a great headphones album. The intimacy headphones provide, lets you take it all in that little bit easier. Take the synth buzzing from ear to ear on "Fixation" or the gloriously dirty throb of the bass in the following track the queasily disturbing, "Save our Souls." There's even a song actually called, "Distortion."

Coming after the terror of "Japanese Headset" (surely a contender for *Silence of the Lambs)* Adrian and Graham's reaction to the death of Ian Curtis finds its way to the surface here as well. With a bass sound tweaked to appear almost like a languorously plucked double bass, "Black Flowers" is a disturbing ode to bygone funerary practices, the synth twisted to mimic a demonic church organ. The track was apparently recorded shortly after the pair heard the news regarding Curtis and provides a fitting end to proceedings.

Throughout *World of Rubber* there's a sense of sickly horror and impending or recent violence, but this is no pretentious gloom-fest; it's far too inventively playful for that.

Industrial before that was really a 'thing'? Maybe.

We can now see their attempt to marry guitars and danceable electronics as the early adopting entity that it clearly was, but at the time it was cast adrift to relative cult audience obscurity. Although I suspect even that fate would have appealed in some way to Adrian. Cherry Red considered another try for a single of "Courts or Wars" but were discouraged by the response to the album and so it never happened.

Talking to Jan in 1996, Adrian was still audibly excited by the project,

"Had it been taken to its ultimate commercial proposition it would have been a very exciting thing in the early '80s. Using certain sounds in a rock context, we were unashamedly 'modern rock' sound-wise - we introduced reggae bass lines and dub ideas to the songs."

Another album was even titled, at least in Adrian and Graham's heads, but aside from an unheralded 1982 appearance of songs intended for that follow-up, nothing happened.

"The next album was going to be called, *World of Bondage* but we never actually got round to making it. We were going to go through all the perversions one by one, it's a shame it was stopped really!"

The reason we didn't hear from Second Layer again?

Adrian, "It was contractual. We were going to sign to 4AD, but they weren't prepared to let the Sound carry on simultaneously, they wanted us exclusively. It would have been nice to be 'anonymous Second Layer' at the same time as the Sound."

Talking about Second Layer is illuminating in terms of the insight it provides to Adrian's way of thinking musically, as well as illustrating how he applied his inspiration and talent according to the project being worked on.

"It's not songs that don't fit, it's a whole new scheme of thinking and I just apply myself to that. The songs develop naturally within that. Most of the songs that develop outside the mainstream of my stuff are written really quickly, almost throwaway, written in ten minutes. It's the sound that matters, I don't care what the song says, not the lyrics or the melody, I'm interested in what it sounds like and that's what keeps that side of my stuff so interesting."

Ultimately it was a question of time that sealed Second Layer's fate,

"Time ran out with Second Layer, it's so hard timewise with touring Europe, so we put all our eggs in one basket. I still wonder if we made a mistake. We couldn't find the time or energy in the end. We gave 100% to the Sound."

So it came down to time and money as these things often do,

Adrian, "If it wasn't so desperate with money and trying to keep our heads above water then we could have done more. If we'd had the odd £10,000 hanging around, we could have done another Second Layer album in a couple of weeks. When I listen now I still think there's something quite unique about Second Layer, a kind of trashiness that maybe hasn't been totally cornered. Graham and I had so many ideas, I mean he was building a 'bass machine' for god's sake, it sounds like something from *Dr No!*"

Adrian was still planning a return of Second Layer even as late as 1996, sadly events conspired against him.

"It'll probably be the last thing I end up doing. The world may not be waiting for it, but we'll take everything to another level. Who knows? It's my one musical regret."

As a coda to the strange tale of Second Layer, there's a short hint to their future in the bonus track included on Cherry Red's CD reissue of *World of Rubber.*

"Skylon" was a song written by future Lush bassist, and general indie legend, Phil King and his then girlfriend Roxanne. Adrian and Graham had been inspired by Heaven 17 and their British Electric Foundation creation and had the idea of putting together an album of other people's songs with different vocalists, Second Layer playing and producing.

"Skylon," (recorded at Elephant Studios with Nick Robbins in 1982) is quite a shock coming smack up against the preceding nightmare journey. It's a wistfully strummed ode to the Festival of Britain, of which the Skylon itself was part, and seems to tell of a failed assignation down there by the Thames. Yes there are synths and a drum machine but this is very different territory for Second Layer. There's a strong feeling of poignancy hanging over the song which had sadly been unheard for all those years, while not written by Adrian it's yet more evidence of his constant hunger for new musical experiences and challenges.

The production role Adrian had taken on with "Skylon" is also important. Adrian had begun production work in 1981 (often at Elephant as usual), then more in the spirit of helping other bands than for monetary reasons.

Phil King himself already had some history with Adrian, having met him through hanging out at Outsiders gigs. Their paths would intertwine many times over the years from Phil's band the Beautiful Losers supporting the Sound, to Adrian producing several of his other bands and finally Phil contributing bass to "Spanish Hotel" on the *Cinematic* album. Adrian even recommended Felt to Phil after the Sound had played with an early version of the band at 1981's Futurama Festival, eventually leading to him joining Felt as bass player.

Phil's memory of Adrian is a familiar one,

"When I was starting out he was always very kind, enthusiastic and helpful. He was a great producer; I was spoiled by working with him first!"

The intricate web of associations, help and shared enthusiasm says a lot about the way Adrian lived his life and energised those around him.

Amidst all of this, it's easy to forget that he had a life outside the world of music. But he did, and as one year gave way to the next he and Julie were doing something couples do when they've been together a little while.

Julie, "At one point in '81 or '82 we were thinking of renting a flat together. I lived at home with my parents while I was at uni. I was at college in Ealing, partly because I was with Adrian and could easily be back in Wimbledon to see him. We did look at some places and Adrian's dad was saying we should buy something. Neither of us had any money obviously. We did go and see some flats but it didn't come to anything. It was just too much of a commitment for both of us. We went with Adrian's dad, my parents didn't like Adrian probably for obvious reasons. He wasn't great with things like meeting parents!"

Julie tells an endearingly cringe-inducing tale of Adrian coming to visit when she was ill in bed at her parent's house. It was mid-afternoon and Adrian was naturally asked by Julie's dad if he'd like a drink. His response? "A whisky please." To be fair he was never one for hot drinks, but still not the way to calm the nerves of parents wondering who this apprentice rock star going out with their daughter was. Adrian didn't see the social faux pas he'd committed in the depths of middle England.

For Adrian some of the politics of polite or maybe just accepted behaviour were opaque at best. Remember this was a person who never learnt to drive, didn't really work outside music and found navigating beach holiday etiquette a mystery, as Julie explains,

"We went on holiday in my parents' camper van, which wasn't Adrian at all! He goes to the beach and he'd be there in his leather jacket. Normal things like that just weren't him at all."

It's important though to understand that this was emphatically not the classic case of a 'rock and roll juvenile' hiding from the world in a bubble of their own creation. There are certainly many, in and around music, who fit that description, but Adrian wasn't one of them.

Julie, "Adrian lived in an unusual world, whereby he didn't feel the need to work and earn money and look after himself. Really, I suppose he was quite fortunate, in the sense he managed to live most of his life like that. I mean, obviously he did make some money from music, whereas most people have to 'buckle down' and get a proper job and, you know, a lot of their dreams just get washed away."

Julie confirms that he was very interested and aware of what was going on in the country and the world at large and was unfailingly kind to those around him whether he knew them or not, giving money that he could ill afford to those who needed it (although getting him to pay for a drink might prove challenging).

This tallies with the picture consistently painted across the range of those who knew him and ties in neatly with the political themes and socially conscious undercurrents that never left his music.

Adrian failed to find a flat to rent with Julie and so, perhaps unsurprisingly, remained at 2 Hillview where he had important business to consider, in the form of writing and recording a standalone single for Korova. Actually he'd already written the song in question with Jan and the band, recording it for a John Peel session broadcast on 16th November 1981.

The Sound's BBC sessions are illuminating and vital in the way they are for many bands who were invited to record them. Put simply; they are blisteringly good.

The Peel session version of "Hothouse," the song that would go on to be released as the Sound's final Korova branded record, is pared back to the minimum, the lyric trimmed to a few lines,

"Feelings pushing through I try to suppress
Content to watch them grow inside their walls of glass
Sweat breaking out I fought to contain
Like the savage roots of this growing pain
I found myself in the hothouse"

Once the song had been recorded with Nick Robbins the lyric had grown to include the following revealing couplet,

"I spent too long looking in from the outside
It's time to get in, it's time to get inside
In the hothouse now I'm in the thick of it
With jungle vines that creep and spread
Feelings pushing through, pushing through"

Allowing for Jan's involvement the lyric seems to encapsulate Adrian's life, as well as being transferable to many of ours. Adrian would often tinker with lyrics Jan gave him as of course he was the one singing them, but in any event he would never sing a lyric that didn't fit with his own experience.

It's very difficult not to picture Adrian as the person existing outside the flow of everyday life, observing through glass, as people do things they maybe don't want to do but are so caught within the parameters of accepted behaviour they do them anyway.

Should he move from the outside and try existing within a world he finds brutal and inhospitable?

It recalls the same kind of outside-looking-in dread articulated by another underappreciated in his lifetime songwriter with his own issues, Nick Drake, via the song, "Hazey Jane II".

"And what will happen in the morning
When the world it gets so crowded
That you can't look out the window in the morning?
And all the friends that you once knew are left behind
They kept you safe and so secure
Amongst the books and all the records of your lifetime?"

You may know the moderately famous picture of Nick standing back leaning against a wall as a blurred figure hurries by on his way to work, swap Adrian for Nick and it would make similar sense. The two artists for whom music was central but for various reasons left them adrift from the tide of 'normal' life.

There's a claustrophobic feel to both the single version and its Peel session predecessor. Both have their strengths but perhaps the session version aces it. Certainly Mike Dudley thought so. In the sleeve notes of the Renascent BBC sessions album he confirms he had written it off slightly as, "a slight song" whereas here he felt it had, "a real new wave pop feel." He also cops to a Stewart Copeland influence in the drumming, which speaks volumes of Mike's ability.

The sinewy, spring-loaded bass that opens the song and the undulating guitar figure push "Hothouse" towards the dance floor but whether it made it there seems doubtful.

By the time it was released on the 28th May (slightly worryingly with a 'live' version of "New Dark Age," as its B-side, were they finally struggling to come up with new material?) maybe it was just a smidgeon less nimble but still pretty great. Catchy too. But in the pop world of 1982 it didn't stand a chance.

Record Mirror's Sunie reached for the Bunnymen references yet again,

"Try as I might, I've never been able to see this lot as more than a bargain-basement Bunnymen. This song does little to dispel that notion: it beetles away quite busily, but to no great conclusion. Success may be 10% inspiration and 90% perspiration, but you shouldn't be able to smell the sweat quite so distinctly!"

We haven't yet caught up with 1982 and the bright and shiny pop climate the Sound were now operating in. By far the best-selling single of the year was a song by an 'old' ex-punk, "Come on Eileen" ruled the year along with records by Culture Club, the Jam, Tight Fight and the Goombay Dance Band, in some ways the usual mix of the weird, wonderful and… indescribable. Even Adrian's beloved Kraftwerk hit the number one slot with a re-release of "the Model."

It often seemed as if anything was possible in the 'go-getter' environment that was building and building in the 'hothouse' of Thatcher's country of contradictions, still high on the jingoistic fallout from the Falklands War.

At that stage in the country's history the calculated cruelty of the market economy was ratcheting up year by year, creating living conditions that were particularly harsh for those in the precarious lower levels of society and bountifully generous to those who didn't need it. Such inequality would affect Adrian in terms of his own existence and would be reflected within his songs.

Even the Sound's endlessly mentioned labelmates finally hit the top twenty with "The Back of Love," a great record released a week apart from the Sound's own chart bid. Given that it was far from an obvious single, why did it succeed and "Hothouse" fail?

For various reasons that naturally had little to do with the quality of the song itself. Firstly, having a record company putting its considerable weight behind the release, initial copies were even made available at a special low price to sweeten the deal. But beyond that the Bunnymen had amassed a considerable cult following by this point and were ready to go overground. That cult propelled the single into the charts, hitting number 32 in its first week ensuring an all-important *Top of the Pops'* appearance helping "The Back of Love" hit a chart peak of 19.

Did the band want a hit? It's a fair question which Graham responded to in his Arcane Delights interview,

"Ha! Yes and no. Sure, it would be good to have had hits. But not by planning it. At least, we never planned a "hit" but we did choose the most likely songs as singles. I wouldn't be against it now."

Graham's response is pragmatic and reflects the tensions other like-minded bands, such as the Comsats, grappled with back then when 'selling out' was still a concept that meant something.

Mike Dudley confirms now that, yes, "Hothouse" was at least an attempt in the direction of getting a hit.

For the Sound it felt like a 'so near yet so far' situation. We can always argue that charts matter little but Adrian was a realist and knew that while chart success wasn't a measure of his or the band's artistic achievement, it would get the record company off their back and ensure more people got to hear his music.

In the music press a narrative was quickly solidifying around the band.

Record Mirror had reviewed their first gig of the year at London's Venue. Mike Nicholls loved the gig describing the band as,

"Like a phoenix rising from the ashes. The Sound break free from their self-imposed chains of despair and strive forward with surging, powerful vigour. They are not pretty and neither is the music."

The gig sounds like the Sound's business as usual position, namely: utterly transcendent, Nicholls' conclusion though was worrying,

"With the current state of play, the Sound will never be huge. Not because their music is excessively esoteric or inaccessible - just too moody and challenging for mass tastes. Maybe by their fifth album the world will have caught up with them."

In amongst the albums, singles and touring we've neglected to mention an event which quite likely had significant and long-lasting ramifications for the band. Some will raise an eyebrow and will tell you managers don't matter, while others will say little happens without them. In the middle, just maybe, lies the truth.

In the Sound's case, in the aftermath of the release of *From the Lion's Mouth*, they had lost their manager Steve Budd.

Steve, "At that point I'd got involved with this kind of self-enlightenment cult (Exegesis). I was very young and it was an all encompassing thing. I was very torn but decided to go my own way and left to join this cult. It was fascinating, books will be written and have been written on it!"

Steve confirms this was a tough time for him,

Graham was more matter-of-fact in his assessment of what happened,

"Steve Budd bailed after the second album didn't sell very well and things started to get a bit difficult. So after that we largely operated without a manager, which I think was a mistake."

Steve's assessment of the position, "It was sad, Adrian's dad and the road manager briefly took the reins at that point."

Steve had left by February 1982.

Whatever your view of Steve's role in the band's progress to date, facing the fallout from his departure via involving Adrian's dad and someone else with plenty of other work to do, feels especially worrying in the wake of an under-performing second major label album.

Losing a person who should be your buffer between art and the requirements of corporate business did not augur well even when that person had limited management experience.

Just to add to the mood of change, their highly liked A&R man, Greg Penny, had vanished to LA.

Just to add to the mood of change, their highly liked A&R man, Greg Penny, had vanished to LA.

What was worse was that WEA were now putting pressure on the band for a follow up album to *From the Lions Mouth*. Note the switch from Korova to WEA. After "Hothouse" the band were quietly moved off Rob

Dickins' boutique label and were now on plain old WEA. It's likely this was because the Dutch arm of the major were now the ones most interested in the Sound's future while the UK maybe sensed the message that hits were not on the cards.

Steve Budd (right), in front of the mixing desk at The Sound's Glastonbury show

Graham, "After that, the record company started to ask for a follow up album and they wanted it 'now'. Adrian and I were at that point working on more Second Layer stuff. So Adrian and I decided to incorporate the Second Layer ideas into work on *All Fall Down,* so you could say *All Fall Down* was Second Layer's second album. Although I know Mike disliked that, Max was OK with it"

Often when a record company begins to lose whatever faith they had in a band, they suggest they go away and record some demos, just to see whether there are any 'hits' in store or whether the game is up. If you're really unlucky the label may suggest you record a cover version or some such horrific idea, at least the Sound were spared that indignity. Don't forget a year later, on their equally uncomfortable parallel path, the Comsat Angels ended up recording a vastly inferior version of one of their own best songs while Jive Records tried, without success, to get them a hit.

Graham, "So we did a demo of it (the album), they didn't really like it but they had nothing else. We were contracted to make another album and this is what we were going to record."

It seems highly likely that "Hothouse" resulted from those demo explorations, catching the ear of an increasingly twitchy record company.

Perhaps unsurprisingly with the passing of time, Mike and Graham's account of events differs somewhat at this point. For Graham *All Fall Down* was not the perverse reaction to being pressured to come up with a commercial record. While from Mike's perspective, writing in the sleeve notes for Renascent's *All Fall Down* reissue, the screws were on,

"The record company were pressurising us to go "corporate rock" - they were disappointed in the meagre sales of *Lions Mouth*. I think they were expecting us to be the instant new Genesis or something. Things were getting nervy, we could feel the weasels closing in. "Get more commercial boys." Fuck that! It was time to go deeper and bite the hand that feeds."

Mike went further in his Penny Black Music interview,

"We fell out with Rob Dickins. We didn't like him. We didn't like the company. We thought they weren't giving us the support that we were due and that if they really wanted a commercial album they had got to put plenty of money behind it which with both *Jeopardy* and *From the Lions Mouth* they hadn't really done. They felt we weren't being co-operative enough and the whole relationship didn't work really, so when they turned around and said 'The solution is for you to write more commercial songs,' we thought. 'Fuck you' and went ahead and produced *All Fall Down.* Ironically, however, they did go and spend money on it by hiring the Manor, Virgin's studio out in Oxfordshire ."

Today Mike simply says that, "It felt to me like the band were deliberately sticking two fingers up to WEA by making *All Fall Down* the way we did."

For Graham talking to the Arcane Delights website it was a different story,

"There weren't conflicts as such, at least not until they heard the final recordings. Then they said they wanted us to make it more commercial, so we went in and added the pounding bass drum on "We Could Go Far" as the only concession. Like I said, recording *All Fall Down* was a lot of fun. The reality was Adrian and I realised there wasn't going to be another Second Layer project, so all the ideas and some of the songs came from mixing the two together. And no, we didn't (ever) go into the studio to deliberately make an uncommercial record. Who in their right mind would do that? Equally, we never tried to make something commercial. That was never a factor when composing music!"

It is of course quite possible for two people in an intense situation to experience it differently and to relate events accordingly.

What was Adrian's view?

Back in 1996, when speaking to Jan, he recalled the circumstances surrounding *All Fall Down,*

"WEA hated *Lions Mouth* so there was no pressure for more of the same. They wanted us to be a pop band! But having said that they certainly didn't like what we then came up with, we got dropped as soon as they heard it. Then they had to re-sign us. They had to come begging back to us, which they didn't like, because the European label was wanting a follow-up. They had to come back and say, "What do you want? We are going to release this."

Although Mike talks of "meagre sales" in reality *Lions Mouth* hadn't done that badly. OK it didn't set the charts alight in the UK but arguably it raised the band's profile sufficiently around the world. If the label had taken a more nurturing approach like say IRS did with R.E.M, then maybe the relationship could have continued. So far they'd bought a critically acclaimed debut for pocket change and funded a post-punk classic, so not a bad outcome but then that's not what business is really about is it?

The cash tills weren't ringing. Adrian was sanguine,

"They had Modern Romance, they were probably happy with them! It's their business to be looking after their investments. But a big company even now should look at what they have instead of trying to change it. Why not exploit what it is? That's what we thought at the time."

The advice Adrian then gives to any band signing a major label deal is simple, but hits at the crux of why so many deals end up disappointing everyone, sadly though it's the artist taking the biggest risk,

"My advice to any band, make sure the company is signing you because they like you, not because they want you to be something else!"

The final word on the intention behind *All Fall Down* must be left with Adrian,

"We weren't provoking anyone, it was just what we wanted to do. We liked it, we thought it was interesting. I always think of *All Fall Down* as something someone like Peter Gabriel would have done."

The reality was that the proverbial 'writing on the wall' had already been daubed before the record was even recorded. WEA had a band without professional management who meant more on the continent than at home and were showing no signs of metamorphosing into something sellable. Worse, they had no recognisable image, weren't cool and even the critics that loved them thought the same. The best that can be said is that today they would have been lucky to have ever got near a major label deal and even if they had, would have been dropped even faster.

Once both label and critics have a narrative it can be hard, if not impossible, to shift them. For writers this is what they hang their review on and in the end get paid for.

Unheralded by a single from the actual album, *All Fall Down* was released in October and immediately abandoned by WEA. It was a sitting target for reviews that indicated some critics were ready to move on.

Melody Maker squeezed in an assessment at the bottom of a page, stuck below a rave review for the debut album from jazz/sophisti-pop band Blue Rondo a la Turk, a sign of the changing times if ever there was one. I'll leave you to debate which album has successfully endured the passing years.

Adam Sweeting was at best unenthusiastic,

"Third time around for the Sound and some things have changed while others remain obstinately the same. Adrian Borland's boys will probably be one of the last of the rock groups as the cosmos shatters into smaller and ever faster moving fragments."

This kind of comment will become part of a familiar theme: namely a band bravely slogging on, despite universal indifference. It's something Adrian referenced, as we shall see, in his statement issued when the band split.

The problem for Sweeting is that the change isn't sufficient, he savages the band for, "a stubborn unwillingness to evolve." Ironically the two

songs he does like, "Party of the Mind" and "Monument," are the only two tracks solely written/attributed to Adrian, not songs intended for

Second Layer. Side two comes in for the worst kicking, allegedly sinking into "a mire without landmarks."

The inevitable conclusion? "Disappointing."

Sounds did award the album three out of five but was scarcely more positive.

Johnny Waller's opening salvo must have stung,

"This is the album the Sound should never have made, didn't need to make, could have made in their sleep and - in a sense have already made twice before!"

"Virtually worthless, stagnant, cliched, overbearing, leaden, competent, uninspiring."

The insults pile up with a sense of disappointment expressed at expecting more from the band. Side two is again singled out as being, "crushingly forced" and having, "no bloody songs!"

Again Adrian's solo compositions are highlighted and 'advice' given to focus there rather than 'compromise.'

Perhaps the most tragic part of the review is towards the end,

"The rock machinery is swallowing the Sound whole and, like a drowning man, the more they struggle, the worse they suffer."

Whatever you may feel about the savaging of *All Fall Down,* those words encapsulate what was happening to the Sound, irrespective of the album's actual merits.

They had been cast adrift by management, their label and much of the music press, labelled as 'too serious' and 'uncool.'

Can you recover from that?

A couple of years back another post-punk cult figure was interviewed for a bittersweet feature in the *Guardian*. Andy Partridge of XTC did achieve those elusive hits but despite many classic albums the feeling of underachievement has hung over the band. Some of his comments could just as easily apply to Adrian,

"It may seem strange to non-UK residents, but location and appearances are so important. One of the reasons we never clicked in England is because Swindon is the joke town,"

It could still feel ludicrous to cite geographical considerations but it's really not. If the Sound had hailed from Manchester or Liverpool and Adrian had been tall and thin would WEA have felt their investment justified the big bucks treatment?

Graham's acidic assessment is no doubt correct,

"The trend at that time was the 'pretty boy' emasculated male... and that's where the money went."

The saddest thing of all is that Adrian knew it.

Back in the Andy Partridge interview the next question for Andy was, who won in your battle with the music industry? The answer, preceded by a hearty laugh, was,

"I did of course! I got a life out of it. They're not sculptors, painters, or poets. All they've got is money. And money's nothing."

Jan asked Adrian what his measure of success was, if you've been paying attention, the answer won't surprise you.

Adrian, "Making a brilliant album, I've always said that. Money can't be your main consideration."

And the thing with Adrian you really don't doubt his sincerity even for a millisecond. The tragic question for him though was whether he was strong enough and lucky enough to survive the route he knew he was taking? We know the answer but that doesn't make it easier to accept.

In the uncharted depths of Youtube, beneath one of the endless Sound songs you can sample there, as millions do, there's a heartfelt comment from a random YouTuber somewhere in the world,

"The Sound was meant to be that cool band in the dark and forgotten corner."

It feels poetic and sadly true, Adrian and his quixotic venture hit home in the end achieving coolness in posterity.

The question now though is, was *All Fall Down* really that difficult and all those other damning things the critics said?

CHAPTER 10

Some things aren't how they should be

All Fall Down, could there have been a more apposite title?

As Mike confirmed the band recorded the album in relatively plush surroundings at the Manor, (normally a residential studio) Nick Robbins produced and future uber producer Flood engineered, alongside Craig Milliner and Steve Prestage.

Graham, "Adrian had done some calling round and managed to get a deal with the Manor where we would work the nights while another band recorded in the day and we wouldn't stay there. So we got it at a third of the price. But then the band recording in the daytime pulled out, so they said would you mind doing it in the day? They also said you may as well stay here as well."

Inspired by some of the Test Department-style proto-industrial 'metal bashers' appearing at the time, Graham brought in some metal poles to hit as percussion. Apparently this raised some eyebrows,

Graham, "We're in this major studio with pieces of metal that we're going to hit, Flood didn't know what to make of it, it didn't phase Nick of course. I know it sounds wacky but it worked!"

No doubt Flood was able to apply the experience gained when Depeche Mode did the same thing a year or two later.

Interviewed by *Melody Maker* in 1985 in piece that sat beneath a wry, Bunnymen referencing title, *Confessions of a Yo-Yo Man,* Adrian told Matt Smith of a tense and surreal recording experience,

"We were drinking far too much when we made it. We went in on the first day and did five tracks all at twice the speed they should have been. One morning I got up and according to reports I was almost blue. Max came down for breakfast and said, 'Hello' and that annoyed me so much I just slammed my fist on the table and yelled, 'Fuck off!' It was a weird time and the album reflects that."

Allowing for a degree of myth-making bravado on Adrian's part, the reality was that although he more or less totally eschewed drugs, alcohol was an issue for Adrian, as in too much, too often.

On the subject of drugs, much later he confessed to Jan that he was, "mucked up enough already" without the added complication of narcotics.

Julie and Adrian

Julie confirms,

"Adrian didn't take drugs at all, but he did drink a lot, which wasn't necessarily helpful."

It's hard to identify exactly when excessive drinking becomes a 'drinking problem' but it was something that Adrian's mum Win acknowledged in the sleeve-notes to the posthumously completed *Harmony and Destruction* album, referring to the "seductive lure of alcohol."

Certainly we've established that the mood surrounding the band was metaphorically and literally akin to 'drinking in the last chance saloon' regardless of the actual quantity of alcohol involved.

As for the rest of the band, drugs did find their way into the lifestyle. No one was immune although Max and Graham journeyed the furthest and ended up dabbling with heroin which perhaps unsurprisingly caused its own tensions, but that was a little way off.

One listen to that infamous title track, sitting there in its baleful pole position, and it all makes sense. The faces of the WEA execs must have been a picture when it came blasting out of the, no doubt expensive, office stereo system.

According to Adrian the song was written in a Belgian dressing room in early 1982. At Graham's suggestion Adrian recorded the vocal outside in the open, photographic evidence of which was included within the Renascent reissue. The effect is unsettlingly intimate rather than naturalistically calming. Ambient noise, a harsh drumbeat, discordant synths and a general mounting tension dominate. The massed 'Manor Choir' delivers the Black Death referencing chorus refrain while Graham's bass tunnels into your soul.

For Adrian, sounding quite measured until the final nightmarish verse, the nation is damned, no one is angry enough and it's two minutes to midnight: collapse is imminent and no one is coming to rescue us.

For Adrian, sounding quite measured until the final nightmarish verse, the nation is damned, no one is angry enough and it's two minutes to midnight: collapse is imminent and no one is coming to rescue us.

As a statement of intent it's miles away from previous Sound album openers, oddly though it's actually bizarrely catchy, in a perverse kind of way. However I think we can safely assume Second Layer still want their song back.

Adrian recording the vocals for "All Fall Down" outside Rockfield Studio

Presumably Rob Dickins wasn't around to suggest an alternative album opener, maybe WEA didn't care by then.

After that onslaught "Party of the Mind" is like the cavalry arriving. Catchy, nimble, a great chorus, almost a nice single. But the jaunty keyboard, yes, 'jaunty,' decorates a song with a unique and very clever lyric from Adrian. Throwing a good party comes easily for some not so much for others, the mood can change in a second and things can degenerate as quickly. For Adrian the invitation is bittersweet, he wants all parts of his character, all moods and feelings to coexist. But it's not a plea for eternal equilibrium and happiness, he was already too wise to believe that could happen. There's a queasy out of balance feeling accompanying the recognition that, "some things aren't how they should be." That sense permeates *All Fall Down* from the broken safety glass on the cover through each and every song.

There's something particularly wrenching about the section where Adrian imagines his companion, reacting to signs of trouble,

"There's a disturbance over by the stairs
And her face looks round for me
Her eyes say something's going wrong"

Maybe it's an admission of the futility of hoping for 'normality,' the haunted, searching look in the eyes of the other person tells Adrian, 'the nightmare is happening again.' Making it hard not to think back to Adrian and Julie at that party, the night after hearing of Ian Curtis' death, Julie realising Adrian's distress and taking him home.

But despite everything it's a humorous song, Adrian happily inviting all, including his "anarchist friends."

The drunken lurching party sounds and discordant guitar that start to envelope the song as it unravels are the final genius touch.

And then some genuine relief. "Monument," sans vocals, later became the band's intro tape, and it's not hard to see why. It has something quintessentially 'Sound-like' about it. The tender tristesse that underpins much of Adrian's writing. Johnny Waller in that *Sounds* review mentioned the awkward lyrical metaphor and I wouldn't disagree, it is a little forced. But you know what? It doesn't matter. Two Sound classics in a row by any reasonable assessment.

Interestingly we're back in Second Layer territory with "In Suspense." Not sure if that's Graham's rhythm generator or just a common or garden drum machine, Adrian's guitar curlicues running around it and then what sounds like the deep tones of a grand piano, but probably isn't. For a Second Layer song it's actually another relatively accessible track, with a bit of tweaking perhaps it could have been a more forward thinking single. I've always thought this was a significantly ahead of its time Sound song, relying as it does on piano as lead instrument for a good portion of the running time. A little echo of "Hothouse's" jungle" 'vines that creep and spread" here though it's "wires" that, "creak and slip."

Adrian's explanation of what the band were trying to do makes sense, there's a lot of variation on *All Fall Down,*

"We were trying to do something different with each track, even "Glass and Smoke," it's a depiction of chaos which is kind of neat, it has its moments. "Monument" is a stand-out and "Where the Love Is." But then someone's favourite track might be something like, "In Suspense" which is more experimental. I like that about the album."

Adrian was right: side two ends with yet another Sound classic; "Where the Love Is." Underpinned by sonorous synth-bass, Mike's resolute drumming overlaid with Max's piano riff and light synth interjections are the perfect set-up for Adrian's cathartic guitar solo. Spines will tingle and the hairs on the back of your neck will be raised, it's that kind of song. Sheer beauty and agony combined.

The desperation behind the lyrics is palpable,

"In a room on the floor with you
I want to be in that room with you

Because it's where the love is"

A fantastic song and the perfect end to side one.

Adrian has proven himself a pretty astute critic of his own work so we should probably take note of this comment made to Jan, referring to *All Fall Down*,

"It lacks something, it's not coherent enough, side two drifts off a bit. It's not as strong as it could have been."

Harsh or pretty much on the nail?

Well side two does begin, not with the usual bang, but instead with one minute of ambient piano and gentle looped rhythm, certainly not what you would normally encounter in the important opening slot, "Song and Dance" does then slam straight into a speeding rocker that acquits itself well. However in the pantheon of Sound songs, where standards are extremely high, it does have the feel of a superior B-side. Not fatal and still very enjoyable in the context of the album as a whole, with lots of interesting buried sounds and textures to enjoy.

Adrian has confirmed he wasn't happy with "Calling the New Tune", describing it as a victim of the democratic approach the band had adopted at that point. For him it was becoming, "80s music, with that funk bass line and syncopated drums." He made sure it was only performed live once.

Heard today it's actually quite an appealing song, with far too interesting an atmosphere to end up as 'random '80s music'. The chorus has a certain hypnotic pull and it works really well at this point in the album, not a stone cold classic but more than solid. And yet when you consider Adrian's view, maybe you can see that he felt the fire was burning a little too tamely for its 3.5 minute duration.

Something which can't be said about the raging "Red Paint," a song that survived in the setlist long enough to strafe the audience at the Marquee and to have pride of place on *In the Hothouse.*

Driven by Graham's bass and including an ominous, low in the mix, murmured humming effect. "Red Paint" feels like an anti-fascist alarm call, so always welcome.

For Adrian however the song was not quite that simple,

"Red Paint" is about politics but not really taking a stance more questioning the herd instinct."

He intended the track as a reminder that, "all problems start from individuals then become mass problems."

Intent and execution make it a highlight of the 'problematic' side two.

I'm sure Graham would have chosen to die in a ditch rather than have "Glass and Smoke" removed from the running order, and I can respect that. You can imagine him grinning from ear to ear as he stabbed at the synth bass.

No doubt Adrian loved the 'middle finger to the world' nature of the piece. And it is a 'piece' more than a song and should rightfully be assessed in that way. This is a 'mood,' not something for people to whistle while cleaning the windows. Judged on those terms it's a success, albeit a potentially indulgent one. But that's the thing with *All Fall Down,* it's all part of the greater experience.

For close to seven minutes Second Layer hi-jack the Sound's album and have a metal bashing party. Lurching back and forth, erupting with noise, "Glass and Smoke" is gleefully full of apocalyptic anarchy. The reviewers had this one wrong, imagine the Bunnymen or U2 daring to even think of sneaking something like this past the record company!? The alcohol and drug reference implicit in the song title tells its own story.

Following it with the sheer, wistful beauty of "We Could Go Far" is clearly no accident, bearing in mind Adrian had admitted to 'control freakery' when it comes to track sequencing.

That its beauty survives the bass drum that thuds throughout speaks volumes. The decision to add that drum remained a mystery for many years until the unadorned original version appeared as part of Edsel's first Sound CD box. It seems the song was the sole result of WEA's concerns regarding *All Fall Down*'s lack of commercial prospects. Clearly someone was desperate to justify their job as it's hard to imagine what possible positive difference such tinkering could make.

Graham, "We were told, 'make the album more commercial.' We said, 'How? It's what we wanted.' They said, 'well, you need a bass drum in "We Could Go Far." ' So we went back and brought the click track up."

Interestingly Jan later received an insight from Adrian into the recording of his deeply resonant vocal - something that involved another clash with Bob,

"Several years later Adrian told me that a row between them before the recording session had fed into the passion with which he sang "We Could Go Far."

The song itself is the perfect end to a strange trip of a record. A premature elegy for the band? Possibly. A warped response to their A&R man's query as to where they saw their career going? Maybe.

Interestingly Jan later received an insight from Adrian into the recording of his vocal - something that involved another clash with Bob,

"Several years later Adrian told me that a row between them before a recording session had fed into the passion with which he sang "We Could Go Far." '

I prefer to think it's a consoling word from Adrian to us and himself, another arm around the shoulder and a message of hope, even though you may not quite believe it yourself.

"Yes, we could go far."

The "yes" carries the emotional weight here.

Hope, it's the thread that runs through all of Adrian's work and is the key to why it endures, in song he could face the dark, acknowledging the pain of existence. Yet at the same time he would draw you in and bring to life a route through, to live to fight another day. The heart would keep beating. To share in that way took so much from him but was essential to who he was, it's just that in the end it was too much.

On *All Fall Down* the hope becomes more fragmentary and distorted, its strength is tested to breaking point but just about manages to hold.

So no, this wasn't the disaster some tried to paint it as, instead it's an often thrilling, always intriguing, journey to the strange place the Sound occupied in 1982.

Adrian summed it up succinctly as ever,

"We were taking something of the Bowie, *Low* attitude. Not that it sounds like it, but the attitude that you mess around with music and try to come up with something else. You take the intrinsic parts and you muck 'em around, move the jigsaw pieces about until it's interesting. In a way, I was trying not to write songs but to write around the mood the band was creating, writing lyrics on top of performances."

For Mike, talking to Penny Black Music, the picture was always more mixed,

"Well, some of the more experimental stuff, like the stuff with the drum machines and so forth, is I feel in terms of the songs, really weak, while other stuff, like "Monument," "Party" and "We Could Go Far", is amongst our best work. There are some great songs on there. Some of it just didn't work though."

As to its fate,

"I think maybe our aspirations were a bit too high. We were definitely getting into that 'this is art' situation, which is always going to be at odds with a major label like Warners."

Graham remains proud and unrepentant, his assessment heavily influenced by the total blast he had making it,

"For me it was the best album we recorded. It was the most fun in the studio, there's so much stuff buried in the mix, it's really complex and not quite what it appears, I love it!"

My advice? Listen without preconceptions, if that's possible: *All Fall Down* is a vital, rewarding part of the Sound's body of work, rankings are meaningless.

1982 had something in common with 1981 for the Sound. They played a major outdoor festival and Adrian, clad in an Iggy t-shirt and quoting

Doors lyrics, caused a bit of a stir.

This time the festival had a 'political' slant. No Nukes, Utrecht was the Dutch version of a festival that had previously been held in Madison Square Garden with various big names involved. For this iteration the Sound lined up with a range of artists including, funnily enough, U2.

Despite being dispassionate regarding the cause Graham loved it, "Personally, No Nukes was the best of all the concerts we did".

Adrian, "Graham and I didn't want to do it, but we had this agreement in the band that if two people did then that was it. Max and Dudley did, so we did it."

Graham, "It was a massive audience. Of course the concert was 'anti-nukes' not just anti-nuclear weapons. We get on stage, we're cheered on, as we're already quite popular in Holland, which was great. Adrian wasn't shy of voicing his opinions onstage. He started summarising his and I's views and is egging the audience on. He gets them to burn their literature. I think he realised how much power you have on stage. It was an amazing moment. The way we came off stage was as well, we didn't finish the song we just got quieter and quieter and then walked off. We left the audience in a hell of a state!"

This is the modern age so you can watch the performance on *Youtube* and a live album was released by Renascent. It's an incredible, barnstorming performance full of power, Adrian's rant about the use and abuse of nuclear technology is preserved intact within an extended nine minute version of "Missiles".

To better understand the mayhem of that night it's worth taking into account the fact that earlier Adrian had been barred from the stage by an overzealous security guard who doubted he was a band member. In addition, perhaps unsurprisingly, a quantity of alcohol had been consumed leading to Adrian being in an unspecified state of intoxication.

Mike, "Adrian was very fond of the drink by then and had been drinking all day. It got a bit out of hand..."

In all honesty I prefer the other songs in the set such as the hyper-intense versions of "Hothouse" and "Winning." But certainly the performance is an essential part of the band's history.

It had a deeper implication for their popularity in Holland. The festival was a big deal and was broadcast live by Dutch TV, raising the band's profile accordingly, after all there's nothing like a bit of mild notoriety to create a buzz.

Which helps to explain the curious fact that throughout Adrian's career he was always more successful on the continent but more specifically in his home from home, Holland.

What caused this? Was there some deep emotional connection with the audience there, well no doubt that was true to a greater or lesser extent. But in fact some of the reasons are more prosaic.

Back in the '80s and '90s the Dutch government subsidised youth clubs in many towns of varying sizes, the aim being to lure people off the streets and away from standard 'discos.' The upside for a band like the Sound was that there were far more options venue-wise throughout the country meaning they could play multiple times over the course of a week. Beyond that, during the '81 - '82 period, the band also played iconic venues like the Paradiso on multiple occasions performing to audiences of dedicated local music fans who of course would spread their love of the band by word of mouth.

These tours were well-funded, well-organised and the band was treated relatively well, whereas not all of that was true about playing in the UK back then.

At the same time the two main Dutch music magazines, *OOR* and *Vinyl* were totally on board from the start, covering the band and giving them suitably glowing reviews. A similar thing happened to the Comsat Angels, another UK post-punk band whose success was far greater in Holland than at home.

This unique combination of factors explains much of the discrepancy in popularity levels - it's not maybe the more romantic answer, but it is a persuasive one.

The impact for Adrian was that when business was looking bleak he always had a place to fall back on, even eventually somewhere to live for part of the year.

Important for a band that now had no record deal or manager and were facing the waning interest of the music press. Graham would argue they had their freedom, but what would they do with it and could they survive?

No Nukes, Irenehal, Utrecht, the Netherlands

CHAPTER 11

There's a new way of life, it's up ahead, looks like an open road, but what's up ahead?

There are those who say the eighties started to go wrong at one minute past midnight on January the first 1980. They would of course be wrong: the much parodied and sometimes loathed decade, for all its shallow indulgence, produced ridiculous amounts of great and enduring music. But for all that, some kind of slow decay seemed to set in as we slid into 1983. The colourful optimism of the 'new pop' began, imperceptibly at first, to tarnish. We started to get a sense of the flatulence to come as the decade wound inevitably down to its shoddy nadir, sometime around about 1988, deep in the post Live Aid hegemony and under attack by the onslaught of DJ culture and the Stock Aitken Waterman plastic pop machine.

But for the Sound there were more pressing concerns than the oncoming recalibration of pop culture.

For Adrian we can only imagine his interior dialogue while he gazed from the window of a cross channel ferry in early 1983 as the band returned from their latest tour of the continent. There are likely moments in most of our lives when it feels as if everything we've worked for is slipping away out of reach, for him this was surely one of those.

The following year he confirmed as much when interviewed by Allan Jones for *Melody Maker*,

"The lowest point for all of us was at the beginning of last year. *All Fall Down* had been the most poorly received album we'd released, WEA didn't promote it at all, they didn't even want to put it out, they thought it was too uncommercial. Then in January '83 they decided they weren't going to renew our contract and we thought we'd really blown it."

It's interesting to see that firstly, the deal wasn't over until January, and then that Adrian was perhaps a lot less blasé or pleased about it than maybe Graham recalls.

Adrian, "I remember we were sitting around our drummer's place in Kingston, discussing what to do next and I thought, we're no better off than if we were four bricklayers discussing this. In fact four bricklayers could probably form a band and be more successful tomorrow than we are now after three or four years..."

It's sobering to think how many bands would have called it a day in such circumstances but Adrian and the Sound somehow picked themselves up and carried on.

Adrian, "We just thought, no: it's too easy to pack it in. It was reassuring to realise our early idealism hadn't been blunted by four years in the music business. From then on it was a case of us starting to rehearse again in someone's front room, just like in the early days, and suddenly it was all there again, the energy and determination, the original spirit of the Sound. It was like a total rejuvenation. We survived. A lot of groups don't."

There's a very telling comment from New Order's Bernard Sumner that comes towards the end of the sleeve notes included as part of Joy Division's *Heart and Soul* box,

"With Joy Division, I felt that even though we were expecting this music to come out of thin air, we were never, any of us, interested in the money it might make. We just wanted to make something that was beautiful to listen to and stirred our emotions. We weren't interested in a career or any of that. Our reasons were honourable."

Replace the words 'Joy Division' with 'the Sound' and this could be Adrian. Indeed at the end of the Allan Jones interview he asks how he would want the Sound to be remembered, his response is no surprise,

"As four people who weren't afraid to put what they felt onto their records."

However if we track back to early 1983 we can see just how bruised and fragile Adrian had been feeling. In a feature for a long gone magazine called *Electronic Soundmaker* the interviewer David Bingham notes a pause in the discussion and senses a dissatisfaction on Adrian's part at the way the interview is going,

Adrian, "I wonder if there's something more cheerful for us to talk about? I mean a lot of what I've been saying has been, 'why haven't we made it type talk,' which is always a bit depressing to read."

He suggests talking about another subject such as why he got into music or what he gets out of it? Not something you often see in an interview, a moment where you feel the veil lifted and a more unguarded response is coming. Although with Adrian I'm not sure he could ever really just do a 'sales job' when interviewed. Nevertheless his comments run deep,

"Alright, well I don't think I chose to do it. It's one of those things in the past that would have been called, 'God's work'. It's the only thing I consider myself any good at, apart from doing an ordinary job and being an unnoticed person."

The use of the phrase, "unnoticed person" is significant. To hear an artist openly articulate such a fear of anonymity is unusual and confirms the feeling that Adrian would have struggled to cope with any form of 9-5 existence. As we shall see, he needed the recognition and attention.

Adrian, "A lot of it is to do with ego type things. I've changed a lot since I started doing this. Before the band I was a very extrovert type of person, cracking jokes all the time and doing stupid things. I don't know if I've become sadder or if it's the fact that I'm performing a lot on stage and putting a lot into it."

The next line is even more striking bearing in mind what we know of Adrian,

"I think you become much quieter in your personal life because that side of you, that energy, has got out; it's escaped and I'm left with being a very quiet person which I never used to be."

Adrian tries to further explain it,

"It's probably a desire to show people how I feel. What is that? Exhibitionism I suppose? But it's better than singing a load of lyrics you don't believe in or being something you're not."

He said a lot in relatively few words and echoed the purity of intention demonstrated by Bernard Sumner.

Talking to Jan in 1996 he seemed to have realised the cost,

"Putting extreme emotion in a song means you have to deliver it on stage in that way."

Adrian goes on to cite a Lou Reed lyric from "Open House" a *Songs for Drella* track where Lou sings of Andy Warhol observing that, "you scare yourself with music."

This lead to Adrian musing,

"Maybe the energy you put into it means you don't have a lot left for life. Scraping away at your own subconscious; it's not always a good thing to do, most people don't in their life. Aren't we brave? blah, blah, (laughs). It's part of the job then you find you have no psychic defences left."

Clearly in the years between the two interviews Adrian had arrived at a hard-won understanding of what his art was costing him.

It had been in his mind for some time, when I interviewed him in 1992 he met me at Wimbledon station and Bob drove us to Adrian's local, the Crooked Billet where our chat took place. On the way Adrian spoke quite seriously of the need to sing more optimistic songs as there was a real risk of his songs becoming a self-perpetuating cycle.

I didn't fully understand him at the time but now it seems much clearer. Despite what some have said, while music was essential and inseparable from Adrian's very being, it wasn't really therapy: it came at a terrible cost.

But there in 1983, from somewhere, he found the strength to continue and on the Sound went.

During the first few months of the year the band toured extensively in Holland, Belgium, France, Italy and Switzerland. But in the later part of this crucial year things quietened down considerably, as Mike Dudley confirms,

" '83 was the point where it all started 'shrinking-in' really."

However before that happened the Sound made it to the USA for the first time. Granted it was only for three east coast gigs in New York, Philadelphia and Washington DC but nevertheless it was an achievement to make it there at all and could have been the start of something much bigger. This was the merest hint of a 'toe in the deep water' of the US market, obviously to make even a dent in the States would have required a huge commitment from the band and whatever label was supporting them. Sadly, although they made one more memorable trip, the USA remained another tantalising 'what if?' situation, amongst the many in the Sound's lifetime.

It's unclear who financed the tour although it's possible it was the last gasp of their WEA deal which, as Adrian confirmed, didn't actually end until January. Either that or the still on board Mick Griffiths pulled it out of the bag.

When I spoke to him in 1991 Adrian confirmed, "I think the first tour paid for itself."

Beyond the career opportunities a trip to the USA brought, these three dates also brought about a dramatic change in Adrian's personal life.

Adrian and Julie on the road

If you pay attention to sleeve notes you may well have devoured Adrian's cryptic song summaries included within the Renascent CD reissue of *Shock of Daylight* and *Heads and Hearts*. Interesting both for what they allude to as much as for what they actually confirm, check the entry for "Longest Days" and also, perhaps unsurprisingly, "Total Recall."

"The Philadelphia Sound - a waitress at Ribits, an invitation to a gig, and the rest wasn't history at all. Hi Earlene. And to think I'd been rock 'n' roll celibate/faithful for four years up 'til then."

It's actually *Rib-its* and was part of a chain of restaurants in the area, now defunct. Judging by the TV ad preserved for 'posterity' on YouTube, probably not the, er, healthiest of establishments but perfect for a hungry rock band, whatever they were hungry for.

What Adrian alludes to is the break-up of his four year relationship with Julie, as a result of a liaison with a waitress, the 'Earlene' mentioned. For Julie who was in the middle of her university finals it was pretty earth shattering.

Julie, "They were on tour in America and he met this girl in Philadelphia. I remember it well as at the time I thought it was the end of the world. He came back and said, "I'm really, really sorry but I've met this girl called Earlene and I'm in love with her."

Adrian himself was massively upset and full of apologies but seemed to have fallen head over heels in love and couldn't treat this as a 'what happens in tour stays on tour' moment. Both he and Julie spent a week in tears before the inevitable final endpoint of their girlfriend/boyfriend relationship.

Julie got through her degree and maintains that Adrian was genuinely traumatised by what happened. The irony is that this event coincided with the band's tour manager quitting. Maybe surprisingly Adrian then offered the role to Julie,

Julie, "I had no idea but everyone said, "do it!" My parents were horrified! It turned out to be an amazing experience."

In case you're wondering, no, Earlene didn't turn out to be the love of Adrian's life and probably ended up the subject of a few difficult and expensive transatlantic telephones calls. But without her we would be two classic Sound songs the poorer, although in this case it was ultimately more Julie who suffered for the art than Adrian. Maybe he was caught up in the head-spinning rock'n'roll experience of visiting America for the first time, he wouldn't be the first, or the last.

Adrian waiting in a hotel lobby in the USA

Still it was another impulsive act on Adrian's part, but one that clearly he struggled with himself, adding to the whirlpool of emotions and events swirling around him in 1983. That he could end a long-term relationship with a person he clearly loved but then enlist her as an employee of the band can be viewed as either mature and pragmatic or, less charitably, calculatingly self-centred and selfish. What is clear though is that Adrian and Julie had a strong bond that would continue for some time yet and there's little doubt she would have taken up such an offer unless it was something that felt right.

The return to the UK must therefore have been quite a crushing descent back down to reality. Once the Earlene moment had passed, focus needed to return to finding a new home for the Sound.

Ironically the eerily similar route the Comsat Angels were travelling brought them to a similar place but with a different stopping off point. The Comsats swallowed hard and signed with an unashamedly pop label Jive Records. The result was a band squeezed into uncomfortable spaces, the discomfort apparent on their faces as they dressed up for glossy photo shoots and allowed outside producers to suggest contemporary production styles that they would grow to regret.

This was not the risky course the Sound would choose to take, although whether it was really a possibility isn't clear. According to Adrian negotiations with various labels went on for eight months, which can't have been easy as the band didn't have a professional manager (the Comsats did, which may account for what happened to them). Virgin, EMI, CBS and A&M allegedly all sniffed around but perhaps unsurprisingly nothing concrete materialised. Some guarantee of commercial viability or willingness on the band's part to take 'direction' and be malleable, must have been sought, something Adrian would have struggled with, as would Graham. Others, specifically Mike, may have been more open to the necessary adjustments this would have meant, he'd made no secret of a desire for higher level success.

But after the WEA deal, and the second fiddle to the Bunnymen game they were left playing, it was a indie-hybrid label operation by the name of Statik Records that came up with an offer the band decided to accept.

Statik was that curious of beasts, an indie with a tenuous link to a major label, in this case Virgin. Still, this was not another 'boutique' label like Korova. Set up in April 1981 by, surprise, surprise, ex-Virgin employee Australian Laurie Dunn, their first release had been an album by Scots post-punk band Positive Noise. The label's tiny offices in West Kensington were a far cry from WEA's comparative grandeur. But Statik briefly had some serious money. They'd struck gold with a hit by Canadian oddballs, Men Without Hats, whose 1982 "Safety Dance" single became a substantial hit in various countries, including the UK where it made it as far as number 6, selling 400,000 copies in the process. A curious record that teetered on the edge of novelty but was at its heart an extremely catchy synth pop/new wave mix.

So the Sound's timing was initially right, the label had some money, for now, and was headed by an experienced industry figure who actually loved the Sound's new songs and wasn't immediately looking to change them into something more 'sellable'.

It was a nice change from Korova/WEA who, remember, were blown away by the Sound's live show but didn't really seem to understand what they signed.

Allan Jones in his *Melody Maker* interview with Adrian the following year confirmed, "Statik loved the songs, wanted the group, it was as simple as that."

In the same chat Adrian sounds upbeat but chastened,

"We were very naive when we started, we thought we could make it just on our ability, the quality of our songs. Obviously, I'd still love to be on *Top of the Pops,* I'd love to play a sell out tour of this country, but if that doesn't happen, it's not the end of the world anymore. As long as the records are good, sometimes that's all I care about."

And the records were more than good, they were great.

Statik provided a modest budget and the Sound arrived at the newly created Townhouse 3 studios (previously owned by the Who) in Battersea.

The Sound's aims were more realistic, although the songs were a world away from *All Fall Down's* dark paranoia. This was the Sound doing a persuasive phoenix rising from the fire impression. When Allan Jones interviewed Adrian for the mini-album release (seriously, it's not an EP despite what some say) he described Adrian as "chastened by those months of doubt," however when asked by Jan how they felt at this stage he challenges that view,

"No, we'd toured *All Fall Down* for a year by that point remember, we'd got that out of our system, I wouldn't say 'chastened.'"

The emotion that seems to drive *Shock of Daylight* is defiance. It's there in every song, even the austere "Winter." But rather than a calculated bid for success this seems like a natural process of identifying the band's strengths and distilling the renewed energy they felt into concentrated bursts. Hence the use of the mini-album format. Although Adrian mentions being short on songs, that seems unlikely. One thing we can agree on, these were songs with a capital 'S,' the exploratory song sketches of *All Fall Down* were nowhere in sight.

Adrian, "They are songs yeah! We were trying to discover what we did best and to try to hit it. And that (*Shock of Daylight*) was what we did best."

The convenient angle is that the Sound delivered the album WEA would have loved to receive from them. But really? They could possibly have found ways to work with it, but it's simplistic to imagine that *Shock* would have changed their major label trajectory.

Recorded in a concentrated ten-day session, Statik brought in Pat Collier to produce. Pat was a veteran of second division punks the Vibrators and had already amassed significant studio experience. He was the archetypal 'safe pair of hands.'

Also on board were old friends from the Tortch Records days, Tim and Sarah Smith then of the Cardiacs. Tim and Sarah would supply essential punchy brass on opener, "Golden Soldiers",

Pat recalled the sessions for the second Cherry Red CD box,

"I was very impressed with the Sound, they were fired-up and well rehearsed. They knew the songs inside out."

This tallies with Mike's recollection of the sessions,

Mike, "We never ever used the studio as a place to formulate the material, partly due to financial considerations, it was always ready to go. We knocked it out, it was pretty efficient."

Pat remembers Adrian as, "quite pushy but in a good way, he knew exactly where he wanted the songs to go" and confirms that the Sound "weren't preoccupied with too many synths" and "didn't fall prey to the worst of '80s production techniques." His ultimate assessment?

"They weren't trying to be too poppy or to be like whoever was in vogue at the time. These are some of the reasons why their music still sounds good now."

Speaking on the C86 Story podcast Graham was realistic about the band's aims.

"We realised we needed to do something a little more commercial and to try to get back what we'd lost after *All Fall Down*."

The outcome was partly by design and, as confirmed by Mike, also in part down to simple financial and time constraints. Not that Adrian was ever going to throw his much valued integrity away on a botched attempt to emulate Depeche Mode.

Talking to Jan he confirmed as much,

"There are areas of music you have to be careful of - some of the demos had us sounding like Simple Minds, which was really worrying. There was a track called "13 Hours" or was it "Half Past You?" (laughs). It was definitely drifting into those areas."

Ironically "13 Hours" (although not the mysterious "Half Past You") eventually surfaced on the excellent *Will and Testament* live and unreleased collection. And yes, there's a trace of Simple Minds there, whether you consider that a bad or good thing is open to debate, but at this remove it just sounds like an excellent song. Some of those contemporary sensitivities now mean little. What we can take from this is that Adrian's famed 'quality control' abilities were, if anything, overactive.

Released in late March/early April 1984, *Shock of Daylight* interestingly also appeared in the United States where it was released through an arrangement with major label A&M, and oddly given a unique American mastering and cover.

If ever there was a Sound record that could have found a life on North American college radio, then this was the one. But lacking the press push it couldn't, and didn't, happen.

Contrast the artwork: The US version is housed in a 'will this do?' cover, probably knocked up in twenty minutes by an intern, the band captured in London posing slightly awkwardly by the Thames. The rest of the world releases are instead given a very intriguing cover shot of a hand pushing apart some curtains and letting a bright burst of sunlight into a room.

The location?

We're at 2 Hillview again, the bricks and mortar character in this story. And the hand? Adrian's. There he is back in his childhood bedroom posing for an album cover. OK it's not a 23 Envelope work of art, but still it's a dressed down image that complements this record perfectly. And the implication of that photo? Well we can be accused of over analysing, with all the benefits hindsight brings, but the feeling of escape from claustrophobic circumstances and turning to face the light hangs heavy. The problem with facing the light is that sometimes it brings clarity to hard truths and difficult realities.

Press reaction was positive, *Melody Maker* were totally on board, with Allan Jones contributing a two page interview the week before release and a large two thirds of a page review a week later. The coverage feels like a genuine 'second bite of the cherry' for the Sound prompted by a undeniably great record.

And what a review,

"This is the way it sometimes goes: a group plays its way into the frame, cheered on by the enthusiasm of the music press, which always likes to think it knows a good thing when it hears one. Albums are championed, success is predicted; record companies look forward to emphatic ticks in profit margins."

Jones goes on to accurately describe the expected trajectory of an under-performing major label signing as they are unceremoniously ushered towards the exit after failing to deliver the success expected by their paymasters.

It's a stirring review that got the teen me to part with £3.99 of my paper-round money without hearing a note in advance. Was I happy with my investment? I think you know that answer.

"*Shock of Daylight* contains probably the most fearlessly outgoing music the Sound have produced since their urgent, ferociously agitated debut album."

Raising some minor concerns about "conservative" production values, the review rightly details each and every song and concludes,

"And this time, the Sound may be in no danger at all of being washed up in fashion's wake."

Note the slight hedging of bets with the use of "may", and feel the sting of knowing he was sadly wrong. Still it's one of the last times in their lifetime that the band would receive the kind of nuanced, perceptive appraisal they deserved. And not even a hint of a Bunnymen reference.

Over at *Sounds* the response was similar, which is probably not a surprise as the writer was none other than major fan Chris Roberts, someone who as a teenager had followed the band around in their early days. Roberts' review again accurately describing *Shock's* escape to the light, however brief it was,

"If *All Fall Down* chipped away at the gothic walls of *From the Lions Mouth*, *Shock of Daylight* nails down the carpet, but nervously pulls open the curtains."

Preceded by a single in the form of "Counting the Days" which even Radio One gave a few sporadic daytime plays, however fleetingly it felt as if the Sound had turned the tide. As it turns out it was a mirage as seen by that desperate traveller in Mike Dudley's, "long desert of the world's indifference".

But right now we can listen and just marvel at what Adrian and the band delivered against all the odds.

Shock of Daylight is a potent mix of desperate lyrics and, with one exception, uplifting music.

To that end could there be a more suitable opening clarion call than that provided by "Golden Soldiers?"

As Adrian's mother Win reminded us, Adrian longed for the heat of the sun, here on "Golden Soldiers" he goes further, feeling the sun on his face and turning that longing to action,

"Sometimes I'd like to smash those windows open."

The action becomes a testament to the heroism and extreme demonstrations of loyalty the person at the heart of the song is prepared to go to. Maybe Adrian was writing about a character but as he told me, that wasn't really his approach until much later when he did experiment with perspective a little,

Adrian, "No, all my songs are totally written from personal feelings, always have been right from the start of the Sound, that's what it's all been about."

It's tempting to see "Golden Soldiers" as Adrian outlining the states in which he really feels alive, as well as being a restatement of his commitment to music and the band,

"I won't give up the good fight".

He's already told us he couldn't be, "an unrecognised person" and "Golden Soldiers" confirms that he wanted to be something more, not solely as an expression of ego but rather of value or worth. Otherwise, what would be the point in existing?

Pounding rhythm, stabs of brass (from Tim and Sarah) and churning guitar, all drive the song forward. Great touches like the deliberately discordant metallic bangs or swelling bursts of organ and manic piano are allowed to punctuate the onward rush at just the right moments.

The double tracked vocal gives an impression of two Adrian's backing each other up, dancing around the military metaphor telling us all he still has the fire inside.

Shock of Daylight is a perfectly sequenced record, just feel the change in mood that "Longest Days" brings. This is the morning after the night before, Adrian has testified of his determination but now like all of us he faces the test of living through days that can be brutally hard and cold. As we've seen Adrian had plenty of days like this in the downtime away from the thrill of making music, in the time when he couldn't blot out the shadows closing in from the margins.

But apart from all that, did Graham come up with a greater bassline than the one that provides the lithe and relentless spine of this song?

Pure bliss. Mike keeps it steady and unobtrusive and Max nails the everyday sadness that is an inescapable part of life, leaving Adrian to reach again and again for the bittersweet euphoria that he manages to layer into his guitar playing throughout *Shock of Daylight*.

What "Longest Days" ends up doing so well is to provide a crutch for those listening, Adrian directly reaches out and says, "do you feel that way too?"

The way it's done feels as if he's turning round and catching your eyes, seeking to give reassurance even if only to say, "I understand and feel it too." It's a simple technique but hard to do well, here it elevates "Longest Days" out of the singer-songwriter confessional towards something more valuable for the listener: catharsis.

And that's the secret of *Shock of Daylight's* staying power across the years.

We can still easily understand why "Counting the Days" was chosen as a single, this is the Sound at their most light and open. Coasting in on Mike's simple drum beat and the swish of cymbals, we quickly ascend to a place where hope is visible and possibly attainable, but this is still Adrian so that hope is tempered by acceptance of the obstacles ahead, this time in the form of mountains and oceans language co-opted by a few of the 'big music' bands of the time but here used in elegiac terms rather than in the service of chest-beating melodrama.

Adrian, "I got harangued over "Counting the Days," a German fan spoke to me and said, 'How could you write such a happy pop song?! You've sold out!' I said 'No, that was how I genuinely felt that day.' "

Grappling with people's expectations, and what you could describe as 'Ian Curtis syndrome,' was something he was well aware of,

"I always think it's interesting when people expect you to be a very doomy person and you're not, people are complicated and multifaceted. Just to draw on one side of yourself doesn't make it a lie. People are surprised I go to football matches and down the pub!"

Adrian was absolutely not a doomy person; a look around his bedroom would reveal lots of comedy videos, *Fawlty Towers,* Rowan Atkinson, Harry Hill and many more plus a varied selection of books, suggesting his claims of not being a reader to be a touch of false modesty. He was, in short, a voracious consumer of culture.

And precisely in keeping with that complex and multifaceted personal reality, we have side two's crucial starting point, "Winter."

Recorded party at Elephant Studios with the almost ever-present Nick Robbins, "Winter" drew some concern from critics who maybe considered it a return to more morose territory, indeed for *Melody Maker's* Allan Jones it was, "stark, ominous, worryingly brooding." Maybe, but as the ying to the yang of side one's equivalent, Golden Soldiers" it worked perfectly, Adrian confirmed as much in the Renascent reissue's sleeve notes,

"Deliberately placed opposite "Golden Soldiers" on the original vinyl, a la Lou Reed's *Blue Mask,* does anyone else miss vinyl track placement? Now it's all so linear and usually downhill."

As Adrian confirms, virtually a solo track, he also jokes about SAD - seasonal affective disorder, as a reference point. As a song it has a baleful brilliance. There's a Second Layer-like feel to the ominous rumbling synth, and the treated acoustic guitar that finally cuts through couldn't sound more stark and alone. Here Adrian just wants to say, "To hell with it, I'll just sleep the (metaphorical) winter away."

But "reason has gone" and old wounds are letting those feared feelings in. It's almost comical to consider *Shock* may be the Sound's commercial apex and that Adrian was aiming for a brighter more upbeat 'sound' but yet still included "Winter." That it works so perfectly shouldn't really be a surprise.

Adrian, "We still took an atmospheric approach on something like "Winter" which is still 'weird-ish' but with a very strong song."

Mike's thoughts today are instructive,

"I just thought he was being fashionably gloomy, my focus was on the music, everything now is with the benefit of hindsight".

It's worth remembering Mike's comment when dissecting an Adrian Borland song.

Then into the final pair of songs that cement *Shock's* impact; "New Way of Life" and its cousin, "Dreams then Plans."

Adrian, " "New Way of Life" wasn't an area that I particularly wanted to pursue but it was nice to touch on it once, to flirt with it. I think Graham would have gone down that road further but we may have ended up with '80s rock.' On the other hand something like "Dreams and Plans" was the other side of the same coin but so much more interesting to me, more grand and noble."

Adrian's comment says more about the sensitivities of the time than about the relative merits of what are both key components of what makes *Shock of Daylight* such a concentrated burst of brilliance. But they do also show how carefully he considered his work and the care that went into ensuring what he presented to the world was true to him and his original intention.

"New Way of Life" possibly has a little in common with "Calling the New Tune," it's not hard to imagine a remix making it single-worthy, while you can hear Graham's bass edging into funkiness. Its final section reaches a cinematic, widescreen transcendence via Adrian's skyscraping guitar solo that just unfurls and unfurls, belying all the doubt and indecision held within the lyric.

Incredibly "Dreams then Plans" may well go even further. It's halfway point with Max and Adrian chasing some kind of musical resolution is pure catharsis in motion. Adrian murmurs, "She is close" and the hairs on the back of your neck respond.

The contrasting mix of fear of the future up against the hope that something new could bring a better way of life, seems a hallmark of *Shock of Daylight* with mysterious figures, whose love could possibly save you, just beyond your reach out in the shadows.

You can only hope it, at least momentarily, provided something of that catharsis for Adrian. Musically, although he didn't seem keen on the comparison, there's a hint of the non-pompous grandeur Simple Minds achieved on *New Gold Dream*, before unwelcome, stadium-filling bombast elbowed its way in.

Adrian viewed *Shock* as a concerted attempt to break away and show people there was more to the Sound than just the serious young men they'd been portrayed as. A fair aim and undoubtedly *Shock of Daylight* is a shift in gears but it's hardly 'lightweight'. The decision to go with a producer who, while experienced, wasn't known for his hit making abilities has safeguarded the album from the ravages of time, doing us all a favour in the process. Just imagine an alternate reality where Adrian looked over at the Comsats and decided to suggest someone like Mike Howlett. There's nothing wrong with Mike Howlett per se, but the temptation to turn the Sound into a Flock of Seagulls hybrid may have been too great, and where would that have left us?

Adrian and Graham

In the alternative, consider what may have happened if perhaps a producer of the ilk of Steve Lillywhite was a viable option? Too close to U2 for Adrian's comfort I suspect, but maybe the extra push they needed?

Anyway, the simple fact is that the budget didn't stretch either to a Howlett or a Lillywhite.

As it was, a fantastic record was made and some critics once again 'got it.' More great gigs were played and the Sound escaped destruction, seeming like they were on more solid ground again. But that solid ground was really anything but terra firma and the future was about to take a turn for the worse.

CHAPTER 12

No one can help me, no one can stop me, it takes everything I've got to stop from doing something stupid

The Sound recorded another record that was released in the first few months of 1984, actually *This Cover Keeps Reality Unreal* sneaked out a couple of weeks ahead of the main event, *Shock of Daylight*.

A collaboration with Kevin Hewick, a musician from Leicester who had existed on the fringes for a few years and had recorded for Factory Records after a support slot or two with Joy Division.

Mike Dudley confirms that Kevin supported the Sound, they got on well so in November '83 went into Elephant Studios with Nick Robbins and recorded enough songs for an EP.

The Sound undoubtedly contributed more than being Kevin's backing band, each member identifiable, with Graham adding an earworm of a bass line to the lead track "Plenty", the kind of quirky but memorable song that could have picked up a bit of airplay had there been a major label in the background.

Helen Fitzgerald at *Melody Maker* loved it and made an interesting comment about Adrian and the Sound,

"The Sound are an excellent and tenaciously confident band whose illuminating passion is governed by the talents of singer-songwriter Adrian Borland, one of the last remaining exponents of a *real* rock'n'roll ethic."

As a student of the greats I'm sure Adrian loved that last bit. But consider, "tenaciously confident", with its suggestion of someone holding on despite everything and still remaining resolute. No doubt the Sound gave that impression but such confidence was being shredded as the months passed.

Living in the UK that year was a dispiriting and turbulent experience. Beginning in March, the miners strike was a horrifyingly violent fight to the death as Margaret Thatcher and her government sought to crush the National Union of Miners and their members. Police on horseback with batons drawn, evidence of undercover military involvement and a general atmosphere of brutal determination to suppress dissent, set a dark tone across the country. Adrian, with his political convictions and sense of social justice, would have looked on in horror and frustration.

1984's charts were a fascinating mix of pure escapism and ominous social commentary. Managing to straddle both categories Frankie Goes to Hollywood warned of nuclear Armageddon via "Two Tribes" after initially advising us to "Relax." Elsewhere Wham were the ubiquitous bright face of mid '80s Britain, although even that hid as much as it revealed. But late in the year famine in Ethiopia overtook everything, resulting in the biggest selling record of 1984, "Do They Know it's Christmas?" Bob Geldof and Midge Ure's Band Aid project would of course then lead to the epochal musical event of the following year; Live Aid.

The Sound were meanwhile spending quite a bit of time outside the pressure cooker that was the UK.

Touring extensively in April, May and June through Holland, Germany, Sweden, Norway, Denmark, France, Italy and Portugal, before winding up with some choice Dutch and Belgian festivals in July and August. It feels like the itinerary of a band with a split personality. In the UK, without record company support, nationwide touring was a thing of the past, instead gigs were more or less confined to multiple nights at their old haunt the Marquee.

The Book of (Happy) Memories, as previously mentioned, was put together in the aftermath of Adrian's death and includes thoughts and reflections from a range of friends, family and people within Adrian's orbit due to their work in connection with the Sound. The brackets in the title were added when it became clear that some of those reflections were a long way from 'rose tinted'. The result is a fascinating but sometimes very uncomfortable read. What the book does remind you is; there are many different ways to view a person's life and that one view does not always cancel out another.

Perhaps the most unsparing 'tribute' is the piece by Dutch promoter and agent Willem Venema who details his feelings both about the band and Adrian as a person and from there delves into the reasons behind the Sound's failure to make the leap from cult-heroes to more 'bankable' performers.

Becoming their booking agent in Holland back as early as 1981, Willem quickly found that the Sound were a reliable draw at festivals and on the kind of circuit where capacities ranged from 1000 - 2000 people, the most famous of those venues being the genuinely iconic Paradiso in Amsterdam. He also noted their album sales outstripping those of U2 and the Bunnymen and registered the frustration this caused Adrian.

It's to his credit that in 1984 the band could still get on the bills at various festivals in Holland and elsewhere, indeed he acknowledges that for a while it was one sold out gig after another. What disappointed Verema was the reluctance of the band, and Adrian in particular, to take the gamble of booking larger venues and to move their Dutch career to the next level. For Adrian the security of guaranteed full-capacity gigs at more modest venues meant the much-needed income they depended on would continue, the risk of playing to half-empty halls was a step too far for him,

"They went down the beaten track: record - club tour - festival, and, maybe I imagined this, but Adrian turned more and more sour with every gig. Every time I

came up with a new plan, Adrian was not at home, didn't feel like it or had crashed somewhere sleeping off his hangover."

The relationship between the two men also soured, Venema suspecting Adrian realised his lost opportunities a few years later but,

"By then the magic was gone."

Venema admits to feeling sorry for the band and has some equally uncomfortable observations to make about Adrian as a person,

"In my opinion Adrian had a few handicaps. He regularly talked way too much nonsense and got tied up in his own ecstasy. He had a girlfriend he never talked about when on tour, he was everybody's friend."

It's an interesting turn of phrase, "tied up in his own ecstasy," possibly one we can recognise from a more positive angle having witnessed Adrian, the eternal enthusiast.

For Venema Adrian's appearance was also an issue, he claims Adrian would come back from each tour more overweight after the excessive alcohol intake.

Nevertheless he still found much to like about Adrian,

"At his best he couldn't be more friendly, he was reasonably intelligent and in some areas fairly erudite".

But the final verdict is heavy with sadness and regret for opportunities squandered,

"I wasn't able to persuade them, and this very promising band missed the career boat. After the rot set I thought long and hard about this: maybe Borland didn't feel like having a career, who can tell? At first I really did think they were better than U2, and I wasn't the only one."

Of course had the band secured actual management then just possibly more nuanced discussions about future strategy would have taken place, but as we know, they never did.

For Venema the ceiling was hit around the time of the No Nukes
performance, after that things changed. Citing Max and Graham's drug

use and Adrian's drunken behaviour, the picture he paints is not a pretty one,

"Adrian started to pull more and more drunken stunts which were bringing the band down. Max started to snort heroin and I think had a negative influence on Graham, only Mike was the model of English sobriety."

Venema admits he abstained from the cliched rock'n'roll lifestyle and so that may have coloured his impression of what was happening around him, but his comments do seem to be born out by the testimony of others who were there, including Mike Dudley who had already had to read the riot act to Max over his heroin use, telling him to control it or one of them would need to leave the band.

In amongst all this Julie Aldred had her work cut out getting the band from A to B while attempting to shield them from the endless offers of drugs that come with touring at the level they'd reached in mainland Europe. As we can see, she was only partly successful.

It was on such a jaunt in mid-summer that year where Jan (Adrian Janes) travelled with the band in a temporary new role,

"I accompanied the Sound in a sort of roadie capacity in the summer of 1984 when they did a short European tour. I regret I can't now quote from memory some of the things Adrian was saying on the ferry over to Holland, but there was a strangeness about certain of his remarks, and the intensity with which he delivered them, which was unnerving and something I'd never seen before. It was like the humorous side of his nature had been entirely, albeit temporarily, switched off."

Mike Dudley today recalls the odd dual nature of communication with Adrian, with subtle, and not so subtle, shifts from enjoyable to 'off' or jarring.

On later seeing a self-portrait that Adrian had drawn Mike felt that,

"It was almost as if he'd captured that other side, the darker one."

Mike looking at Adrian's self-portrait

How much awareness Adrian had of these shifts we can only imagine, but being out on tour would never have been the kind of environment for sober reflection or rest and recuperation. Equally Jan confirms the changes in manner could just as easily vanish and be replaced by normality,

"Yet I remember, once we had landed and were in the van, how good a mood he was now in, calling across to people in a car alongside us to ask if they were going to the Park Pop festival (where the Sound were due to play)."

When you look at the Sound's itinerary for the second half of 1984 you can feel the jarring effect it must have had on all concerned, zig zagging from the little England oddness of playing the Surbiton Assembly Rooms (alongside the Cardiacs), to a few days later appearing at a couple of festivals in Holland, including Sneekwave, back to London then to finish the year four dates in the USA, financed by Statik. Those four US gigs were this time split between east and west coasts, a cool 2807 miles apart.

In the Renascent *Shock of Daylight/Heads and Hearts* reissue sleeve-notes Adrian identifies new song, 'Whirlpool' as being, on one level at least, about the surreal stresses of touring. While there was more going on here than just another mundane complaint about the rigours of touring on a shoestring, nevertheless the lyrics and unrelenting vortex of the song tell us something of what he and the band were experiencing,

"Night follows night here, daylight just hurts eyes and gets in our way, but we go gladly with smiles like the madman who lurk in the whirlpool".

The strange duality of touring: boredom interspersed with 90 minutes of extreme adrenaline highs.

In amongst all of that there was as usual a new album to record. Bear in mind there hadn't been a full Sound album released for two years, a long gap between releases back then.

In November the band returned to Townhouse Studios to record what would become *Heads and Hearts.*

Funnily enough, that wasn't the original title. The band had initially said the record would be titled, *the Giddy Limit,* something that was reported in the music press at the time. A now rarely used slang phrase meaning behaviour that reaches the furthest boundary of acceptability, as well as having an additional self-pleasuring connotation. Mike Dudley recalls it as a band in-joke changed to the "more significant sounding" *Heads and Hearts.*

This time production was handled by a new name, American Wally Brill. Brill had been working in A&R for A&M Records before moving into production work. The band could no longer recall how he came to produce the album but actually the link goes back to 1983 when a singer named Annabel Lamb, whose music skirted the edges of new wave much like the more successful Hazel O'Connor, had recorded a version of "Heartland," inviting Adrian to contribute and appearing with him, lurking at the back, on BBC music institution the *Old Grey Whistle Test*. Her take was competent but lacked the fire of the Sound's original, not that it was likely she'd better it. Adrian himself wasn't massively impressed.

Nevertheless the track was released as a single, but naturally didn't chart.

Lamb's producer and husband, at the time, was Wally Brill. And there the connection was made, one that would have a second act somewhere further down the line.
Brill recalled meeting Adrian in the early '80s while still working for A&M in London and later coming across *Shock of Daylight,*

"I absolutely loved it and to this day "Golden Soldiers" is one of my favourite songs of all time."

Wally's enthusiasm was the reason *Shock* made it to a US release via A&M, so his appreciation of the band seemed genuine.

His recollection of those early encounters with Adrian is illuminating and paints a vivid picture of Adrian's demeanour in mid-1984,

"My first meeting with Adrian was shall we say, 'interesting' I can't recall it in full but I do remember our second meeting very clearly. He came up to the office because he wanted to talk to me about something. It was a hot day but he was wearing this green leather jacket and he obviously hadn't bathed in a long time, his hair was matted and he looked like a homeless guy."

Julie on tour

Adrian was apparently carrying a bottle of Blue Nun, a German white wine notorious at the time for its cheapness and later famous as Alan Partridge's favourite tipple, cementing its descent into tackiness. As to the green leather jacket, the less said the better.

"Adrian was swigging from the bottle and was obviously drunk, he was talking about something. It was a remarkable meeting! It didn't dissuade me from working with him, he's an artist, it's just character."

Brill confirms Adrian's enthusiasm and highlights a lack of pretension. His overall impression was a familiar one; here was a bright, intelligent person for whom music was the centre of everything but who didn't live up to the visual 'standards' of the MTV era,

"So on the surface of it, Adrian wasn't pretty. Adrian was real. There was nothing glamorous about him. There was never going to be a photo session with gauze on the lens where he looked like some romantic figure. That wasn't him. He looked like what he looked like, and that was it. It was a little tragic, and it was a little stupid in terms of the industry, because as I recall at the time everybody wanted 'beautiful'. And so if you look at the artists that did succeed in that period, most of them were very telegenic or photogenic. And the ones that aren't sort of disappeared or had cult followings."

Brill had a love for the music and some understanding of the band's strengths, it's interesting to hear him focus on what he perceived as their individual strengths, praising the "texture" added by Graham's basslines and the ability and ideas that Mike contributed.

But for him Max was an unheralded strength within the band,

"His invention and creativity were really special, I've recorded a lot of keyboard players but never one who 'plays the spaces not the lines'. I found it thrilling; he was part of the reason the Sound were unique."

Coming after the refreshed return that was *Shock of Daylight, Heads and Hearts* should have been the muscle behind the next push. Instead what it turned out to be was a complex slice of melancholy where love songs merge with existential questioning. Frustration and disappointment running not far below the surface of a relatively glossy production. I say relatively because this is still a long way from the kind of awkward compromises many of their contemporaries were submitting themselves to in an effort to please their paymasters. All of this has left *Heads and Hearts* too often damned with faint praise over the ensuing years.

Mike Dudley has mixed feelings about it,

"It was like recording with Hugh Jones in that we're playing under the influence of what someone else thinks we should sound like, except unlike Hugh, who had a lot of control and had his own sonic signature, recording with Wally was kind of like that except we could do more of what we wanted to do. That was because he didn't have a lot of power and control to project as a person. It sounds OK, in that it's all 'there' but you couldn't listen and say oh this is a 'Wally Brill production.' Rather it's what it is as a result of all the people trying to get their own way against each other."

For Mike the end result was slightly disappointing,

"It's emotionally flat I think, sometimes you react to a piece of music because of the way it sounds and I feel like that with *Heads and Hearts.*"

But intriguingly Adrian's comments to Jan indicate the outcome was in line with his aims for the 'sound' of the album,

"I think it's probably the most musical of our records, if you asked the average person in the street what music is, they'd probably think *Heads and Hearts* was our most straightforward and musical."

But Adrian does echo some of Mike's reservations regarding Wally Brill's production approach,

"We're not uncooperative but we are a pretty stubborn band. You can make suggestions and if they're good we'll take them, but we're not going to do them if they're rubbish. People weren't going to play things they didn't believe in. We want a producer to help us get there, not to hinder."

Still there's no indication the album was a disappointment to Adrian, beyond the comment,

"The mix could be a bit more rock'n'roll."

The album was preceded by a single released, quickly after recording, in November 1984. Statik had stumped up for a rather nice 23 Envelope sleeve, famous for creating the 4AD visual identity, they created a new logo for the band and would design the eventual album cover.

"One Thousand Reasons" was a pop song, obviously the Sound's version of what that entails and a notch down in commerciality terms from "Counting the Days," but still something that could translate to radio play and it did get just a little from Radio One plus some music press advertising from Statik. The song's yearning chorus was catchy but it's difficult to imagine the daytime radio listeners taking to the pensive melancholy of the verses. Their loss of course, but then the talk of hearts put "on ice" and the unresolved emotional turmoil of someone weighing up the pros and cons of a life changing commitment would always appeal to a more 'selective' audience. Wally's talk of Max's ability to 'play the spaces' is in full effect here, it's beautiful stuff. The single was extended and came with two excellent B-sides, enough to sustain fans until the following March when *Heads and Hearts* hit the shelves.

Chris Roberts once again managed to grab the review copy at *Sounds,* awarding five stars and describing the album as, "a classically romantic affair," full of "fractured love stories." This passage of his review if particularly relevant,

"As these fractured love stories bleed out their realistic, action-numbing tension, there's a distilled coming-to-terms with such dilemmas as hopeless energy and frustrated desire."

As is his description of the Sound as a band and the production quality of the album,

"A unit so tightly meshed that power comes through restraint and economy rather than histrionics. The production is invisible, boosting nothing, imposing upon nothing, just presenting what's there. Which is eleven extraordinarily vivid songs, seven of which are as beautiful as breath. Sad that the weakest, "Whirlpool", opens, but in the unpretentious, searing honesty of "Restless Time", the sullen, grinding "Under You", and the dignified grandeur of "Wildest Dreams", "Burning Part of Me" and "Mining for Heart", there's more than enough to cherish 'til you perish. I could go on…"

It's a nuanced review that while betraying Roberts' great love of the band still skewers some of what makes *Heads and Hearts* unique.

In contrast over at *Melody Maker* the narrative was downbeat and concerned. That concern was for the band's future and would be the story that played out in the press over the next couple of years.

Martin Aston cites *Shock* as a welcome comeback, but for him *Heads and Hearts* marked an unwelcome return to, "the furrowed brow and confusion of *All Fall Down,* lacking the "streamlined clarity of its predecessor."

It felt as if the critical view was that it was time for the Sound to take a great leap in the way the Bunnymen had with *Ocean Rain* or Simple Minds with *New Gold Dream.* But the band had eschewed those grand gestures and instead were digging deeper into the feelings and undercurrents they were so good at articulating.

Aston went on,

"Still restless, jagged and shot through with a tense emotive urgency. *Heads and Hearts* is identikit Sound, swirling around in a musical cul-de-sac."

Praise was given for "Whirlpool" and "Love is Not a Ghost," before the ominous conclusion,

"No-one's asking Borland to cheer up - I'd much rather hear someone challenge the turbulent dramas of today rather than gloss over them with lipstick and kisses - but despair is such an unrelenting cancer, and it's affecting the music too. "I can see a distant victory," says Borland. Here's hoping the wait doesn't consign the Sound to the point of no return."

As we've seen there was much wrong with the culture of music writing back in the '80s but equally there was a depth and thoughtfulness to some of the work, whether you agreed with its final conclusions or not.

That wasn't in evidence a few months later when in a live review *Melody Maker* accused the Sound of being on the verge of sounding like, "a latter-day Dire Straits" but it was there in Aston's troubling commentary. Despite his, Mike's and a fair few other fans and pundits' views, *Heads and Hearts* is a mature gem that dives deep into difficult emotional terrain, illuminating corners that many would rather leave in the shadows. Perhaps that's what causes issues for some who prefer their Sound either raw and defiant or anthemic and righteous. To embrace *Heads and Hearts* is to open yourself up to feelings that may not be welcome and likely won't be happily resolved.

As for the production, it's been described as 'glossy,' on reflection I'd prefer maybe, 'translucent.' I always think of the album in terms of its excellent 23 Envelope cover; although have no idea whether the designers, Nigel Grierson and Vaughan Oliver, listened to the music or not. I'd certainly like to think so. The use of a 'frosted' effect and the aquamarine colour palette, as well as shots of green and orange, suggests a very particular mood, only heightened further by the existential implications of a figure viewed from behind staring out across a frozen landscape.

Nigel Grierson of 23 Envelope recalls how the design came together,

"Vaughan had told me that Adrian had been in touch about a sleeve, and asked if I had anything applicable already. I suggested that image which I'd taken on a trip to the Alps. The depersonalised nature of the image, by virtue of it being of a figure from behind, meant it could lend itself to a sleeve (ie. it could be of anyone). Whenever I was doing documentary type photographs, I'd always have one eye on the lookout for something more abstract or textural that might make a good sleeve. I'd liked the context where the chairs felt like they were floating around on a white canvas. I'd also breathed on the lens to soften and abstract the image further. My initial idea was to scribble something across it like it was a personalised postcard from somewhere. We didn't want to do the obvious - a neat image mounted on a plain background with small type, and decided to move it towards something more textural, at the same time as keeping the original graphic integrity of the image.

Vaughan did the final design using the same image enlarged as the background, with the 'broken' weathered typeface look. I don't remember much consultation with Adrian or the band. We just said

'There, what do you think of that?' and it was done."

I suspect when Adrian saw the cover he was more than happy with how the songs of *Heads and Hearts* would be represented.

The aqua-imagery continues into opener "Whirlpool," with its metaphor of opposing currents rotating out of control sucking down those unlucky enough to be caught in their drag. Whether about touring, or the pull of a life that can't be rationalised or held at bay, the tense and disorientating swirl of the song is driven to additional levels of unease by some free-jazz saxophone squeals added courtesy of the late Ian Nelson (then a member of the excellent Fiat Lux and brother of Bill Nelson. Ian joined the band at a couple of Marquee gigs that March, arriving late for the first night and rushing straight on stage sax in hand).

Was there an escape? It's not clear and that's a theme across the territory explored on *Heads and Hearts*. These are not songs with neat 'Hollywood endings.'

In 1991 I asked Adrian for his favourite Sound song, without hesitation he confirmed,

"Definitely "Total Recall." There's something about that song. It's brilliant, it's the way it goes from E to A flat. It's just not normal, it really builds up to that chorus. It's emotional, it's angry, it's a song about what you often feel when you're in love, you actually spend a lot of time feeling angry, I do. Just when you first start, before it gets boring!"

That lonely bass, Mike's rimshots, Max's light as mist synth and then Adrian's circling guitar, leading up to chorus where the sadness takes flight and we are in a place where hope still just about exists. Adrian's Renascent reissue liner-notes suggest a link with that US tour and its emotional entanglement, but the song is non-specific enough to be once again, universal. "Total Recall" articulates a desire to return to a point where communication on a deeper level was secured and longed for possibilities were within reach, we don't know whether that "distant victory" was won, but can hazard a guess.

Adrian harboured some reservations about the result but refers to this version as one of many, indicating his attachment to the song,

"The *Heads and Hearts* recording didn't sound quite as big as I wanted it to. But then that was just one version - it should have been a bit slower and grander for me."

He would have another chance to realise his ambitions sooner than he may have expected but that was a little way off in the future.

"Under You" dives further into an emotional foment. The crystalline beauty of certain passages, especially that blissful coda, aided again by interjections from Ian Nelson, rubbing up against a stark, becalmed sense of anxiety. The lyrics are a litany of troubled soul-searching where the highs are always followed by terrifying lows and in the end no one can help you unless you are within the orbit of the 'person' whose light heals all, however briefly. It's the time alone that chills.

Adrian apparently envisaged a gospel choir in the mix and confirmed the underlying theme of salvation through a meaningful relationship,

"I had/have this serious concept that all human/spiritual life can be embodied in a simple one to one relationship..."

Not sure about 'simple' being achievable but still it's another piece of evidence towards the view of *Heads and Hearts* being an album of love songs, however twisted and conflicted.

Mike felt the song was, "a bit glum" and was concerned by lyrics on some of the other tracks, in particular the "darker side" alluded to on "Wildest Dreams." He did however love Ian Nelson's contributions and had pushed for him to contribute,

"It was my idea to bring him in, he was a brilliant player and contributed a lot to that album. Some people didn't like it because they thought it was 'too jazzy' but that didn't bother me."

"Burning Part of Me" has long felt to me like part of a pair with "Under You," although its yearning highs are that bit higher and maybe its lows aren't so disturbing. Lots of great musical detail; from the low rumble of Graham's bass to that swelling synth and then the rush of the chorus. Why a pair? Well, once more the protagonist has found warmth in a place that will ultimately destroy him/her. On a more prosaic note, what was the 'red' being burnt up? Money maybe? Adrian jokes about being 'not so subtle' so just possibly.

The unintentional response to a Spear of Destiny song, "Love is Not a Ghost" could be the most emotionally upbeat track on side one. Listened to on headphones it's full of nice little sonic touches and could easily have been a single with an atmosphere a lot less chilly than "One Thousand Reasons." Here's Adrian walking the streets, likely a little the worse for wear, defying those who say, 'love is dead' and in the end lapsing into a burst of "Molly Malone", while Ian Nelson's sax sounds more conventionally rousing than at any other point on *Heads and Hearts*, the song's climax touching Springsteen territory.

That should be no surprise, Adrian was a fan as he confirmed in an interview now posted on the *Heads and Hearts* blog,

"This will shock you, but I think Bruce Springsteen is great. His songs are not just about 'cars and girls!'

It's funny to think back to a time when the musical red lines were so firmly drawn that Adrian anticipated surprise at the admission he was a Bruce fan, it actually makes total sense and the results would make their way to the surface again in a few years' time.

Flip the vinyl and in pole position on side two is the dark, disturbing sprawl of "Wildest Dreams" one of the Sound's most underrated tracks. Beginning with the all too significant line,

"Hiding in daylight, biding its time, the monster that wakes in your sleeping mind."

A carefully arranged song rich in detail and nuance that became even more potent in its live incarnation. It's hard to think of many of the Sound's contemporaries who could have pulled off the creation of a sinister soundscape like this without tipping into some gothic pantomime. Wally Brill was so right about Max, sometimes he was the Sound's secret weapon, his synth hovering just above the surface adding the exact amount of necessary atmosphere, deepening an already tense and worrying mood. And yes, as Adrian says, Mike does seem to "imitate a ticking device."

Oddly first single "One Thousand Reasons" is relegated to second place, knowing Adrian's understanding of running order psychology, this must have been a deliberate choice and casts an odd spell over *Heads and*

Hearts' second act.

Adrian was far from happy with "Restless Time" - he felt it had totally failed to reach its potential and only came alive on stage over the course of 1985. As he said,

"A pretty fucked-up song, we hated this version of it!"

Apologising to Max for letting it past his "censorship of crap" Adrian felt it was emasculated by the watering down of his guitar solo. Listening now, it's harder to understand his dissatisfaction, until that is, you compare the studio version with one of the various live takes available. Live the guitar solo draws blood, in the studio it's polished and put away neatly in the body of the song. But clearly, it's not 'crap.'

"Mining for Heart" had a working title of "Julie" and is a song that was written in the aftermath of that 1983 US trip. It's a strange unsettling piece, a long way from what you would identify as a 'love song', and could have been something that wouldn't be totally out of place on side two of *All Fall Down,* the difference though is in the production that leans heavily on the interaction between Adrian's clipped guitar and Max's deep and woozy synth part. Within the Sound's catalogue there's nothing else quite like it, Adrian was happy with Wally Brill's input,

"Mining for Heart" - I thought that was a really good version, I think Wally really got into the atmosphere of that track, maybe better than I would have done. He brought an angle I hadn't thought of."

The character of side two is further tweaked by another track without parallel in the band's song history, "World As It Is," a song about trying to grit your teeth and accepting an imperfect world; something Adrian would never do. An odd sounding track that runs on an energetic dum pattern from Mike and has some very '80s stabs of synth noise plus a spy-theme-like micro-brief piano break. It feels like an interesting B-side rather than a strong album track, perfectly enjoyable but at two minutes eight seconds, more of an interlude.

Adrian admitted to a steal from that old friend, "Raw Power," but when the result is as different as this, I think, we can forgive him.

As the gorgeously bittersweet "Temperature Drop" begins its journey to the end of the line, it's hard to imagine two more different Sound songs rubbing up against each other.

Chosen as *Heads and Hearts'* second single several months later in June 1985, "Temperature Drop" is a beautifully constructed track about the end of a relationship. Coupled with a strong B-side, "Oiled," that had been played live on multiple occasions, it was in many ways a strong single but was up against it in 1985's technicolor pop world.

Adrian was happy with it, as he explained to me in 1991, confirming it was an "end of love song",

"It's about leaving somebody. That's a good song, 'Fire turns to frost, dreams are lost as it dawns on you', that's a good line."

We can speculate whether it was part of the fall-out from the end of Adrian and Julie's long-term relationship, however some of its lines read like a warning to future partners,

"The same way I feel it when it starts, so I know when it stops." Brutal truth maybe, but consistent with Adrian's 'heart before head' approach and either romantically impetuous or callously cruel, depending on your point of view or particular experience. As album closers go, this seems to have been chosen carefully, softly taking us out of a troubled journey while delivering difficult truths along the way.

Adrian, "For much of that album, the first person singer, me, is the victim a lot of the time on this record. At the end though he's the person saying, 'it's over.' It's written from real life. It's a 'hard' song, I can fuck someone up as well. That's *Heads and Hearts'* reality. It's the twist at the end of that record. No one is better or worse, they are all capable of doing that to someone."

When I spoke to Adrian in 1991 this is how he ranked the Sound's albums,

"The best Sound LP is *From the Lions Mouth,* well that and *Thunder Up* and maybe *Heads and Hearts.* We always had that 'building up to something gap', we always had to build up to our classics!"

So Adrian was undoubtedly happy with *Heads and Hearts* well after the dust had settled and doubts had an opportunity to set in. Any subsequent suggestion, otherwise, appears to be misguided.

It's a great record but as a step forward in the Sound's *career* it was a disappointment after the new hope that surrounded *Shock of Daylight.*

Bemoaning the much smaller interview coverage granted by *Melody Maker* one year on, Adrian seems understandably frustrated. No doubt he didn't like the chosen strap line that asked, "Is the game over for the Sound?"

Adrian, "There's an obsession with success and the charts. It's not how good an album is, it's how high it gets. Music isn't a competition! People are saying, 'Why do you carry on if you haven't had this success?' I don't look in terms of 'success' or 'failure' and it surprises me that journalists who are so hot to pick up on a band when they 'sell out' ignore those who refuse to. We're still making valid, thoughtful music. What the hell's wrong with that? Isn't it enough in itself? It is for me."

The interviewer Mat Smith is understanding but outlines the harsh realities of the marketplace, eliciting this telling response from Adrian,

"Obviously you have to sell enough records to justify your existence, but we do. In Europe anyway."

Ironically Adrian provides his own Bunnymen reference after a discussion of idea pilfering from the Sound's songs. Describing *Heads and Hearts* as fatalistic and the 'downside' of the coin compared with

Shock's swashbuckling heroism,

"I often feel like Mac's "Yo Yo Man," always up and down."

He seems both to relish and rail against the perception of the Sound as underachievers who have stuck to their guns,

"Everyone seems to be trying to tell us that we should stop. All through Europe we've been getting comments like, 'Don't you think the 'concept' is now complete?' "

It's a subject he would be drawn back to again and again right up until his statement when the band finally split, for now he vociferously held on to control,

"We don't need people asking if we're going to continue 'til the end of the cosmos. We'll stop when we want to, thank you very much!"

That March the Sound had ventured outside the capital and played in Leeds and Birmingham. The crowds away from London were disappointingly small and the rare excursion beyond their safety zone was clearly a sobering experience for Adrian. An exchange captured on the *Heads and Hearts* blog reveals him in a more vulnerable, less fiery mood,

"The only way to get anywhere at all now is by having a hit single. It's getting harder and harder to get anyone just to come and see you play, it's a bit depressing really."

So the search for a happy medium of success and artistic fulfilment continued: the Sound seemingly a major label band on an indie label,

But in a world taught to crave happy filmic endings we need to be careful of what we wish for in terms of an alternative outcome for Adrian and the Sound.

Let's consider a world where they looked the part, played the game, had a heavyweight manager and in turn saw the right levers pulled at the opportune moment by a compliant record company with the necessary funds. What would have happened? Does what we've learnt of Adrian's strengths and weaknesses paint a picture of a man who would have thrived under the pressure and amidst the demands of major success? It takes a certain type of person to cope with that in an industry that offers little emotional care and support. We shouldn't pretend otherwise: Adrian would likely have been crushed by the demands of the success he, paradoxically, needed to continue with what he loved.

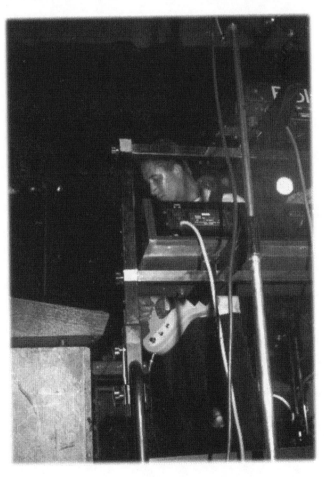

Max playing guitar and keyboards

CHAPTER 13

Well our prides in shreds, because we've smashed our heads, again and again against a wall that never bends

As we've seen Adrian had delivered what was in essence an album of love songs, certainly it's producer Wally Brill thought so,

"If you listen to *Heads and Hearts* he's talking about connection to someone else, with a few exceptions, that was an album of love songs."

When unravelling Adrian's music you are usually dealing with several related strands, including, but not restricted to; emotional entanglements of the romantic variety, (more commonly known as 'songs about girls') internal emotional conflict and feelings stemming from the pain of his illness. Beyond that politics weave in and out, sometimes in plain sight, on other occasions hidden.

Like any good Venn diagram there are various crossovers between those sources of inspiration and a number of ways in which one influences another.

The day to day practical mechanics of Adrian's life clearly had a strong bearing on all these areas. He was still of course living with his parents at 2 Hillview and looked after by his mum Win who took care of all the stuff most of us have to get used to doing for ourselves.

Mike tells an instructive tale dating back to that Scottish tour in 1980,

"We were touring in Scotland and I cooked myself a fried breakfast, Adrian said, 'Cook me some of that' and I said 'Fuck off, do it yourself.' He said he didn't know how. I showed him how to fry eggs and he did it, he fed himself, probably the first time he'd ever done that!"

As to why this state of affairs was allowed to endure Mike is candid,

"He was just lazy, he allowed himself to stay home with his parents and let them do everything, cook and wash etc, so he could play guitar and write songs. When he was in the band, he was used to people doing everything, he was looking for a substitute mum and dad to do it all."

It's a picture confirmed by Graham Bailey in his *Walking in the Opposite Direction* interview,

"Adrian liked to have people do things for him. He wasn't good at being anything other than a musician and a writer and I think that comes from being a single child where everything is done for you."

As we've touched on, in the world of music this state of affairs isn't unusual, it's a place full of arrested development. Although in Adrian's case it felt more a product of his upbringing than a 'rock star affectation' where adult life with its responsibilities and expectations is put on hold, sometimes permanently.

Nevertheless such a way of life can still have a knock-on effect on a person's emotional maturity, something we can see in the tortuous state of Adrian's love life. Since the end of his long term relationship with Julie he had taken steps to ensure she remained in his orbit through her road manager role and had regularly fallen in love with girls who had appeared briefly in his life, something you could call the, *'Earlene factor.'*

Mike, "We'd turn up somewhere and he'd meet some female who'd come to see the band and two hours later he's asking her to marry him."

Something where the rock star rule of 'what happens on tour, stays on tour' very definitely applied. Again it's not an unusual thing to find when looking at the strange life of a touring musician. Later in life Adrian himself discovered that he had fathered a son through a brief liaison that occurred as the band toured Europe. Although he did later make attempts to contact his son, pre-internet, his efforts were unsuccessful.

None of this makes him a 'bad' person, or undermines his art, but it is a factor that must be taken into account if you want to try to understand him.

1985 rolled inexorably on with the Sound on the road for most of April and May throughout Europe including a blistering slot at the Seaside Festival (standing in for the Cult) in Belgium where Adrian was interviewed as part of a TV broadcast and asked about where the Sound stood in relation to the current music scene,

Adrian, "We fall between people who want harder, more 'extreme' music and the pop groups because we're neither one nor the other, we're not middle of the road, we're just in the middle. It's just the music we want to play."

Adrian interviewed at Seaside Festival

As usual Adrian was often the best person to articulate the quandaries he and the band faced. The next step they took was probably not one you would have predicted. Two gigs at the Marquee were booked for

27th and 28th of August, nothing strange about that of course, the band played there more than at any other venue in the UK, however audience members arriving at the club on those nights were greeted by a note on the door confirming that both shows would be recorded for a live album.

The temperature over those two summer days in London, hit 80 degrees Fahrenheit, so imagine what it was like in a non air-conditioned sweat-box like the wonderfully scuzzy old Marquee, a place where your feet glued themselves to the floor and a visit to the toilet was an absolute last resort, strictly at your own risk.

Anyone lucky enough to witness one, or both, of those gigs probably won't recall those details but will just remember the glory of the music that was delivered from that iconic (before the word was 'ubiquitised' and debased) stage over the two nights.

As Mike says in the Edsel CD box set liner-notes,

"I think the Marquee captured some of the best of the Sound live. The feeling is there, they were great gigs, I almost forgot they were being recorded."

It was like a dream: a band revered for their live 'shows' playing a quasi greatest hits set to the people who loved them.

One of the nights was reviewed by Mat Smith in *Melody Maker*. It's a beautiful review, capturing what was clearly the excitement Smith felt, but on the other side, the frustration at what he knew was happening to the Sound's career. Describing Adrian in vivid terms, "as much a visionary as Morrissey or Mac, he just doesn't stick a bunch of flowers up his arse or employ a pretty boy pose."

"How people can remain immune when the sheer power searing off the Marquee stage is enough to push even the most cynical observer through the back wall and halfway down Wardour Street is beyond me.

But they do".

It's a lovely thing to read a review where your vivid experience is mirrored to such an extent: it could feel lonely, especially in those pre-internet days, loving a band that too many had never heard of.

Smith's final paragraph is bittersweet,

"Another Sound gig, another set of superlatives and still the great unwashed waste their shekels on the next great white hype. Sound fans have long since learned to live with injustice but on a night when the stifling heat of the Marquee is multiplied a thousand fold by that generated by the band on stage, it's hard not to be bitter. It's your loss sadly, but sadder still, it's theirs too."

What can I say, other than that I experienced one of the nights and yes, it was transcendent like few gigs manage to be.

When it came to mixing what was a very well recorded album, Adrian would be working with someone who'd had significant involvement in some of the music that had soundtracked his musical evolution, as he explains in the sleeve-notes of Renascent's reissue,

"Craig Leon who had co-produced the first Ramones album, credentials enough for me, mixed the album with me in Holland. 16 tracks mixed in two days which is fast."

Craig Leon's CV features many albums beyond the Ramones, including Blondie, Suicide, Richard Hell and more. His partner Cassell Webb is also an experienced singer, songwriter and producer.

Craig explains how the link-up came about,

"Cassell had signed with Statik Records in the UK and was preparing her first album for the label. At the same time Laurie Dunn, the owner of the label, asked me to mix the Sound's live album, *In the Hothouse.* I knew a couple of the albums that were on Rob Dickins' Korova label as well as *Shock of Daylight.*"

As we shall see Adrian got on well with Craig and Cassell and went on to work with them in the very near future. It's not hard to picture Adrian chatting with Craig nine to the dozen.

Craig, "We did talk about the other projects we'd worked on. Like most musicians in the immediate post-punk era he was interested in the lower East Side NY bands of the previous decade. He had a great affinity for the Velvet Underground who were probably a strong influence on him. However, he never really copied or channelled any band in particular. He had his own distinctive approach to both writing and playing. I also remember that he held his bandmates, the Sound, in great regard."

It's an open secret that many live albums, either credited or uncredited, feature varying degrees of overdubs, but not *In the Hothouse.* Adrian confirmed how the recording was treated in the mixing process,

"The powerful drum sound was achieved using gates and harmonisers (a method we used at gigs anyway), guitars and keyboards were left virtually raw, so it really does represent what we sounded like in the latter stages of our existence."

Worries about the band having sped up, high on the adrenaline of the live moment, proved unfounded and the result was a genuinely classic live album.

The double vinyl felt like a grand statement of defiance and possibly a thank you to all who knew just what a live band they were. Highlights? The whole damn thing, although it's hard to beat Adrian's Patti Smith ad-libs in "Heartland" or the occasional snippets of on-stage chat, 'We're gonna be knackered after this...' "

Statik ran music press ads that could be accused of hyperbole, 'Finally a live album from a band acclaimed for their dynamic concert performances - it'll burn your brain', but actually feels about right. Four individuals on a stage, united in one pursuit, doing what they excelled at, plus an audience that understood that and loved them for it. There's a sense of the crowd knowing they have discovered this rare thing and not quite believing their luck or that the rest of the world remained in ignorance.

Mike puts it more succinctly,

"We did what we always did at the Marquee; play hard and sweat a lot. We always put everything we could into the music live. Because we meant it, we weren't fucking around, this was proper, we wanted you to know it, so we worked hard."

And what a great cover, a design you could be forgiven for thinking had come again from 23 Envelope but was actually created by Graham Bailey.

Mike, "The design was done by Graham, he was going through a period of being interested in photography. I remember being really impressed by the set up, he did it at home. All the curtains and stuff, the wind blowing it and putting the photos on top of that. He was really creative with it, it was my favourite album cover. The photo of the band on the stage was actually taken at the Paradiso."

In the Hothouse was released in the final week of November, coinciding with a London gig at, for once, the Hammersmith Clarendon.

Incredibly Chris Roberts managed once again to take the reviewers' chair for *Sounds,* awarding five stars out of five, while over at *ZigZag* magazine Mick Mercer summed the album up adroitly,

"Foam-mouthed into the fray, the Sound caught in striking form live."

Describing a gig experience as, "the fray" seems totally appropriate when speaking of the Sound because it really was an, 'intense competitive activity,' as the dictionary definition confirms.

However *Melody Maker* journalist Dave Thompson chose to deviate from reality and turned in one of the most embarrassingly asinine reviews I've ever seen.

Beginning the review with the phrase, "Someone I fear is taking the piss" and referring repeatedly to 'Hot House' rather than *Hothouse,* Thompson mocked the notion of the Sound for doing something that, in his view, was the "mastubatory" preserve of superstars; releasing a live double album. In his assessment, as the band would never be superstars, the release was pointless. But it's his description of the record as, "dull, uninspiring and soulless," that truly beggars belief, it's an 'upside down world' moment and seems the exact opposite of everything the Sound always were.

It stands as the most ludicrous review the band ever received but still must have hurt and/or infuriated at the time.

But there were more important things for the band to consider as the year faded, firstly that Clarendon gig, their penultimate show of the year.

Two-thirds of the setlist was made up of new material (if you include "Prove Me Wrong"), even the show opener was new, "Fall of Europe," a future B-side. Several highlights of *Thunder Up* were played that night, even a song, "Through and Through", that wouldn't be officially released until the *Statik Years* CD box of 2023. It was another reliably blistering gig and didn't suffer in the slightest for the high quotient of unfamiliar material.

Little did the audience realise what would happen next, or how long it would be until they'd hear any of these songs on record.

In the news section of an early December issue of *Melody Maker* the following short announcement was made,

"The Sound have left Statik and are looking for a new deal. A spokesman for the label said, "We can no longer promote them in the style they need." The band, who've just released a double live album, *In the Hothouse,* are midway through recording a new studio LP."

The widely quoted story is that a financially challenged Statik went under and the Sound were one of the casualties, Mike has said,

"As far as I'm aware, the owner Laurie Dunn simply 'did a runner.' He'd ploughed a load of money into the Sound but of course the records bombed commercially so I guess he ended up thinking, 'Shit what do I do now? Ah I'll bugger off back to Australia.' It really was like that, one day everything was fine and the next he was gone and we were left high and dry."

I suspect events moved quickly and memories have blurred, but it does seem clear the Sound had already jumped ship before Statik's collapse, which in any event didn't happen until later, probably sometime in 1986. The Statik spokesperson's comment seems loaded with possible implications. Or, just possibly, it sums up the simple reality: the Sound needed the financial muscle of a bigger label if they were to make the requisite headway, but that ship had long sailed.

The strange coda to the Statik-era occurred some years' later. Laurie Dunn had taken the band's master tapes home with him to Australia. Mike speculates that maybe his conscience weighed on him and he decided to 'gift the masters back to Adrian.' The intentions were good but the customs paperwork wasn't, it seems Laurie didn't complete the required forms correctly and the package was impounded by HM Customs and Excise, subject to payment of whatever fee was required. Normal process would involve contact with the addressee but if that did happen then seemingly Adrian didn't respond. The result? After the time limit ran out, the masters were simply destroyed.

It's a horrifyingly cruel, but bureaucratically arbitrary, fate for an artists' work to be treated in such a way but that's what happened.

Despite everything, the Statik period wasn't wasted. Firstly, the band had been saved from a labelless wasteland by a sympathetic and enthusiastic label that did its best to support and promote them. In that environment they'd created some of their best work. That it went no further wasn't really the fault of either band or label.

For Adrian there was one more good thing to come out of the period.

While working on *In the Hothouse,* Cassell Webb and Craig Leon had asked Adrian whether he'd like to contribute to Cassell's new album *Llano,* to be released in 1986 by Statik and recorded at Wisseloord Studios, Hilversum, Holland where *Hothouse* was mixed.

Craig, "We heard the song "Total Recall" on the tapes of the live recording and loved it. When we met Adrian he told me that he thought the song could be performed slower and more pensively than the version on the live album so we took that on board."

As we've seen Adrian had always had in mind a "slower, grander version" and so this must have been music to his ears. With that song in particular it feels as if Adrian viewed it as having multiple iterations and treatments, where different textures and approaches could tease out alternative layers of meaning and emotion.

Cassell herself had some awareness of Adrian's work so it seemed a natural step to work together.

Cassell, "I'd heard some of his songs but I wasn't totally aware of how much work he'd done. I thought he was a great guitarist and had incredibly expressive ideas. With "Total Recall" the live version was a bit more frantic but I felt the lyrics were brilliant."

Craig, "In my view Adrian was a masterful guitarist and a great songwriter who had yet to reach his full potential. It's difficult to develop a totally unique guitar style. Very few players are capable of doing it, but he managed to do just that. Though I play guitar and have played a lot on various records, particularly Cassell's, I wanted to work his guitar playing into the style of the record that we were making in 1985 and make it a part of the environment, so I stuck to keyboards on those sessions."

Praise indeed coming from someone with Craig Leon's experience.

In 1991 I asked Adrian what he thought about Cassell's version and he was markedly more enthusiastic about it than he'd been about Annabel Lamb's, "Heartland,"

Adrian, "No that was good, it was like slow-motion."
Me, "I like the album,
Adrian, "Yeah I do too, especially "Wandering Ones" and "When The Rain Comes Down" very lonely, beautiful music."
Me, "I can hear your guitar style in there..."
Adrian, "Yeah there is 'Adrian Borland' in there, I really did help on that LP. I co-wrote a few of the songs. I'd definitely like to make another album with her."

It sounds as though the experience was enjoyable for all concerned and must have been rewarding for Adrian at a time when the future was once more uncertain.

Craig, "We didn't have a great budget (the usual dilemma!) and therefore not a lot of time to do either project so it was basically work all the way. We did spend quite a bit of time out of the studio with Adrian since we enjoyed each other's company. He visited us quite a few times at our house in West London."

Cassell confirms, "Adrian and I would walk and talk. We helped each other with our music."

There's no doubt Adrian would have been watching and learning throughout, and the kind of record *Llano* turned out to be maybe suggested directions he would later consider in his solo work.

The album itself was probably purchased by a fair few Sound fans on its release early the following year and although very different from the Sound, there was enough Borland DNA in there to satisfy, with his guitar sound unmistakable. Anyway aside from that it's a lovely album on its own terms.

Named after Webb's birthplace in Texas, the opening title track is beautiful, Adrian's guitar adding a tension that contrasts nicely with her folk-pop stylings. He brings his classic Borland-style uneasiness. The combination of the two artists is genuinely intriguing, it's unarguably Cassell Webb's record but bringing Adrian on board does what many collaborations fail to do: create something distinctively different. Here he successfully adds a colour that probably wouldn't have been there in the same shade had Craig Leon handled the guitar duties.

Clearly Craig was absolutely right about Adrian's guitar playing as his involvement is evident again from the first notes of "Voices to Rivers."

Although not co-written by Adrian the lovely "Everytime I Get Around You" was probably the lightest, most commercial song he'd been involved in to date and may have tested how open minded some Sounds fans were, but not as much as "Gypsy Solitaire" which has a touch of Laurie Anderson about it.

On safer ground, from a Borland perspective, "Wandering Ones" is an expansive epic with Adrian also on backing vocals. The song makes its way to a suitably violent crescendo where Adrian lets rip for the one and only time on *Llano,* but up until then it rests on a very similar strummed guitar churn to that which underpinned a Sound song that was debuted live at the same time; "Shut Up and Shut Down."

And what of "Total Recall"? Well it's a minimal ethereal marvel, beautifully drawn out in slow-mo and featuring a different emphasis in terms of the delivery of the lyrics. There's a strange feeling of it almost being the other party in Adrian's original speaking back to him in sadness at the failure to commit and make something from a briefly snatched opportunity. The chorus swells beautifully and no doubt Adrian smiled to hear his song become 'slower and grander' like he originally envisaged. The ending feels celestial as did the *Heads and Hearts* version, but there's a subtle difference compared to the Sound's take, Cassell sounds more reassuring, less desperate, the denouement more hopeful for the future. Whatever residual feeling you feel left with, it sounds like a classic reinterpreted, and that's because it is.

No one knew it at that point, or even when *Llano* was finally released the following year, but Adrian's path would take a very different turn before the decade was over. Away from the Sound's post-punk signature to something few fans would have anticipated or, in some cases, wanted. In reality the signs were already there if you were paying attention. Just consider that almost 'bouncy' new song, "Prove Me Wrong," debuted via the *Hothouse* album: there was a conflict amongst the Sound's new material that saw competing feelings of despondency existing next to a clear urge for escape to a more positive emotional state. Does art imitate life or is it the other way round?

Oscar Wilde was reliably insightful on the subject saying,

"Life imitates art far more than art imitates life".

For Adrian the emotional turmoil boiling up inside him found an outlet in his art, but was that art engaged in a self-perpetuating feedback loop? Physically and mentally draining and dragging him towards a precipice at a pace that terrified Adrian and would eventually shock those around him.

Sadly the dramatic events of 1986 would reveal the true extent of the challenges he faced in maintaining not only a grip on what was left of his career, but of his life itself.

Adrian and Max

CHAPTER 14

Vampires flying off into the sunset

How to describe the musical landscape of 1986, the tenth anniversary of punk? Well, while the nostalgia machine hadn't quite completed its history reframing 'magic' yet, the process was, nevertheless, well under way. Writing in the *Observer* at the time, future *England's Dreaming* author Jon Savage was caustic about the year's retro-punk focus,

"Punk is now a costume on the very clothes rack of youth style it set out to subvert. Its 10th anniversary is turning into one of the media obsessions of the year, yet just as the past is rewritten in the language of the present, then so is a series of complex and contradictory signs (about which no one can agree) reduced into a sludge of nostalgia and style recycling."

It was true then and a hundred times more so today. For Adrian and the Sound the bitter winds of musical change were blowing all around them. Having successfully used the opportunities that came with punk, and then to have managed to escape its confines via the opportunities of post-punk, the Sound had subsequently missed the 'big music' boat that certain of their contemporaries, such as the Bunnymen and Simple Minds, had jumped aboard. In some ways we should be grateful when we look at the creative dead ends both those bands hit at pretty much precisely the time the Sound found themselves back in the wilderness.

Their closest travelling partners in musical life, the Comsat Angels, had by this time burned through two major label deals and would soon begin their third. A spell that started with much optimism but would end a few years down the line with an exhausted sigh and a ridiculous new band name. It was an experience that almost destroyed the band.

The Sound were back out there looking for a record deal. Graham is honest when assessing the situation at the Arcane Delights website,

"I guess we were slightly desperate to find a label after Statik went bankrupt."

The band were looking for a new home in a rapidly changing musical world. Post Live Aid the charts had evolved away from the environment of the early to mid '80s, with its infiltration into the mainstream on the part of all kinds of synth-pop and post-punk. Notwithstanding the years' top selling single from the Communards, the best sellers were a queasy blend of novelty rubbish; Cliff Richard and the Young Ones, film themes, Berlin, and glutinous MOR such as Nick Berry and Chris de Burgh. It wasn't a very pretty sight. In the world of indie the Smiths ruled and a new surge of often ramshackle guitar bands was about to rise that would be named after the *NME*'s *C86* cassette.

All a long way from the Sound's musical world.

Although the final Statik press release claimed the band had begun recording a new album that wasn't strictly true, Mike Dudley confirms they were still at the stage of writing and rehearsing at this point. We know of course they had plenty of new material, so much that some would end up bumped to B-side status or even remaining unreleased until the *Statik Years* box.

Also around this time Julie Aldred ended her stint as their road manager. It's hardly a surprise; 1986 saw the band play only nine documented gigs compared to the close to 50 they'd played the previous year. For once the shows they did play didn't involve a visit to Holland, instead comprising a couple of Belgian and Spanish festivals, a short Spanish tour and one UK gig, their second upstairs at the Clarendon in Hammersmith.

Mike Dudley has already confirmed there was a distinct sense of things, "winding down."

It must have been a tough time for all of them, but especially Adrian. Mike's sleeve-notes for *Will and Testament* provide a sobering and emotional picture of the Sound's final two years. Think back to his remark regarding the band entering, "the long desert of the world's indifference," well they were plodding into that desert as 1986 dawned.

On a very practical level money was getting tight. Well it was always tight but during the WEA years there was an easing of the situation. After that, as Adrian once explained to me, they learned to be prudent, which for a band with no manager was quite an achievement,

Adrian, "Any income that came in from advances or gigs, especially festivals that paid quite well, would go into the band's account and then we'd pay the equivalent of around £4000 a year for each band member. Once that ran out things got pretty impossible."

Some limited help was coming. Even during the *Korova* years the Dutch arm of WEA had been far more enthusiastic about having the Sound on board than their British colleagues. With UK options exhausted could there be a lifeline out there on the continent? The answer came in the form of a Belgian indie label called Play it Again Sam.

Set up in 1983 by Kenny Gates and Michel Lambot, the label was still relatively new but had already signed an interesting range of industrial, electronic and post-punk artists such as Front 242, Legendary Pink Dots and the Young Gods amongst many, many others, still today remaining a pillar of the European indie scene.

Graham wasn't so keen,

"PIAS (Play it Again Sam) was a major mistake. Total crooks."

Still, bear in mind the sheer craziness of the fact that the Sound NEVER had an experienced manager. Despite that, they managed to get a major record deal, a further contract with Statik and now another, albeit minuscule, indie deal.

Graham, "We managed to interest Play it Again Sam, not sure how. We had begun to feel we were banging our heads against a brick wall. But we thought, it's good we've got a label, let's make some albums with them. I never paid much attention to what was happening with the business or the mechanics, maybe I should have! Later it became clear that we should have looked closer at the contract. As usual the musician is at the bottom of the pile."

So it was time for a record.

Jan, "Did you envisage *Thunder Up* as being the final album? "You've Got a Way" certainly feels like that, listening to it now."

Adrian, "It's definitely 'vampires flying off into the sunset' isn't it, "You've Got a Way"? The big Hollywood ending! I'd never thought about that."

More than ever before the implications of committing to pouring everything into the making of a new record were likely weighing on Adrian. The doubt as to whether there would even be another album was looming while life was providing too much time for reflection.

In 1996 Jan asked Adrian about this whole process. As he responds there's a very real sense of him turning the facts over in his mind while deciding how much he can say, in that once it's said, it confirms what he fears and becomes somehow concrete.

"I'm drained after completing an album, emotionally and mentally. It's becoming a big problem for me to get myself together quite honestly. It comes from putting too much into the music - you just end up fucked-up."

The reality for *Thunder Up* was that Adrian was, by his own standards, pretty 'fucked-up' already.

Although Julie Aldred had long ceased being Adrian's girlfriend and was no longer working for the band, she was still regularly in contact with

Adrian.

Julie, "I'd gone on to get a job in local government but I still saw Adrian quite a lot socially. But he started to get more episodes of, I suppose, depression and usually his mum would give me a ring if he got really bad. She'd say, 'He's really struggling at the moment, you know.' "

It feels very sad to imagine how worried and desperate Win must have been, watching her son's health and behaviour worsening.

Julie, "She would say, 'Can you come round and have a chat with him?' I still think they thought I was a good influence in some way. I don't think she knew who else to call. Obviously I'd known him for a long time and we were still great friends. So I'd go round and try to talk to him."

Adrian's behaviour was starting to include increasingly erratic episodes as Julie explains,

"There was an incident where he was in Wimbledon and he was wandering round knocking on people's doors because he was paranoid that someone was following him, I've no idea who. I remember him telling me about these conspiracy theories that seemed real to him."

It was during December 1986 that events reached a crescendo leading to Adrian's hospitalisation at Springfield University Hospital in Tooting, south London.

The hospital dated back to the Victorian era and opened in 1840, its main red brick buildings appearing quite grand belying it's original purpose as a, 'pauper lunatic asylum.'

Julie, "The incident where he was sectioned was when he attacked his dad. He went to Springfield Hospital. That was the first very serious incident. He actually tried to attack his dad in the middle of the night. He wasn't at all a violent person which makes it all the more terrifying. Bob called the Police and they sectioned him."

Bob Borland spoke at length about the events when interviewed for *Walking in the Opposite Direction,*

Bob Borland speaking about Adrian

Bob, "He'd behaved very weirdly that whole day. At lunchtime he warned me to be careful as he said, 'someone is trying to kill you.' Adrian was recording at Elephant Studios and went from there to Leman Street Police station. He asked them to lock him up in a cell because he didn't want to be accused of a murder."

Of course the police refused but did call Bob and Win to warn them of Adrian's behaviour. Later, at four in the morning, Adrian took a mirror out of its frame to use as a weapon and then tried to rush into his parents room. Win was luckily half-awake and managed to stop him at the door.

Until that time Adrian's parents hadn't really been fully aware of what Bob described as Adrian's, "abnormality." It was at this point that Bob began to trace a possible trail through Adrian's lyrics.

While in hospital Adrian made his first of six documented attempts on his own life,

Julie, "I went to visit him and it was heartbreaking because they drugged him. In there he smashed a window and he tried to cut his throat with a piece of glass, leaving him with the scar he had on his neck."

Staff asked what drugs he used and Julie explained to their surprise that he wasn't a drug user and this wasn't therefore a drug related episode.

"He improved and they let him come out for a day at first in our care, he was in there for several weeks. He eventually came out and they put him on whatever drugs they prescribed. But I know it dulled his musical creativity which of course led to him wanting to come off."

Graham Bailey has confirmed that the drugs left Adrian like, "a zombie," the result being that someone as artistically driven like Adrian felt no choice but to stop taking the medication, setting up a cycle of behaviour that would continue until his death.

Graham, "He would just take himself off the drugs and then he would drink shitloads."

Graham recalls the events described by Julie and Bob,

"He tried to kill his parents, I didn't witness it but he told me. He was given the option of being arrested or getting psychiatric help."

During that period Graham remembers Adrian having a particular fixation with Jim Morrison and the Doors, whose "The End" includes the Oedipal referencing line,

"Father? Yes, son? I want to kill you. Mother I want to..."

Who knows how deeply, or if at all, this inspired or actually influenced Adrian.

"I don't think anyone else visited him in the mental institution. He was shuffling along in a gown, he knew who I was but the lights were on and nobody was home. He was changed forever after that, he couldn't create on the medication, so he would come off."

As we know Graham was not Adrian's only visitor but he does paint a disturbing picture.

Different people refer to Adrian's condition in different ways. Adrian himself calls it 'nervous depression', his dad, schizoaffective disorder, others refer to variations on those descriptions. Sometimes there's a frustrating lack of clarity, you can only wonder how Adrian himself felt. Sadly it's not unusual in such situations.

What has to be borne in mind is that people don't necessarily talk to each other enough about this stuff at the time. Often the various 'participants' (in Adrian's case, family, friends, fans, band members etc.) in a person's life will have different, partial or fragmentary recollections and accounts of events and their understanding of what was happening will vary greatly. It's the nature of life, it's messy and it's often only in hindsight that we gain a better understanding of what really happened.

Schizoaffective disorder is sometimes confused with schizophrenia and although it does share some symptoms and likely causes, there are particular and important differences.

We can easily see how the symptoms fit what Adrian was going through: hallucinations, delusions, 'feeling flat', confused thinking, symptoms that come and go and serious mood changes such as depression or mania.

It's the fact that symptoms fluctuate and the focus on mood disturbance that distinguishes schizoaffective disorder from other conditions.

And the causes? Sadly research continues, however there appears to be a clear genetic component, which in Adrian's case makes sense bearing in mind the apparent history of mental illness on Bob Borland's side of the family.

Beyond that we are looking at 'triggers' that can cause the onset of the condition where a person may be genetically predisposed. We can rule out drug use, but of course not alcohol overuse. We can also rule in stress, one of the main prompts for a person suffering schizoaffective disorder's debilitating symptoms.

If we want to try to understand how it feels for a person experiencing these symptoms, then Bob's memory of Adrian saying that, "It felt as if my brain was 'on fire' " is probably as close as we'll get.

Bob's interpretation was that the communication between Adrian and the other 'person' in his brain was so intense, that was how it made him feel.

Having watched Adrian through his life to date we can see a person with huge energy, enthusiasm and talent, but also with a personality that meant he felt he always had to win and to be seen to win.

We have also witnessed an only child from a supportive family, but with an often combative relationship with a father who wanted Adrian to succeed whatever that may mean. How much pressure this put on Adrian we can only speculate, but certainly the fiery nature of their father-son relationship is confirmed by the accounts of a variety of people in Adrian's life.

Graham Bailey has been robustly candid with his views. We do however need to have in mind that he and Adrian were estranged at the time of Adrian's death, partly as a result of apparent approaches made by Graham in relation to a dispute over money.

Nevertheless Graham was Adrian's friend from way back in childhood so his opinion is at least something to consider. When interviewed for *Walking in the Opposite Direction* he posited his own view,

"I don't think it was a mental condition. I mean, I'm not an expert, I'm just going to give you an opinion that might piss people off. His father was on his back his whole life. Hard, like really hard, you know, wanting him to succeed. And he didn't. He was never 'doing good' by his dad. That's where all the arguments came in. It was always, 'it's not good enough.'"

It doesn't really need me to point out that families are complex entities and that to make judgments involving people who are no longer here to comment is fraught with difficulty. It does however feel clear that Adrian's behaviour was a manifestation of a mental illness. That it was affected by the course his life took, seems, on the balance of probability, to be highly likely. Like many aspects of life, an intricate web of factors work together to create the eventual reality that the individual experiences. With Adrian, for better and worse, his art and his life were intertwined in a way that makes it difficult to see where one ends and the other begins. Great art resulted but the price was high and he was starting to understand that.

It's extraordinary to now focus on the fact that, amongst this horror, Adrian was making a record. The sheer force of will required must have been huge.

In such circumstances the familiarity of being back at Elephant Studios, with the ever amenable and supportive Nick Robbins back on board, was surely a source of at least some reassurance for Adrian at a time when he must have felt he was being torn apart. There's a sense of circles completing and a band back to basics, both through necessity and by choice.

Nick was asked about Adrian's state of mind while he worked with him,

"Adrian was at various times an alcoholic, and I have to say that it never seemed to me to affect what he did when he was in the studio. He always seemed completely in control, and it was a great surprise to me when I would hear from Bob, or someone else, that there had been an episode and he'd had a real problem because I didn't really see that in the studio, I just saw someone who was getting on with the job."

It seems to have been a mixed picture and possibly depended on the individual's perspective, Nick would of course have been focussed on making the record as good as possible. Jan visited Elephant to see how things were going and was troubled by Adrian's apparent state of mind,

Jan, "Towards the end of the *Thunder Up* sessions in 1986, I had gone along to the studio and again Adrian was in that strange brooding mood. He and I went for a drink but this didn't seem to relax him. As you may imagine, I was quite perturbed that a friend I'd been close with for over 10 years was acting so oddly. I rang his home a couple of days later to check on him. It was his dad who answered, obviously upset, and told me that he was in a mental hospital."

Despite all of this Adrian and band were keen to continue; they had some fantastic songs, but as Mike explains this wasn't a case of a 'new beginning' more unfinished business,

"No it wasn't really a new start. It was more a case of 'Keep going, guys, don't stop, just keep going'. You know, we needed any deal we could get, and Play it Again Sam was the only deal we could get, a small deal with a small label, we still needed to do what we needed to do. So despite the fact that it was an obscure little Belgian label, with not much money available, we could go in and record, we could make an album, we could maybe carry on playing, so let's do it."

Mike's next comment tells more about the situation they faced together,

"It certainly wasn't a new beginning, it turned out to be a last gasp, Custer's Last Stand."

But don't for one minute imagine that meant their hearts weren't in it, this is the Sound we're talking about after all, so when their backs were against the wall they were naturally going to go out fighting, as the song says,

"It's the acceleration group
With the acceleration groove
Formation fighting
Four into one"

The first glimpse of the sessions came in the form of a single, "Hand of Love", released in May 1987 and coinciding with a handful of Dutch, Belgian and UK dates. Yes, it was that final pair of incredible Marquee gigs, announced in the *Melody Maker* gig guide with a triumphant and far from normal, "They're back!" from whoever was putting it together that week. Because, you see, Sound fans were like that.

It may not have been quite a Bowiesque level of reinvention but "Hand of Love" was a new wrinkle in the band's catalogue. Opening with a measured acoustic strum and a sparse drumbeat, Max's keyboard part then enters hesitantly and has a lovely simple twinkling naivety about it. It's a warm and humble song that has echoes of the Velvet Underground at their sweetest. It's also an unabashed redemptive love song.

At the time it felt a brave choice as a single and probably wrong-footed a few people.

There's a lot of bruised tenderness here: just take that opening line,

"When nothing is going your way
And nothings going right
You're walking with an angel in your dreams
But walking the night in your life"

The song talks of redemption and hope but in an atmosphere of doubt for the future and betrayed trust lying in the past.

Here was Adrian pushing himself to create something that defied people's expectations and succeeding. Ironically it's not that hard to imagine the record getting some airplay due to its superficially 'pretty' sound. It's a track that didn't need, nor get, a big recording budget and benefited as a result.

But there may have been other motives coming into play here which will make more sense in a years' time: suffice to say Adrian was looking for a way out of the intensity of the music he'd been making for the duration of the Sound's career. He felt that in scaling back to a more acoustic based style, the music made would be less demanding to replicate on stage. "Hand of Love" was an early manifestation of that new approach, right then it was an outlier but soon it would be the norm.

Ironically the lyric, when dissected further, flirts with optimism but its hope and redemption seems fragile and possibly unattainable. Even at his most catchy and commercial Adrian slipped an uneasy emotional neutrality into the sting in the tail of his songs, you wouldn't find easy answers here, often making it hard to pump your fist or wave a flag in the air as those who inhabited stadiums yearned to.

Coupled with another two excellent B-sides, "Fall of Europe" and "Such a Difference," that had been debuted at the *Clarendon,* and placed in a sleeve that referenced one of Adrian's recent crushes, it was a strong release but couldn't realistically 'cut through' the musical distractions of 1987.

Thunder Up was released in June. Mike Dudley confirms that at least, "some effort" was put in promotion-wise but frustratingly the label ignored the band's suggestion for the artwork.

A friend of Mike's put something together featuring a design based on a Russian Revolution era propaganda poster in the style of Alexander Rodchenko featuring a girl with her hand held up brandishing a piece of paper. I suspect the label baulked at the licensing fee that may have been payable and instead went their own sweet way and left us with the worst Sound record cover by some considerable distance, depicting a clown on a trapeze with a very nondescript typeface for the band's logo. Oddly in Canada there was an alternate, equally random design depicting a close-up of an aircraft's propeller blade and engine.

It was a great shame, especially when you consider the origin of the record title: *Thunder Up,* is taken from the Dutch, 'donder op' in essence the equivalent of, 'fuck off." In Mike's friend's design the *Thunder Up* would have terminated in a defiant exclamation mark perfectly chiming with the mood surrounding the album. A missed opportunity for a striking and memorable piece of artwork.

Never mind, the music within gave us some of the Sound's best songs, despite what some fans and critics may have said over the years. In many ways *Thunder Up* suffered some of the same odd commentary that has sometimes coalesced around the misunderstood *Heads and Hearts,* occasionally being described as 'too pop' or 'tired' and lying in the shadow of previous album peaks. But gradually the tide has turned and this record's greatness appears more widely accepted.

There's a limit to how many times you can use the word 'heroic,' but when writing about Adrian and the Sound, those restrictions need easing slightly. Charging out of the gate "Acceleration Group" is an extraordinary call to arms at the point when everyone is saying you're down, you're out and the game is over. Despite it all you go back for one last push. Every line hits home and musically the track was a heads down rush to the finish line.

Maybe these words could serve as the Sound's epitaph,

"The flames will flicker
And the wanting will waver
But there's something in this somewhere
That's going to go on forever"

As we hit the song's end and Adrian's clipped, "That's it" is heard, it's implicit this is the band giving their all whether anyone cares or not.

Mike's *Will and Testament* notes again hit that nail on the head, "This song was a self-energising crank-up to try and boost the future." For the live version, it was,

"Performed at just the moment when the tank, already running on fumes, finally stopped on empty."

Remember it wasn't just Adrian who had put his life and soul into the Sound, all four members had devoted their lives to the crusade.

Adrian spoke at length to Jan about the making of *Thunder Up* and carefully explained the band's thinking as they were going into the studio,

"We went back to producing ourselves and said, 'Why do people like us live so much?' We had a perception that we were more popular live than on record. How do you get that on a record? Well, record a lot of it live, whatever essence or magic you can conjure up with the silences and the empathy, try to get it on the album."

With this aim in mind, and with Nick Robbins facilitating what the band wanted, most of the songs were cut almost entirely live with possibly a vocal, guitar or keyboard overdub and no 'drop-in's' where a mistake or poor element of a track is replaced.

Adrian, "We even left mistakes on deliberately, because if we start cleaning it up then it's not live anymore. It was deliberate to leave in the chatter, like "Hand of Love" has this long sustained chord at the end and if you turn it up you can hear Dudley saying, 'Good take!' Then "Baria Alta" starts. Little things like that can help the flow of an album."

Mike, "That was my idea, leaving in all the studio chatter."

It works, adding another layer to a complex record.

After the lighter mood, on the surface at least, of "Hand of Love" then come the strange currents of "Baria Alta," another song unlike anything the Sound had committed to tape before. Bizarrely described by one reviewer as an attempt at reggae, the track drifts up along the steep cobbled streets of Lisbon, through the heat and dust, searching for relief and yes, a drink.

It's Mike's favourite track on the album,

"It should be Bairro Alto (upper district), but back then you couldn't check these things on Google! At the time it was a sort of 'night-clubby' place in Lisbon and Adrian spent time there because he could get a little drinky at any time of day. It was summer and really hot."

Reggae it definitely isn't but it is a highly atmospheric track feeling as if it's constantly ascending to the "high place" of the lyric, Max gives us a gloriously hazy synth part, and yes, Adrian starts by singing about a location where you can get a drink at any time of day but along the way drifts off into musing on something more thoughtful and bruising,

"I've hardened up to what this place has offered up so far

I've lost some sensitivity maybe you can see the scars

And when I found out what counts in this place

It still couldn't erase the smile that's on my face"

The reality was that Adrian hadn't really "hardened up" enough (can you ever?) and the scars he sings about were all too real.

"Baria Alta" makes way for a musical thunderclap; in the shape of the titanic, "Kinetic."

More or less as it was recorded, live in the studio, "Kinetic" starts oddly with what is actually Mike's final drumbeat of "Baria Alta," Adrian loved the effect and described what happened next as "a shifting of gears." Illustrating Thunder Up's schizophrenic nature perfectly, "Kinetic" is a pulsing ball of unstoppable momentum as befits its title.

All four members lock-in and deliver a spine tingling rush that sees Adrian looking at his 27 years on the planet and concluding that it's time to move, to break out, to escape. It's an incredible lyric that moves from exhortation to recrimination as he addresses another person or that other part of himself and refuses to waste his life.

There's even humour as he warns,

"You kiss me, you touch me, you don't know where I've been."

And then a non-pompous crucifixion reference, as Adrian refuses to allow the nails in his hands and feet to allow him to reach for the answer that lies tantalisingly just out of reach.

Mike talks correctly of "Kinetic's," "earth-swallowing groove" and, as he also says, yes, it is, "as they say these days," a 'banger.'

If you don't have a copy of *Will and Testament* then you really do need to get hold of one, there you will hear a suitably all conquering live version recorded at the Paradiso on that penultimate night of the Sound's live career: 4th December 1987.

Ragged round the edges and utterly, spellbindingly ecstatic in its illustration of what this band was about. Wait for 'the drop' when Adrian murmurs the album's title, time stops, but not for long.

When you're wrapped up in the temporary cocoon of that forward motion, you don't have to consider your destination and the voices in your head are, for a few minutes at least, drowned out.

The 'sound' of *Thunder Up* has come in for some criticism and has always felt oddly 'thin,' something the Edsel remaster seemed to improve slightly.

Mike has mentioned that the reason for the underwhelming sonics was linked to the album being recorded direct to DAT (digital audio tape), technology that was introduced that year and remained in use until the early noughties.

Nick Robbins however, is keen to put the record straight,

"With reference to the sound of *Thunder Up,* it's been said that it was the first time we used digital recording and that perhaps it didn't benefit from that. Well, in all honesty, it wasn't. We didn't use digital recording. It was done on an analog tape recorder. The mixes were then, at the very final stage, put on to digital. The problem was that I'd got very excited by a piece of equipment called a Sonic Maximizer and stupidly I put the whole record through and thought it sounded wonderful. But I think, looking back on it, it was probably a bit of a mistake."

A 'sonic maximizer' is a rack mounted effects tool that filters the sound but while boosting the bass and treble it can suck out the midrange. So listening to *Thunder Up* maybe that's the answer - one online commentator sums up the risks of using one, "If you play in a band, your sound will disappear into a fizzy, loud mess."

A persuasive illustration of the issue is provided by the barnstorming second single, "Iron Years". Just compare the Hugh Jones single remix to the original album track, not only do you get to hear Adrian in the fade sing of "melting down the iron years" but it's also thicker and more expansive. Try it; you'll like it. Sadly, Adrian confirmed the cost of having Hugh remix one track was as much as the whole album's budget for a producer.

"Iron Years" was a good single choice, anthemic without being overbearing, the brassy (synthetic) hook an effective earworm. Echoing "Total Recall's" evocation of time passing, "before your very eyes" the "iron years" of hard slog were very much where the band were at that moment.

The song soars, but Adrian sounds more convinced that the person he's offering support to will find the hope that, to him, seems just out of reach. Musically upbeat but lyrically more problematic, hallmarks of *Thunder Up.*

An old friend begins side two: "Prove Me Wrong," premiered at the Marquee in August 1985 and previously released in its live form on *Hothouse.*

On the surface a short and eager to please 'bouncy' pop song that could also have made for a decent single but, like "Iron Years," there's an undertow of frustration and disappointment. Here the protagonist has reached some kind of apparent acceptance of loneliness by focussing on the "logic of a lonely life" where, "if no one sees things your way, you can still see them alone." A challenge is then laid down for an unnamed third party to "prove me wrong", the "I want you to" suggesting the opening bravado of the song is built on weak emotional foundations.

The lyric could in fact be equally applicable to a band feeling they were hurling themselves against a brick wall of indifference career-wise.

Whether or not Adrian was busy with an internal discussion or not, these songs also offer considerable consolation for listeners. Look back at that quote from *Sounds'* review of *Jeopardy,*

"The Sound are pro-youth, pro-loners/losers/individuals, pro-love, pro a reason for looking up and going on."

Adrian was certainly fulfilling that manifesto on *Thunder Up* even if he struggled to believe it himself.

Mid-way through side two and we wander into very different territory. "Shut Up and Shot Down" was forcefully debuted at the Clarendon in November 1985 and is another unusually structured song that trades in an atmosphere of pre-electrical storm unease. Indeed Adrian himself memorably sings of feeling "like summer thunder."

Today Mike feels his playing was a bit clumsy and that the track came over better live. Perhaps he's being overly self-critical as the band take us masterfully through a song that weaves within a maze of moods and textures, from seething anger to pent up release and back to a brittle 'peace' with the threat of violence hovering like the heat haze.

Mike, "It's all about living in Thatcher's Britain. Everything's closing down; it's our "Ghost Town" really. The 'power' is saying, 'Shut up, sit down and take it, do what you're told.' "

Britain in 1986/87 felt that way; although there are some who would argue, convincingly, that we are back there now. (Mike references the Specials' classic single that made it to number one in the UK singles chart back in 1981, the record managed to accurately portray a country torn apart by riots in multiple cities.)

In amongst the political turmoil there's also a disturbing image of Adrian feeling, "Like a would-be murderer who knows it's not the way." Bearing in mind what we have heard about Adrian's psychotic episode during the recording of *Thunder Up,* such a lyric just adds more resonance to a song that is already knee-deep in menace.

But then it seems the storm has broken and a shadow has crossed the sky to blot out the sun. Certainly that's how the chill that descends during "Web of Wicked Ways" feels, even its lyric references the resulting shudder.

Mike describes the song as "sinister, like a spider crawling across a web". Maybe it epitomises the strange dichotomy at *Thunder Up's* bruised heart because when the chorus slides into place there's a gentle feeling of brief respite. As Max works wonders with unusual keyboard textures while Adrian seems resentful of the feelings dragging him down,

"It's a sin to have these sad days, lying in a bed of bad ways."

Listen out for Adrian' almost hidden background vocals on the chorus, "it makes you hang your head and cry."

Thunder Up's final one-two punch is shattering.

"I Give You Pain" is another outlier in their songbook. Pulsing with a worryingly repressed energy and featuring a lyric that toys with what, on the surface, may be sadomasochistic themes, Adrian finally lets loose with throat shredding screams and lacerating feedback. It was even more immense live, appearing in that form on the 12 inch of "Iron Years." Looking at that lyric now, with its talk of the settling of a "secret score," it may really be a manifestation of Adrian's internal self, warning Adrian of the pain that will come, "subject to object you."

The noise abates and Max's plaintive piano takes centre stage for the gentle beginning of the absolutely fitting finale of "You've Got a Way."

Yes, the 'vampires' were finally flying off into the sunset as Adrian memorably put it. It really is that "big Hollywood ending". Mike recalls Max working hard on the 'string' arrangement that elegantly drives what seems to be a relatively straightforward love song to a, likely idealised, person whose presence can "shoot the night right through with the light of day."

Adrian's ever ascending guitar solo leads us into the ether and leaves us there as the synths subside. It's a hell of a way to go out.

Adrian, "I was so fucked-up when I was making *Thunder Up,* it was clear to anyone there that the writing was on the wall."

This wasn't the case of a band who can't get it together in the studio, but rather one living on borrowed time, their momentum still carrying them forward even though they've stepped off the cliff into a void.

Adrian,"It wasn't a group falling apart on the record, it was a mind falling apart after we'd got it on tape. It was the strain of getting it down, the psychological effect. Music does funny things to the mind when you get too embroiled in it. The spiritual element of music that you can't define takes you over. I think many people experience that. You lose your defences; you've broken them all down to write those words."

This is the place Adrian inhabited once *Thunder Up* was completed.

Understanding that makes what happened next less surprising and all the more inevitable.

Stills from 'Iron Years' video clip, filmed in the Paradiso, Amsterdam

CHAPTER 15

Push me to the breaking point...

If you poke around online for a few minutes you will find people who don't like *Thunder Up,* which is their prerogative of course. But you will also see myths perpetuated that suggest the band weren't keen either.

Not true.

In 1996 Adrian confirmed to Jan that he "really liked *Thunder Up.*" In an interview with *Limit Magazine* in 1998 he went further,

"Ultimately I find *Thunder Up* the very best Sound album, because it sounds like the band 'live' in the studio and, in a way, it actually was."

Mike was equally happy, as confirmed to *Record Collector* in 2002,

"It was recorded in the teeth of all the problems that caused us to break up, on a budget of tuppence and a shirt button, yet contains the best songs we ever wrote and Adrian's best lyrics".

While in the same article Graham describes the album as their, "crowning glory."

Back in June 1987 *Thunder Up* was out in the world and the press were doing their job.

Melody Maker proved most astute with a fantastically on the nail review from Mick Mercer. Mick accurately describes many of the qualities that made the band as great as they were celebrating their return after, "two years of 'silence'."

His praise for the Sound as, "Never what you expect, never lumbered with one lyrical lynchpin" very much describes what we've seen in the lyrics of *Thunder Up,* he goes on to cite their "blank image" as "hiding frosted weariness," confirming that the Sound were, "conventional only in set-up". This deeper appreciation of what we all know were some of the Sound's crucial strengths allows Mercer to question the validity of some of their contemporaries, specifically mentioning the band who were still a fixation for Adrian; U2.

Mercer's conclusion is memorable and entirely justified based on *Thunder Up's* contents,

"The Sound, by *refining* their despair, simply amplify their magnificence and magnify the intensity of expression. They've never been bad and they've never been better. Play it incessantly."

In the 1985 interview now available on the *Heads and Hearts* blog Adrian talks about the press and confirms,

"I read all the reviews we get, it's interesting what people say about you. But band's taking what journalists say about them seriously is never healthy."

Despite what he said back then, I'm sure Adrian got some satisfaction from Mercer's fervent prose, certainly more than he would have felt reading some of the other reviews.

Over at *Sounds* Mat Snow gave a grudging thumbs up but strayed into lazy, often puerile, territory.

For him Adrian had always been, "a stodgy looking man fronting a stodgy looking band," from which he believed a, "silvery romantic spirit was trying to escape."

Likening them, unflatteringly, to a "brick shithouse" who "didn't look much cuter" he sized Adrian up and decided he was, "the perennially pissed off teenager, huffy about the world's woes and why he hasn't got a girlfriend, in short an uptight, woolly-minded git."

Citing the band's reduced financial circumstances as assisting them in making the most of their talent, possibly a fair point but it was hardly the first time they'd done that, he concludes,

"I could learn to like this record, but I don't expect to ever get a laugh from it."

You could ask, "Why quote such negative nonsense?" Well, sadly it is important because the Sound's predicament in June 1987 can't be appreciated without it. Whether you like the situation or not, the press set the tone of how a band was perceived, for better or worse.

As can be seen from another grudging assessment at the short-lived *Underground* magazine. There Alex Bastedo described the Sound as, "largely forgotten in England, but still attaining giddy heights in the Lowlands". Still he does agree the band had turned in a, "sterling performance" but felt there were, "crass lyrics, one dimensional vocals and an absence of killer hooks."

The sign-off line carries an unintentional pathos,

"When Borland really gets his act together again they'll be brilliant."

Only they had been and still were brilliant, despite everything the world had thrown at them.

Adrian had bemoaned the lack of space given to his *Melody Maker* interview promoting *Heads and Hearts'* release, so his reaction to the brief few paragraphs granted within the news section this time round must have been a mix of despondency and anger.

The piece describes the Sound as "an anomaly; a hangover from the early eighties, when rock was enjoying what could transpire to be its last real renaissance, with the Bunnymen, New Order, Simple Minds and U2 all pushing to the fore."

There is a lot of truth in that statement, the implication that the Sound were left on the platform at the station as the train pulled off for sunnier climes, is a bitter one.

Despite being a favourable piece that talks of *Thunder Up* as, "Mean, moody, bombastic and thoughtful in one," much is made of the band's plight. A "muddy mix" is put down to the "low budget production" and the failure of the band to follow U2 up the charts is put to Adrian, he must have loved that.

Adrian, "People have said the Sound are the archetypal struggle band, but it's actually quite enjoyable."

Although the writer notes Adrian's chuckle, I wonder whether that was only after a bottle or two of German wine.

"The archetypal struggle band."

Adrian always had a gift for the snappy phrase and really did the writer's work for him here, he could have swapped places easily and would no doubt have been very entertaining dishing out judgement on the latest hype acts. It's a shame that never happened.

Oddly enough *Thunder Up* wasn't the only album Adrian released that year. Perhaps in a way it was, because for the other he adopted a pseudonym, Joachim Pimento. The band was the almost legendary Honolulu Mountain Daffodils, consisting of a group of Adrian's friends from his local pub, the Crooked Billet each appearing under an assumed name. The line-up was: guitarist-keyboardist Zoe Zettner, guitarist-vocalist Lord Sulaco, guitarist-percussionist Daiquiri J. Wright, guitarist Franklin Silverheels and bassist Smoky Alvaro.

Bearing in mind Adrian's prolific work rate it feels incredible that he managed to be involved in the release of three albums and an EP over the next five years:

Guitars of the Oceanic Undergrowth, Tequila Dementia, Aloha Sayonara and *Psychic HIt-List Victims.*

How to describe the Daffodils?

Well Adrian did talk of them when Jan interviewed him in 1996,

"I have a really dark sense of humour and I attempted to inject it into the Honolulu Mountain Daffodils. It was basically a group thing of friends who would sit around in the pub and say, 'Let's form a band!' "

Probably a common occurrence, but in this case they actually did it.

Adrian, "It was a whole worldview, as nihilistic and hedonistic as hell! Probably best summed up by the lyric of "Fahrenheit 451" that's almost like the worldview of the band encapsulated."

As a song "Fahrenheit 451" talks of the end of the world being acceptable if there was, "tequila coming out of a tap."

Adrian, "It was oblivion over reason! It makes sense, there's part of me in that lyric, it wasn't all a joke there was some autobiographical truth in there. I was writing obscurely about my real life experiences."

Some of that involved tales of Adrian being offered 'mescaline smarties' something that in reality probably involved LSD rather than actual mescaline. Don't try it at home unless under medical supervision...

So the Daffodils didn't eschew the angst entirely and also managed to sneak in a cheeky Suicide sample,

Adrian, "I Feel Like a Francis Bacon Painting" is quite an angst ridden song with some throwaway lines, complete with its Alan Vega/Suicide sample from "Frankie Teardrop."

Your enthusiasm for their music may depend on your capacity to feel you are in on a private joke but, as a Sound fan, you will at least want to hear it. Have in mind what would happen if a group of people with rather great record collections got together and chucked all their influences into the mixing pot. Sometimes it worked, other times, not so much.

Adrian, "It's so in-jokey it's unbelievable, the *Melody Maker* asked us if we were 'elitist' and we were. We didn't give a damn as we didn't have to sell any records. Not that we necessarily did with the Sound, but we were aware of our audience, with the Honolulu's we didn't have an audience to think about! It wouldn't have been worth doing if it wasn't extreme and weird, but it was still rock, not avant-garde."

Adrian's priceless final assessment,

"I wanted it to be something Iggy Pop could play while having lunch, something he would be happy with!"

Iggy was never far away from his mind, but behind the humour it's clear this was still another way of Adrian channelling some of the darkness he felt enveloping him. With the Honolulu's he was making it less frightening, via a strong dose of Dada with its anarchic acceptance that life has little meaning. But Adrian couldn't keep that up for very long: he still believed, and up until the end would always seek that deeper meaning in music and in life.

While most of England was probably "sleeping in the sun" Adrian and the band were thankfully still in a position where they could play in front of large crowds at European festivals.

The Sound played Parkpop twice, 1984 and 1987

Appearing at the Parkpop festival in The Hague, the band were one of the headliners with crowds numbering some 30000 or more. Adrian was interviewed for TV after the Sound's storming set and was, on the surface least, upbeat about questions around whether this was a "new start" for the Sound. When asked if there was more optimism in the music, a look passes across his face that suggests he knows that's not strictly true, he instead cites a new humour in the latest songs.

"It's not so good really. We're not commercial enough for the English charts and we're not quite strange enough for the slightly more esoteric independent charts. We're caught between two stools, trying to do good songs in a rock form. It could change with just one record, in England all you need is one hit and everyone knows who you are, it could change overnight. I think we deserve it."

As a music fan himself, Adrian was increasingly becoming aware of the limitation of the format within which he was working. In that tiny *Melody Maker* feature he had moved the question of whether the Sound were, "out of date" towards a wider one, of whether rock music itself was out of date. As he willingly agreed, "Because that's all we are really - a good rock band."

Some of that artistic restlessness would soon find an outlet.

As the Parkpop interview winds down, while still on camera, he stands to leave and raises his drink, "Here's to Parkpop '88."

While there would be a Parkpop the following year, the Sound would not be around to appear.

Continuing their short run of summer festivals the band also had Spanish and Dutch dates pencilled in for November and December making this, on paper at least, a much busier year than 1986. In addition, a handful of new songs we're taking shape, including, "13 Hours," "Distant Drums" and "Will."

In the meantime, Play it Again Sam hadn't given up on *Thunder Up*, releasing the "Iron Years" single remixed by Hugh Jones and sounding so much better on 12 inch. The record label even financed a video filmed, fittingly, at the Paradiso. Notwithstanding Graham's feelings towards them, Play it Again Sam did seem to have a degree of faith in the band even at that late stage.

Melody Maker now featured Chris Roberts as one of their writers and he gave "Iron Years" a suitably rave review. Describing the Sound as, "Dignified survivors" and *Thunder Up* as, "criminally overlooked." But perhaps best was the correct observation about "Iron Years" that,

"Pathos oozes from every fluid joint. The Sound have an innate grasp of said quality, knowing when to understate and when to scream."

Sounds however piled on the intimations of failure narrative so beloved of some of the papers,

"When you think of The Sound, you tend to think of stadiums, blood red skies, new gold dreams and so on, and then you remember that the Sound were that bunch who never made it. For maintaining a sunny disposition after all these years, for cranking out the rock'n'roll against all the odds, for battling on regardless, they are to be congratulated."

As for the actual music? Nada.

In the face of such attitudes, off to Spain the band went. The aim was to follow up on the previous years' trip, there was still a decent audience for the band there so the visit made sense.

The story from here on in has an almost dreamlike quality, floating to its inevitable shambolic outcome. Along the way the participants' accounts differing here and there as they try to make sense of what happened, to them and those around them.

Graham, "Then we had that awful tour in Europe. Things weren't quite so good but we were still hanging in there. But the first gig was at a place called The End in Vitoriain Spain. Ad rian just flipped, he thought it was an omen."

Vitoria-Gasteiz, or Vittoria, is the capital of the Basque region in north-eastern Spain, The End was a popular club in the 250,000 population city.

The date was the 7th of November 1987.

It's ironic that on the night the Sound were filmed by the Spanish TV channel ETB 3 and also interviewed briefly. One song survives and can be seen on YouTube: perhaps fittingly it's a version of "Total Recall."

And it's an excellent version, but then Adrian was still a professional. You can scrutinise the footage for clues, yes he tweaks the lyrics here and there and modifies the melody line a little, but all appears in order, the crowd is a good size and appreciative.

As Graham has previously mentioned Adrian was on a serious Doors kick and so the coincidence of playing a club that shared the name of a particularly significant Doors epic was too much for him.

Graham, "The Door's "The End" and here we are playing at a club called *The End*! He just lost it, I couldn't handle it."

Mike has the events of that period etched on his brain,

"It was difficult. With hindsight, I realise that you never really knew which Adrian you were talking to. A person with schizoaffective disorder sometimes has this personality and sometimes another. How do you deal with that? None of us really knew."

You can feel the pain and confusion of people having to deal with something that was outside their direct experience. And of course, youngish men, being youngish men, there probably wasn't enough open discussion going on, because, well, you just don't do you? Later it seems obvious but at the time events just 'happen', in reality by then there was little they could have done.

Mike, "Adrian at the time had moved on from thinking he was Ian Curtis to thinking he was Jim Morrison. He had this fantasy about being Jim Morrison in the real reality as opposed to the false reality where he was Adrian Borland."

It won't be lost on anyone that Ian Curtis had also been a big Doors fan and it has been said that both Curtis and Morrison were people who showed very different sides of their characters to the people close to them. Life seemed to be moving in concentric circles.

Events had taken a surreal and disturbing turn during that day when the band sound-checked.

Mike, "In the afternoon we were doing the soundcheck. The dressing room was under the stage and I was in the hall with Max and our road manager at the time. Adrian and Graham were in the dressing room. The road crew was winching up the lighting rig and that was making a squealing and rattling noise. Graham came up and said, 'I'm worried about Adrian, he's being really bizarre and thinks that the noise he can hear is part of a conspiracy and that aliens are coming to take him away. He doesn't want to come out of the dressing room.' "

Eventually the band managed to persuade Adrian to come up and do the soundcheck but all was clearly not well, as Mike explains,

"Whilst he was sound checking the mike and guitar he seemed to be in a totally different place, not really aware of what was going on around him. He said I want to do this gig at The End because it will be 'the end'.

The band all knew he had previously tried to kill himself,

"People were panicking, they didn't know what to do, the road manager had no experience of this and Max and Graham were just looking at each other, all at sea."

Mike knew the tour would have to be cancelled but the decision was made to go ahead with that night's gig.

Shortened gig complete, the following day the rest of the tour was then called-off.

Mike, "The next day it was Adrian and me on the plane back home to his parents' place. There was a bit of me being the oldest so I'd do it. I remember sitting on the plane on the way back, it was a night flight and Adrian was by the window. He was looking distractedly out of the window and said, 'I just want to make sure this is actually happening'. He was under the impression that I wasn't me, that I was one of these people he was afraid of, a sort of construct to look like me."

Mike took Adrian back to 2 Hillview,

"When we got there he was still unable to sleep and suffering from a psychotic episode, so I sat up with him. Julie was there and Win and Bob. The doctor tried to help by giving him an injection but he wouldn't let him. I think about three a.m. he eventually went to sleep. I was woken up in the morning by my door opening and Adrian trying to get in. I'd put my suitcase across the door. I tried to explain to Adrian that it was for his protection not mine. I didn't want him to put himself at risk of trying to, 'do me in'."

Adrian went back to Springfield Hospital for a relatively short stay.

Mike confirms the band had to complete the Dutch leg of the tour as they simply couldn't afford to cancel it, and Adrian seemed to be OK with doing that. It appears there was some confusion over the Dutch gigs with them being cancelled then rearranged, no doubt creating some annoyance and doubt in people's minds as to what would actually happen.

On the 1st of December Max and Adrian went into the studio to record a 2 Meter Session. Now legendary, the show was conceived and presented by Jan Douwe Kroeske. Max and Adrian performed atmospheric acoustic versions of "Iron Years" and "Hand of Love," later to be released as part of the excellent *2 Meter Sessions 1987-1995* album. Adrian sounded in good spirits with no hint of what was to come.

The night before what turned out to be their final gig, the band and some friends went out to an Asian restaurant to celebrate Adrian's birthday, perhaps unsurprisingly alcohol played a starring role. Fun for those in attendance but not, I suspect, for the restaurant staff who sadly had to witness some pretty boorish rock'n'roll behaviour,

Graham, "Bear in mind we were all extremely drunk. There was a big group of us out celebrating Adrian's birthday, Adrian gets up to leave and trips over a chair. He's drunk and falls over into a fish tank, breaking it and sending the fish all over the floor. It wasn't intentional but we ended up getting chased down the street by staff with knives."

Fan and friend of the band since 1981, Patrick de Leede was on board for this tour and was selling the T-shirts, sometimes sleeping on a band members' hotel room floor.

Another job for Patrick was procuring illegal substances for bands,

Patrick, "But not for Adrian! He never took anything, only German white wine!"

The events of those few days are burned into Patrick's mind and still provoke an emotional reaction, Today he recalls what were the last days of the Sound,

"Adrian was weird, he was a different person. He was always talking of Amsterdam, the Paradiso. Everything was concentrated on him doing that show. I had a feeling, something's not right here. He was paranoid and telling stories about people stealing his lyrics, including U2."

Not uncommon themes for Adrian, but at a level of intensity that was worrying. As far as the gigs were concerned,

Patrick, "There was so much energy at that final Paradiso gig. I've never

Posters advertising 8 of the 11 gigs The Sound played at the Paradiso

felt that much energy before or since. I had a gut feeling that something was exploding in Adrian that day. After that he just kind of collapsed mentally."

Graham wasn't happy with the quality of the shows the band was playing on that tour and felt Adrian's medication was impacting his performance,

Graham, "He was playing but just going through the motions."

The Sound playing the Paradiso

For Mike the recollection is different and matches Patrick's assessment,

"So we did that tour. The second to last gig (4th December 1987) was at the Paradiso, which was a fantastic gig. We played really well and everyone was over the moon thinking things were back on course. Adrian was acting relatively normally. Then the next gig, at a club the size of the Marquee in Zoetermeer (the Boerderij), was packed. Halfway through the show he just unplugged his guitar and walked off stage in the middle of a song. We just stopped playing and walked off into the dressing room. He was sitting there blank faced very still, like a facsimile of himself. As if he'd been hollowed out from inside. We didn't know what to do but we called off the tour and I think Max took him home that time. And that was the last gig we'd ever do."

The Boerderij is still there today, with a healthy calendar of upcoming gigs, although in a new building a little bit further down the road. The 400 capacity club was as good a place as any for the band's last hurrah.

out and tell the audience the gig was over. But I knew: this was the end of the Sound. It broke my heart."

With hindsight we now understand that Adrian was seriously ill.

"We had this meeting and in between the last gig and the meeting I formulated a plan where we'd just 'suspend' the Sound and give Adrian some space. However long it takes to get some help and sort himself out and then we'll reconvene and carry on with the Sound, assuming that would be possible. We'd played in Holland with Fiat Lux (Ian Nelson's band) who we got to know quite well and I thought why don't we get together with them and do a little one-off project. People thought that was a good idea and so we had a meeting. But Adrian was straight away saying, 'It's been difficult and I think they're after me because of what I write in my songs, so what I'm going to do is write happier, poppier songs and everything will be great if we carry on like that.' I looked at the others and they said, 'OK Adrian, that's what we'll do.' The moment they said that I thought I've had enough of this, I can't go on and Adrian can't so I just said, 'OK guys, sorry, but I'm leaving the band.' Adrian said, 'OK you know where the door is.' "

Patrick also recalls the gig,

"Adrian was completely not there in his head. They played a few numbers then Adrian threw down his guitar, began a tirade over the mike and walked off stage. I went backstage and then we had to come

Although Mike didn't leave the room until the end of the meeting it must have been a shattering moment. But consider his position as part of a band with two heroin users and a frontman who was in the throes of serious mental illness as well as being a, just about, functioning alcoholic.

Poster advertising the gig at the Boerderij, Zoetermeer

When interviewed for *Walking in the Opposite Direction* Graham was clear that the end couldn't be avoided,

"We couldn't carry on anymore. Everything that was, now wasn't. We were in such a state of decay as a band, I was off the rails myself at that time, not mentally but 'I wasn't performing well as a fine upstanding citizen' shall we say!"

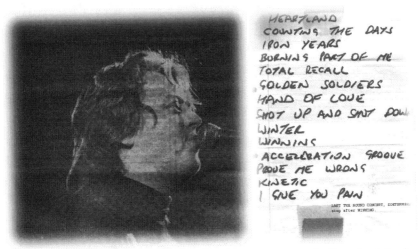

Adrian, photo taken during that last gig in de Boerderij and original setlist from the Sound's final gig

Mike Dudley's account of events highlights Adrian's wish to change his music because of the effect he perceived it was having on his mental condition, something confirmed by Graham,

Graham, "We all came home and then Dudley announced he was leaving the band, which he said was for Adrian's health, suggesting that if he left, the Sound would finish. Which it did and sort of didn't. To give him his full credit it was a huge hole, we couldn't replace Dudley. After he left we did audition a couple of drummers. Adrian wanted to go acoustic, he wanted me to get an acoustic bass and he'd play acoustic guitar. I wasn't interested, so I was out and that was it. Adrian wanted something where it was tempered down so the energy and endorphin levels were less."

In 1991 when I asked Adrian why the band split his answer was open and frank,

"Because I had this nervous depression, a nervous breakdown, so that's why we split. I've suffered from it several times since then."

Speaking to Jan in 1996 he elaborates and adds some further detail that neither Mike nor Graham mention,

"We went on tour and come the end of the year I just got nervous exhaustion and then in Vitoria someone spiked one of my drinks and I just got really out of it. It was a place aptly called The End. I got one of these drugs in my drink. I was alright for the gig, but in the morning I could barely crawl out of bed, I was stumbling around looking at myself in the mirror thinking, I have a gig in five hours' time. It wasn't a good way to start a tour. It just got worse from there, I flipped out in Barcelona so the whole tour was cancelled. I can laugh now but it wasn't really funny."

Adrian's memory includes making it to Barcelona which doesn't seem to have happened unless the flight home was from there. In addition he slightly downplays the mental health aspect by citing drink spiking. As for the Dutch tour he confirms the financial issues as being a factor in having to go ahead.

"We managed to get back the final Dutch leg. We were under a lot of financial pressure to do that or we'd have been three grand down. The last full gig was in the Paradiso. But the final moment on stage with the Sound was at a place called the Rock and Roll Farm near Rotterdam in a small town (not really a 'small town' in reality, the population was over 120,000). I sang "Winning" and it sounded so hollow I just had to walk off stage. Because of my state of mind; I was just 'out to lunch.' I just thought, this is bollocks, 'winning'! I didn't want to be some cabaret act churning out something you don't mean. Then we got all the hassle from the journalists. The DJ played "Ziggy Stardust" straight after, which with me being left-handed, was quite apt. In Ziggy's case, "When the kids had killed the man, I had to break-up the band.""

Well thankfully "the kids' hadn't killed the band", but it was over.

Jean-Paul van Mierlo was at the gig as a fan,

"Adrian Borland, my hero, in my hometown, in my home venue, I'd waited for this for years, but then...walking off stage half-way through the set. All the people around me asking what, why, how long? Later on we fans understood; this was the last ever gig of the Sound. And many more years later, in fact in 1999, I really understood."

It wasn't the heroic last stand a fan might have imagined but rather a messy unsatisfactory end to the career of a band who made a name for themselves via the commitment they showed on stage.

The Dutch press was scathing. One paper ran a piece suggesting the Sound had been forced to complete the tour, including playing at least an hour at the last show, in order to be paid in full. The band and road manager's talk of vocal problems and violence in the audience were ridiculed by the paper.

Worse was the highly unflattering cartoon of an overweight and drunk Borland sitting at the bar saying, "What a gig!" While the band counter by saying, "We only played an hour", Adrian responds by telling them, "It doesn't matter, tell the audience I lost my voice."

It's not a pretty picture and of course doesn't reflect the genuine torment behind what happened. The damage must have lasted into Adrian's solo career - promoters get twitchy when they see stories like this.

Ultimately the idea of Adrian and the Sound playing under the yoke of contractual obligation is not one that anyone who loved them would want as an epitaph.

Talking to Jan, Adrian reflected on the fallout that followed their return to England,

"Once Dudley had left, Graham wanted to do something different with a new singer and name and I just thought, well you can but I'll do my stuff. I was interested for a week and then no, I was in a very bad way but I knew I had more to offer as a songwriter."

Adrian therefore conceding his poor mental state and, by 1996, he could reflect and realise it was the right thing at the right time,

"I think it's good it ended there. Max had already contracted AIDS, but didn't yet know it. So in a way the writing was on the wall whether we knew it or not. It was as good a point as any. The next album would have been a deliberately new sound for me, brighter. When I look back I thought we'd hit this ceiling for so long and never really reached the second floor, it wore us down psychologically. Never being able to break out of this moderate success, just staying the same, it wasn't going anywhere, the same places every year playing clubs for 500-1000 people. Which sounds great now, and it is nice for a while, but after five years you've done it. I don't know if we'd carried on whether we could ever have broken through, but we didn't have the energy left."

Adrian felt the load was heavier on them because of the lack of professional management, undoubtedly true.

The Sound wouldn't be the first band, or the last, to fall to pieces under such circumstances. Could a proper break and sympathetic medical treatment for Adrian have saved them? Maybe, but beyond his illness, deep down Adrian knew the time was up. He was having serious concerns about where he could take the 'rock format'. Those concerns were valid. The music scene of the late '80s wasn't hugely sympathetic to a band like the Sound, the reviews referring to them as relics of a previous era would have continued until any press coverage likely dwindled to a trickle.

In the news section of the 13th February 1988 edition of the *Melody Maker* there was a brief paragraph that acted as the Sound's obituary, echoing Adrian's frustration at the 'ceiling' the band had hit,

"The Sound, one of the indie scene's longest serving bands, have split up. Singer/songwriter Adrian Borland is pursuing a solo career. He told the *Maker* this week: 'Basically we went for as long as we could without it becoming a joke. The stance we took didn't exactly get us nowhere, but it was obvious it wasn't going to get us any further.' "

An excerpt from the lyrics of one of the final Sound songs, "Will" (note: there were actually two different songs with this same title demoed) show the sheer weary agony Adrian was feeling. Written after the

WILL   Borland 1987 Monumental/Sabam/Editions C.

V1) I FELT THE RAIN, KNOW HOW THAT FEELS
COOLING MY HEELS IN THIS COOLER FOR WHEELS
IT'S STRANGE OUTSIDE BUT IT'S STRANGER IN HERE
WITH A LITTLE VOICE YOU DON'T ALWAYS WANT TO HERE
CH) BUT IT'S THE WILL, THE WILL
PUT ME WHERE YOU WANT ME, BUT I'VE STILL GOT, GOT
THE WILL, THE WILL
PUSH ME TO THE BREAKING POINT, BUT I'VE STILL GOT, GOT
THE WILL, TO GO ON
I'VE GOT A SIMPLE LITTLE SONG (THAT) I SING ALONG TO

V2) I WOKE UP AND IT FELT LIKE HELL
AND THE DRUGS YOU'RE ON MEAN THAT YOU CAN'T EVEN TELL
BUT SOMETHING GOT INTO ME
A LITTLE FACE YOU DON'T REALLY WANT TO SEE
CH) BUT IT'S THE WILL etc.

Adrian's handwritten lyric sheet for 'Will'

aborted Spanish tour and touching on his time in hospital, the song joined two other new tracks played in those last days ("Distant Drums" and "13 Hours") that give a tantalising glimpse of what the next Sound album could have sounded like,

"I felt the rain and how that feels
It's strange outside
But it's stranger in here
With a little voice
You don't always want to hear
It's the will
Put me where you want me
But I've still got the will
Push me to the breaking point
But I've still got the will
Got this simple little song
That I just sing along
And it goes like this
I woke up and it felt like hell
And the drugs you're on
Mean you can't even tell."

It's a tough listen, Adrian always said if you wanted to understand him listen to his lyrics. Well here he seemed to be desperately trying to convince himself he could go on. One listen to the live version from that Paradiso gig, Adrian's voice raw and cracking, will tell you: he couldn't have gone on.

A new beginning wasn't just advisable - it was essential, both for Adrian's mental health and his musical future. Two elements that he now, all too painfully, understood would always be interwoven.

The Sound at one of the many gigs they played at the Paradiso

CHAPTER 16

It's, um, formative okay?

In amongst the many hours of interview footage gathered in the making of the *Walking in the Opposite Direction* documentary, there's a quietly revealing comment from Mike Dudley,

"Adrian's the sort of guy who spent most of his time trying to make the world around him fit his idea of how he thought it ought to be. Not just politically, but everything. The way people behaved around him, the colour of the wallpaper, everything. That was his obsession. He wanted the world to fit in with him rather than the other way round."

To walk though life in this way is to invite disappointment. When Adrian finally crashed the Sound into the brick wall they'd been battering themselves senseless against for years, it wasn't a move fully within his control. But maybe deep down he'd been seeking a reset, a way to exert some command over a life that had left his direct control, one he really didn't like the look of, full of painful internal and external conflict and massive stress.

Certainly from early in 1988 he'd been recording demos of songs that were likely intended for the Sound but reflected the new acoustic direction that Graham had, perhaps understandably, baulked at.

It's no coincidence that in the desperation of a song like "Will" we hear Adrian singing of a, "simple little song." Well, what would come next was his vision of that simpler, brighter kind of music.

Over the years there have been a wealth of Adrian's demos traded amongst fans, as well as the large number of cassettes sitting in the archive carefully managed by Jean-Paul van Mierlo and the Stichting Opposite Direction foundation.

Among them is a humble cassette tape from very early 1988. Eight songs including a couple that got lost along the way, it's a reminder of just how prolific Adrian was, as if there was a tap that was never really turned off.

Leading the way is a deceptively bright and breezy acoustic strum called "Light the Sky" the kind of song that "Hand of Love" pointed towards but lighter than anything the Sound ever recorded. But despite all that there's still those lyrics: darkness, weakness and broken dreams and, in the end, Adrian again puts his happiness in the hands of another person.

"I need *you* to light the sky."

A new start but some of the old issues can't be banished that easily.

Nevertheless it seems incredible to see Adrian pick himself up and move on so quickly. He even played an acoustic gig that March at the Mean Fiddler in Harlesden north London, appearing on a bill with indie band Red Harvest, one of the numerous acts he'd carried out production work for.

Although when I discussed it with him a couple of years' later, (having heard a bootleg where he sounded less than happy onstage) he said he really didn't rate the performance,

Adrian, "The Mean Fiddler? No, I hated that! It was a perfunctory performance. I've given up that solo stuff, all that 'malarkey'!"

It's quite revealing that a few months into being a solo artist there's a sense he was already yearning for band dynamics.

Nevertheless, the speed with which Adrian returned to music making was admirable, but there's a lingering doubt as to whether he'd really faced the realities of his situation. In 1996 Jan asked him a question that indicates he may have been wondering the same thing, his query, possibly unintentionally, referencing the unreleased "Will,"

Jan, "Did you feel much different in yourself at that stage? Was it an effort of will?"

Adrian, "No, it wasn't an effort of will. I've always been an optimistic person and it was just a question of drawing on that side of myself rather than the other one."

We've seen that Adrian was capable of great optimism and enthusiasm but there's a hint of a person in a degree of denial when you take in those words and contrast them with the wreckage of 1987. But who would want to deflate such feelings?

Adrian's life was certainly entering a new phase. Firstly he now had an energetic, young manager, Rob Acda, who also happened to be a huge Sound fan. Rob was a Dutch musician who had branched out into management and live booking, he was only 28 when they started working together. Tragically his life was cut short when he died in 1994, prompting a dedication from Adrian in the form of "In Passing" from future album *Beautiful Ammunition*. Today his foundation sponsors a music award in his name for young bands held at the venue when he was a booker, Haarlem's Patronaat.

It wasn't too much of a surprise to see Adrian turning to Holland for the next stage of his career. Despite the bitter way the final Sound tour had ended, it was still the place he was best understood and appreciated. We were now at the stage where Adrian was largely unknown in the UK but had the status of 'cult rock star' in the Netherlands.

Initially visiting for a holiday, Adrian ended up beginning an arrangement where he would spend up to half the year living there, staying part of the time in Haarlem lodging in his managers' attic. In effect Adrian became a wanderer spending time with a range of friends in various towns and cities across the country. For all Adrian's problems once more we need to remember that a lot of people liked him, no, more than that: loved him. He was above all a very enjoyable person to have around, full of humour and enthusiasm (that word again) as well as having a disarmingly vulnerable side.

In Haarlem, as well as manager Rob, he also spent a lot of time staying with his friends Sonja and Marco who grew close to him.

There are many memories, testimonials and comments from a large number of people talking of their interactions with Adrian, in amongst all of them there's no one who talks of disliking him. Yes people did experience some difficult moments in their relationships, but that didn't tend to cancel out the overwhelming positives.

However it's also worth remembering Mike Dudley's comments about the way Adrian dealt with the world, in particular his need for people to look after, and do things for, him. It seems that it was Adrian who was the focal point in these friendships and that others, willingly, worked around him. Some of this may well have been a manifestation of his illness and the need for comfort and relief with people who knew him. In return he was an entertaining guest and could sprinkle a bit of cult rock-star 'stardust'.

When in Amsterdam, as well as a girl called Sabine, Adrian was also friends with Margriet. His nickname for Margriet was 'Bobby' the reason being that like the old image of an English policeman, she seemed to always be around to look after him.

Margriet would accompany Adrian to the Paradiso (where it became a tradition that she would lay a rose on the stage while he played) whereas Sabine would be in attendance at the Melkweg. The venues were close to each other and the women lived within a short distance, but Adrian kept the platonic friendships separate.

Sabine speaks touchingly of how she remembers Adrian,

"I found him not only very intelligent but vulnerable too, especially if you were talking to him one on one. You also noticed that he was just a very nice person and that's actually always been the case."

With Adrian this wasn't a common case of inflated rock-star ego, far from it, he was a refreshingly down to earth character who was much more likely to be self-deprecating than self-aggrandising.

Dutch journalist and friend Joke van Gemerde summed up the contradictions succinctly in the *Book of (Happy) Memories,*

"Adrian was a complicated personality: irritating, funny and sometimes movingly vulnerable and *never* boring. He never pretended to be better than he actually was, he just couldn't."

Another Dutch acquaintance, Tinka Hofmeijer wrote to a friend and tried to explain her feelings about knowing Adrian, a section was also included in the *Book of (Happy) Memories,*

"Adrian is probably one of the most complex and frustrating people I've met. Most of the time he's very selfish and when he's in a terrible mood you can be sure that everyone around him is. I've seen him being mean to others and he can have a very heavy temper. I know him as a sarcastic, cynical person with a strange sense of humour. Still, I like him a lot. In spite of his dark sides I just can't hate him. After a good conversation with him he has the gift of giving me more energy."

It takes courage to be so brutally honest at the same time as being quite tender in your feelings towards a person. For Tinka it came as a shock to reread these words years later but there's no harshness there, just love and respect for Adrian, faults and all.

Asked about the 'Dutch phase' of his life during an interview, with Dutch Radio KRO's Leidsekade Live promoting 1992's *Brittle Heaven,* Adrian explained how it came about and also how he would later meet his new band the Citizens,

"Well I sort of came over for a holiday and decided to stay, I met Rob Acda my manager and he introduced me to the Sjako! guys. And then we got Victor (Heeremans) on keyboards, which was a very natural thing you know, it just clicked straight away. We did one song in a rehearsal studio and it was something like, okay let's start a band."

Adrian with the Citizens

When I spoke to Adrian in 1991 he was clear about the pull Holland exerted,

"Yeah, there's a much bigger audience over there, much more enthusiasm. There are always good crowds at the gigs. I'm actually quite well known in Holland. That's the reason I live there, apart from getting away from Wimbledon for half the year, which is nice."

By then the attic living arrangement had ended but I asked Adrian what it was like and whether he had learned any Dutch,

"I stayed in a little attic room. It's OK, apart from the occasional bouts of loneliness when everyone's at work and I'm doing nothing. The language is a problem. I can't speak a bloody word of Dutch!"

Once more Adrian was in a situation where he was, to a degree, disconnected from everyday life. And no, he didn't learn the language, Mike Dudley would not have been surprised at the lack of accommodation for the ways of the society he was living within. Then again he wouldn't be the first Englishman to studiously avoid the effort of learning another language.

Adrian's work with his new band was still a little way off. Right now there was a new album to plan.

The good news? Play it Again Sam were still on board, so Adrian had a label ready to release his songs, something that couldn't be taken for granted and would have likely been a challenge to find in the UK.

In 1991 I asked Adrian about his relationship with the label,

"Well they've stuck with me, I mean they're not terrible to me, I think Kenny (Gates) is more involved with other things now, but I mean at least I helped get the label off the ground, so they sort of owe me one, I also did a lot of production work for them in the early days. They've done all right for me so far. At least they're putting my records out, which is more than I can expect of the major labels in this country, who really couldn't give a shit! It's hard to get your music heard, you know."

For what he was planning Adrian needed a record company behind him. He was true to his word: the next record would not be a rock band playing live in a room in the way much of *Thunder Up* had been. His aims were far more expansive and would only grow as the months passed. Naturally, being on an indie, the budget would be pretty restrictive but luckily for Adrian he knew a lot of people and could call in a few favours.

One factor that would carry over from *Thunder Up*: the always trusted Nick Robbins would be manning the desk at Elephant Studio.

Nick, "After the Sound split, Adrian rang us at the studio to say he wanted to make a solo album and would we like to help him? Of course, we said yes, we'd love to. And so we had an initial meeting with him where he told us that he would like some, what were really, top session musicians to be organised and he had the songs ready."

As you would expect Adrian was very good at articulating his vision for what would become *Alexandria,* Nick quickly realised this would, in some ways, be a very different recording experience,

"We set about organising various musicians with him and planning the sessions. At this stage I just assumed that his songs would be fairly similar to the Sound, but in fact of course they were quite different and his whole mental space was very different."

But certain patterns of behaviour hadn't changed as Nick explains,

"Of course he was often stressed in the studio when making records because they meant so much to him, it was even worse when he was on his own making a solo album."

When talking to Jan in 1996 Adrian recalled the experience as being enjoyable,

"*Alexandria* was quite easy and good fun to make. It was nice to have different people coming in and out of the studio for 28 days and getting a different take on your songs."

But for Nick it was less so,

"I hadn't realised that by this time Adrian was beginning to have some real problems, and during the making of *Alexandria* he was a nightmare, not because he was offensive or anything like that. He never was, but because if you've ever been in the studio with somebody who has just far too much energy and a lot of problems, then you'll understand just how difficult the making of that first solo album was."

Nick appears an eminently polite and friendly person so is too discrete to go into further detail, but his residual feeling of slight regret is still palpable,

"It is a little bit disappointing. I don't think it (*Alexandria)* sounds as good as it should have, and some of that is down to the fact that Adrian wore me out, he would work such long days and he would have so many things to say all the time that it became very difficult to concentrate on my part of the job."

As it was *Alexandria* was only partially mixed by Nick, the remaining tracks were passed to *Shock of Daylight* veteran Pat Collier,

"I think that's possibly one of the reasons why he then asked Pat to finish the mixes, or to do another set of mixes, because they were a little disappointing to be honest. Sadly, he didn't ask me to remix it, which I would've liked, but there we are, that's life."

Nick didn't work with Adrian again, but wasn't bitter and remained massively respectful of Adrian's talents,

"I thought he was one of the best musicians I've ever worked with, without doubt."

After a look at the roll call of musicians appearing on *Alexandria* you have some sympathy for Nick. It must have been a complex series of sessions to organise.

Adrian described the nature of the process to Jan,

"*Alexandria* was a question of chance meetings with Anthony Thistlethwaite and him liking the tapes and them coming down the day after touring with the Waterboys. Of course then there were all the session musicians and working with Danny Thompson, an ultra experienced jazz bass player (veteran of a myriad number of sessions including Nick Drake, Richard Thompson and John Martyn). It was great having him play on "Deep Deep Blue." He played with Orbison and that song was written with him in mind. He had the freedom to do what he liked within the structure of the song and was listening to the lyrics, not the chord changes."

However it wasn't always easy to curb the improvisational instincts of someone like Danny. Future friend and collaborator James Walton Ingham recalls Adrian regaling him with tales of the *Alexandria* sessions and the recording of "Beneath the Big Wheel,"

Adrian, "He wanted to do all this improvising but I only wanted three notes! But Danny wouldn't do it, every time he got to the take he'd suddenly start improvising. So we waited for Danny to leave and just sampled the three notes. That's what runs through the track."

Adrian was right incidentally.

The album ended up featuring close to 20 additional musicians including four backing singers, string players lead by John Metcalfe, and even a contribution from former Sound member Max somewhere in there.

A few of those involved were recruited in unusual ways, including Adrian's friend Audrey,

"Adrian was going through one of his more stressed-out periods. His mental state always deteriorated when he was recording. Anyway, he managed to break his left hand in the middle of recording the album, and I ended up in A&E practically all night with him and the next day he had to go back and have it plastered. He insisted I went with him again, even though I'd only had about two hours' sleep. When we finally emerged from the hospital, he decided to tell me he was due in the studio and again insisted I go with him – he knew the reaction he was going to get and needed me for moral support. When we got there, everyone obviously immediately saw the fingers to elbow plaster cast, so you can just imagine the reaction...he was due to do some guitar-work but guitars were obviously out of the question, so it was decided that backing vocals were the order of the day. I'm just sitting there, totally exhausted and minding my own business, and Adrian marches up to me with the immortal words, 'You can sing a bit. Make yourself useful.' "

Notwithstanding the stress Adrian loved the overall experience, although never again sought to involve such a supporting cast, whether due to economics or choice.

He explained what he was trying to achieve with *Alexandria* when granted a full page interview with the ever loyal Chris Roberts in *Melody Maker,*

"I wanted a brighter situation. You end up performing songs night after night, so if you start off in a very dark intense claustrophobic musical area it rubs off on you after a while. This could be what got to Ian Curtis. If you surround yourself with a heavy, gloomy thing in the end it comes back at you, like a picture you painted jumping to life and almost throttling you. So I thought the best thing I can do, if I'm going to carry on, is *lighten up.*"

There's a lot implied in that paragraph: the direct comparison with Curtis is worrying. Adrian went over and over the implications of the music he made for his emotional state but never fully succeeded in breaking the chain of effect, maybe it was an impossible task.

Alexandria was the 'A' of a proposed A-Z of solo records, the title inspired by a possible mishearing of a girl's name on a bus to Catford. Although Adrian managed not to fall in love with her, she unwittingly provided the album's evocative name. He did also concede it had a bright, sunny, 'beginning of civilisation' sense to it when viewed in retrospect. Before confessing to Chris Roberts that theorising like that was probably, "all bullshit, isn't it?"

"Light the Sky" led the charge as his debut solo single in September 1989. You can see why; its determined strum is reliably stirring and conjures up images of Adrian out in the great wide open striding purposefully in sensible knitwear. Presumably that was the intention?

For some Sound fans it may have been something of a shock in its unashamedly poppy nature.

Sounds reviewed it and were unconvinced, describing it as, "rustic rock" that should have been Adrian's 're-entry' but instead was, "a rather mundane, empty love song" quipping that it could end up as a soap opera theme tune. Ouch.

Overly harsh undoubtedly, on record "Light the Sky" was an excellent opener but immediately outclassed by the classic that followed.

"Rogue Beauty" deserves a place on any Borland best-of. The strings really stun here alongside Danny Thompson's acoustic bass, Graham missed out when refusing a go at the instrument. A minor gripe: the programmed drums naturally miss the sensitivity of Mike Dudley, still it's stirring and sees Adrian back on the hunt for that mythical communion with another human.

These two songs were among the first written in the aftermath of the split with Adrian feeling they showed a more, "conscious optimism, whereas a year later I was starting to feel the withdrawal effects."

Future single "Beneath the Big Wheel" is another lovely song, Danny Thompson's bass lithe and supporting of a track that uses an evocative metaphor to critique the cruelty of a society driven by profit and greed.

"Nothing's fair and nothing's fairly earned when you're on the big wheel."

Adrian misses his turn and ends up watching from below, collar turned up against the cold. Although there's hope in its final words, still that instrumental coda feels chilly and tense as Adrian's guitar crashes in for the finale.

"Community Call" teeters on the edge of being a little boxy and clunky but Anthony Thistlethwaite's sax drags us up and along and soon we're shoulder to shoulder with Adrian in the fight against loneliness and people who are, "Out for themselves, they don't see the pain you give someone like me."

"No Ethereal" is one of the songs coming from that period where he was feeling "withdrawal effects" and it's not a stretch to imagine the Sound turning in a persuasive version as it feels closer in structure to something that might have found its way onto *Heads and Hearts*. Lyrically the clincher is the feeling behind the line,

"My only hope on this lonely night is that you will hold me through the next cold decade."

There's an emotional fragility there in Adrian's voice, if you listen closely, that may raise a lump in your throat. He was right: it would be a "cold decade".

"Other Side of the World" takes us into chamber pop territory and has a suitably stately beauty. Once more Adrian is looking askance at the suffering in a world most never see, you wonder if this was his more subtle response to the blustery side of Live Aid.

Simon Walker's violin leads us into "Crystalline", a song of summer possibility but with a telling mention of the "shaken ghost left far behind." Key line?

"Sometimes I think, sometimes I choose not to."

Adrian described "Shadow of Your Grace" as, "a helpless situation, but it hasn't got that heavy ponderous feeling; it *suggests* rather than emphasises it." It's an unashamed regretful end of love song with a candid admission of culpability,

"I'm standing in my own work and I'm knee-high in waste."

Again "Weight of Stuff" teases a little more of the Sound's dynamic with a lyric of frustrated desire for renewal and new starts, mind you the

Sound hadn't featured clarinet since Bi left...

Alexandria's sky-scraping heart should have been "She's My Heroine." Adrian describing it as the album's "safety valve," letting off steam as the record, up until then, only threatens to do. A tribute to his beloved Patti Smith; it's close to great. But maybe this is where the reasons for Nick's concern about the mix become clear, just when you want it to take flight the song remains stubbornly earthbound, that it was much better live is no surprise.

And then we have that Orbison inspired finale, "Deep Deep Blue." Written weeks away from Roy's death, Adrian genuinely wanted to get it to him, but time and industry contracts beat him. To say it's worthy of such a master will confirm its rightful place as the bluer than blue closer to a brave and ambitious record.

Hidden away in the sleeve-notes there was a revealing admission from Adrian,

"It's, um, formative ok?"

Full of his usual humour, and maybe betraying some of his nervous anticipation of the reaction from fans and critics, the reality is, mix concerns notwithstanding, he more or less pulled it off. *Alexandria* added a new palette of colours to an already wide-ranging catalogue. Listening back now it's a rich and moving piece of work.

Adrian's assessment as later given to Jan is a warm and accurate summary, but then it was his album,

"It was actually meant to sound quite happy for me, quite bright and hopeful, not that all the lyrics were. I still think it was a break with the past. I think the Sound probably could have adapted to those songs and it would have been a new phase of the Sound, and we'd probably have shaken off another load of fans who'd just got into *Thunder Up*! But I've always done that, it's a bit like a rodeo staying with me. Anyone who went the distance and genuinely liked everything is a very interesting person. Maybe only me! The Sound split and so what would have been the point in carrying on and sounding like them? I do wonder what would have happened if the Sound had been given those songs. We might have sat down and decided to make a lush orchestral album. There's no reason Graham and Dudley couldn't have played that. The main difference was the tone. It's slightly lighter and more optimistic compared with the heavy stuff the Sound did. Definitely more deliberately pop than the Sound ever were."

Dressed up in a quite literal but not unpleasing cover provided by the Play it Again Sam in-house designer, (look, it's a lot better than a clown on a trapeze) *Alexandria* picked up largely positive reviews.

However you do start to wonder what Adrian would have done without Chris Roberts at *Melody Maker,* not only did he carry out their interview but he also secured the album review.

Roberts raised concerns regarding the production, wasn't impressed with "Light the Sky" and was underwhelmed by a couple of other tracks, but overall gave *Alexandria* an enthusiastic welcome, beginning the review with the statement, "The man is back!"

His conclusion was hopeful but, with the benefit of hindsight, unintentionally unfortunate in some of its use of language,

"It's, um, formative ok? mutters the sleeve, *Alexandria* sees Adrian Borland, one of our sanest irresponsible lunatics, mapping out a path from the Sound to a new fury. It's taking shape, gathering momentum. Insurrection, resurrection."

The late great David Cavanagh covered the album for *Sounds* and awarded three and a half stars out of five. His was a measured but welcoming assessment that mentions hearing Adrian, 'hold court' in a Wapping pub where he talked at length of the music press 'hounding' him while preferring the "prettier" Ian McCulloch. As an anecdote, knowing Adrian, it has the ring of truth about it.

Cavanagh described *Alexandria* as an opportunity for Adrian to speak,

"Softer and softer, wearing his leather jacket tucked up against the cold and broadcasting to those who'll listen. A great deal more power to him."

The problem was; far fewer people were listening.

I asked Adrian about *Alexandria*'s performance sales-wise and he confirmed that in Europe it sold between 5-10,000 copies, while in the UK around 1000. Problems with distribution were mentioned but in the language of *This is Spinal Tap,* it may simply have been a case of his appeal becoming, *"more selective".*

The post album single, "Beneath the Big Wheel" wasn't going to take over the airwaves but it did get favourable reactions from *Sounds* and even the *NME.* However Adrian would have needed a strong disposition to read *Melody Maker's* shocking take-down that ended with the facetious advice,

"Adrian mate, go get pissed, or laid or something. Have fun."

Alexandria deserved more. It was a bold move that took bravery and determination from Adrian but probably received the cold shoulder from some Sound fans, if they even heard it.

Last word should go to a slightly exasperated Adrian back in 1991,

"I was pleased with it, some people said to me they're not quite sure what it is because it's not rock'n'roll, it's not folk, but I said surely that's great, to do something that you don't quite know what it is? But they go, "No" because they like things to be more straightforward. I think if people aren't sure what it is, then I might actually have achieved something and made a really in-between, crossover album, like a kind of orchestral music, folk and rock mix. And you're saying you don't like it because it's not one or the other!"

The *Melody Maker* interview would turn out to be his last with the established UK music press. From here on in life would get harder, Adrian would adapt, but it wouldn't be easy.

327

CHAPTER 17

I threw it all away, it's the only way I know

And so the 1980s vanished in the rear-view mirror. Adrian had been through a lot in that garish, often misunderstood, decade. But where was he now? Well there was one constant in his life; while he spent more time in Holland, back in 'Blighty' Margaret Thatcher was still in power, She and her followers had succeeded in reshaping the UK over the course of the previous 11 years.

The main tenets of 'Thatcherism' must have seemed anathema to Adrian and everything he believed in, shrinking the state so that help for citizens would be pared back to the absolute basics and letting the 'free' market do its worst aided by the removal of regulation and controls. The country is still paying the price.

We already know what Adrian's political stance was, so can imagine he must have felt disconsolate as he gazed back across the channel.

As he said to me, "I just don't like Thatcher's vision of it, I hate the Tories!"

And where did he now stand in terms of the relentless tide of musical change that was still surging at that point in the 20th century? Well it wasn't a landscape especially sympathetic to what he was doing that's for sure. The explosion of dance music driven by the rise of Detroit techno had changed everything. As the '90s arrived there were once again stirrings in the UK independent scene with shoegaze and indie-dance poised to eventually infiltrate the charts. None of those worlds really offered a home to him.

The final paragraphs of that Chris Roberts *Melody Maker* interview saw Adrian musing on where he stood and finding some recognition from his peers, even seeming to confirm the U2 being fans rumour,

"It *does* cheer me up when I hear that Bono's got all my stuff, when Wayne Hussey from the Mission comes up to me at a gig and says, 'Hello, I really like *Lions Mouth*,' when I'm standing waiting for the House of Love to come onstage and they tap me on the shoulder and say how much they like my guitar playing... It's not an ego thing but it is nice. I write music in isolation, but I make it for consumption. There's a stance, a vital attitude, which I still have. The most important thing is that the songs are *greatness.*"

The Bono reference came from a conversation Adrian had at Wisseloord Studios while mixing *In the Hothouse.* A new Irish band called Cactus World News were in the studio next door, recording their debut album for MCA, having released a single on Bono's record label Mother. It gives some secondhand credence to the claim that the U2 frontman may well have been a fan.

I bumped into Adrian that night when the House of Love had praised him. It was the Creation Records, *Doing it for the Kids* all- dayer at London's Town and Country Club on the seventh of August 1988, apparently the hottest day of the year. He was in high spirits and no doubt enjoyed the band's incendiary race through Iggy's "I Wanna Be Your Dog."

Adrian, "Did I tell you how I met Terry Bickers (incredible original House of Love guitarist) at the Town and Country Club? I was waiting for House of Love to come on and I got a tap on the shoulder and it's Bickers saying. 'Hi Adrian, I really love your guitar playing.' And I said, 'That's weird 'cos I'm waiting for you to come on and I really love your guitar playing!' "

For Adrian the experience was strange but incredible, and clearly gratifying.

Also on the bill that night were legendary indie eccentrics Felt. Describing Lawrence and his band as 'eccentrics' almost feels like mentioning the sky being blue, but I'm setting the scene for Adrian's incursion into their world.

Adrian's production career had potential, he had a pretty decent CV with Felt's final album *Me and a Monkey on the Moon* probably the most well known record amongst a decent selection of indie releases that he had a hand in.

When in 1991 I asked him about his production work and in particular the 'Lawrence experience,' he laughed when recalling it,

"It was an absolute nightmare! Lawrence was the producer really, there's no way anyone's going to tell Lawrence what Felt's going to sound like. But I think I really focussed them. There was a review in *NME* that said Felt have never had so much direction, cue - mention Adrian Borland, but not in *NME*! Christ!"

During the recording Lawrence's strange behaviour was of course in full effect,

Adrian, "At the time Lawrence was going out with a girl with curly hair, he nicknamed her 'Bubblehead.' Anyway it's dark in the studio and we're recording vocals and Lawrence suddenly just stops dead and says, 'Is Bubblehead in the room?' Everyone just fell about laughing."

Adrian survived the eccentric sessions and later even turned up playing guitar on Lawrence's next project, Denim's debut album, amusingly credited as 'Adrian Amsterdam.'

It's a great record, as are the first two Borland produced albums by the ridiculously underrated Irish post-punk band Into Paradise. Their front man David Long recalls how their link-up came about,

"When Keith Cullen from Setanta Records signed Into Paradise, initially for an EP, he said he was thinking of getting Adrian Borland to produce it and wondered if I had heard of his band the Sound. Now, to answer

Keith's question, yes I had heard of the Sound. Myself and my childhood friend, Shane O'Neill (of the wonderful Blue in heaven) were in a three piece band called Amuse and we saw and heard the Sound for the first time on the *Old Grey Whistle Test* when they played "New Dark Age." We were blown away by them and then got our hands on *From the Lions Mouth* and we played it to death. But it was years since I listened to them when Keith suggested Adrian as producer."

Keith Cullen had not long set up Setanta and was a little in awe of getting Adrian involved, as he confirmed to Paul McDermott in a piece for Medium,

"When I started a record label, trying to get through to Adrian Borland from the Sound to produce Into Paradise was a big deal."

Keith today recalls tracking him down via directory enquiries, speaking to Adrian's mum over the phone to finalise arrangements, much like I did when arranging my fanzine interview. His production fee was very modest, always helpful for a new indie label.

Adrian ended up involved with the debut Into Paradise EP and then two albums, including their major label debut, recorded and released during a brief spell on Ensign Records,

"This was 1989 and the EP was called *Blue Light*. It was recorded over two days in Elephant Studios, Wapping with Adrian producing and Nick Robbins engineering. The two days with Adrian and Nick worked out great, Adrian was full of enthusiasm and came up with some great production ideas. Then Keith offered us an album deal and we went back to Elephant in July for ten days to record our *Under the Water* album with Adrian and Nick. Again Adrian was brilliant to work with, he did an excellent guitar solo at the end of "Here With You," in one take in the drum booth for the natural echo in the room. He came up with key changes, backing vocal melodies, hired timpani drums, Rickenbacker 12 string guitars and was nearly always first in and last out."

The experience was overwhelmingly positive for Dave and the band,

"We all got on really well during the whole time. So all I can say really is that the first EP and first album, he was a pleasure to work with."

When it came to summer 1990 and the recording of their next album *Churchtown* the situation was very different, Dave is honest and candid about what happened,

"We signed to Ensign and they wanted our next record to be recorded in a big studio, the Church in Crouch End. Then we had to pick a producer. Out of loyalty, I choose Adrian. This was a mistake. I should have listened more to the others and gone with someone new. We as a band weren't in a good place and Adrian wasn't in a good place. Making the album was hard work. Nobody's fault really. We didn't even have enough songs for an album and so we were picking riffs from old rehearsal tapes, while in the studio, to turn into songs."

You can feel the regret and frustration hanging over the memories even all this time later. *Churchtown* still turned out to be an excellent record and received some rave reviews, that much to Adrian's annoyance once again didn't mention him.

Keith, "He was great for the recording but mixing-wise I don't think Adrian was so strong."

Into Paradise survived for another few years back on Setanta, following their major label period, but never worked with Adrian again. His production career petered out shortly afterwards.

Back in early 1990 Adrian embarked on three months of gigging through Holland, Germany, Sweden, France, Italy and Switzerland including a couple of rare UK gigs (plus an excellent Bob Harris Radio 2 session) and even, over the summer, some Dutch and Belgian festivals. It was almost like the old days.

Except that he had a new band, the Citizens of the *Alexandria* album credits.

Introduced to him by Rob Acda, who had been their manager, Adrian's new bandmates were members of the band Sjako! a Dutch trio including Thijs Vermeulen (bass) and Wouter Planteijdt (guitar). Adding Victor Heeremans on keyboards and Jaap Vrenegoor behind the drums, who had also played with Sjako! (Although Roland Zeldenrust played drums during the first three months of the 1990 tour).

Adrian with Wouter Planteijdt playing in the Patronaat

Adrian had successfully tested the waters with a few Dutch gigs late in 1989 before embarking on the more extensive dates. Perhaps surprisingly both *Melody Maker* and *Sounds* despatched writers across the channel to review the 15th December 1989 gig at the Patronaat in Haarlem

I wonder whether it was Rob Acda who arranged this or a concerted effort from Adrian to pull in some favours?

Totally unsurprisingly it was Chris Roberts who wrote *Melody Maker's* excited report that appeared in their first issue of the new year.

Describing the show as Adrian's first proper gig with his new band since the end of the Sound, the review is a great evocation of the reliably transcendent experience of a vintage Borland gig, complete with ad-libs from Patti and Lou and a lot more guitar than on *Alexandria*.

Roberts concluded, "Another lion's mouth roars again."

Over at *Sounds* Keith Cameron had an equally great night,

"The criminal self-deprecation vanishes and the sweaty-countenanced rock anti-hero of old takes over, as ever outside the fickle constraints of fashion."

The only worrying observation concerned the Citizens. Cameron noting a suggestion of blandness, blaming, "The competent band of Dutch hired hands" suggesting they blunt "the delicate pull" of some of *Alexandria*'s more elegant songs.

Still it was an excellent pair of reviews and must have pleased Adrian when faced with the pressure of a full scale return to touring. However Cameron was right about the Citizens; of course they were excellent musicians, but they weren't the Sound. To be fair - who could be?

As far as Adrian's romantic life was concerned this period of touring coincided with a new relationship, one of the longer and more significant in his life existing as it did beyond the 'first flush' of attraction.

He had met a girl called Resi and the two were together between October 1989 and April 1990, their first encounter was at a party held by Bert and Monique. Bert was the bass player of Dutch band Immortal, who had played with the Sound several times, and Monique was Resi's best friend. Resi herself knew of the Sound and liked them, but was by no means a hardcore fan.

Now an accomplished artist, Resi was interviewed for *Walking in the Opposite Direction* and paints an intimate picture of life with Adrian,

"I found him, in a certain way, very attractive, he was also very intelligent. It was his humour and the topics we discussed, we'd also play a lot of language games. It's my own theory that he had a thing for numbers and figures."

Resi also noted Adrian's aim for an alphabet of solo albums. Looking back perhaps it was another small way of imposing order and control amongst frequent chaos.

Echoing comments made by Julie, he continued to be a romantic partner,

"He wrote to me telling me that I was very beautiful. He was also very sweet and gave me a lot of attention. Right from the start I got lots of presents, attention and love from him. It was fun. And I also think I took very good care of him. I had a nice house and I could take him there and cook for him. I was taking care of him. We were in a relationship from October '89 to April 1990, so that's not terribly long at all and at that time he wasn't in the Netherlands all the time either, but when he was there then he had a good home."

It's probably true to say that we all like to find a place where we feel safe, comfortable and looked after, but with Adrian it was something more, a recurring pattern within his life. He was seeking a haven where he could recover from the difficult times and maybe, beyond that, hoping for a form of unconditional love similar to the affection and care lavished on him by Win.

Resi, "Yes, he certainly felt comfortable in Leiden and that was partly to do with Monique, because as well as me, Bert and Monique were also absolutely home to him. He would often crash there too if he needed to recover, or if things were really not going well with him he knew where to find them, but also if things were going well. He just liked it. I remember he got really excited when you called the area code which was 071 and that was kind of forever connected in his mind. Then London changed to the same code during the period that we were together which he thought was kind of fantastic. And of course both begin with an 'L.' He just felt at home."

Resi describes an Adrian we know well by now, one who would travel to Leiden with his guitar and little more than the clothes he was wearing, waiting then for her to take the initiative and do his laundry. What would have happened otherwise is worrying from a sanitary perspective and certainly the nature of the arrangement wouldn't survive modern gender role analysis. Resi concludes that bodily cleanliness was not a prime concern for Adrian...

Her parents owned a small sailing boat and it was suggested they go out for a trip. Echoing Julie's experience of Adrian on a beach stubbornly dressed in his leather jacket, he turned up in totally inappropriate attire for time out on the water. Leather jacket, leather shoes, the day's newspaper stuffed in his pocket.

Resi, "In retrospect I think he must have felt very uncomfortable and he went on the trip just to please me. He may even have been scared. While we were on deck he sat inside reading his newspaper on his own."

It's Adrian's vulnerability that comes through in situations like this, fraught with very English awkwardness and embarrassment. Any of us who don't always comply with convention, or fulfil expectations, can surely identify with how he must sometimes have felt.

As Resi confirms Adrian was very different to her in many ways, but they still got along well, mind you, Mike Dudley would have been very disappointed to hear her say,

"He really couldn't cook, he couldn't even fry an egg."

Mike's on-tour cooking class had clearly faded from Adrian's memory. But it seems he understood he wasn't great in some areas and then sought to compensate in other ways, such as surprising Resi with gifts he couldn't really afford,

"If we went out for a walk and I looked in a shop window and said, 'That's a nice sweater,' an hour later it would be gift-wrapped on a table ready for me at home. It was really an act of love. He didn't have much money at all and what he did have he often spent on me."

However Resi confirms that it wasn't a lack of money that especially bothered Adrian but rather an absence of recognition for his music.

"He felt he wasn't really being recognised for his deepest creative effort, for his music and how good it all was. He always hoped for more recognition."

In amongst this pressure she confirms he made a determined effort to hide the truth of his illness from her, although some signs of what could be interpreted as either jealousy or paranoia had been apparent from time to time.

The strain for Adrian eventually proved too much and reality exploded into the open one evening when he appeared at her home in the midst of a psychotic episode, charging around the house repeatedly shouting that he was Jesus and generally acting in a manner that was worrying enough for Resi to think she may have to call the police. It didn't come to that and Adrian left, likely then spending the night out roaming the town.

Naturally she was very scared that night and although she and Adrian returned to good terms afterwards, it marked the end of their time together in a romantic sense.

338

Looking at the fallout from a relationship that perhaps was always balanced unequally in terms of relative importance to the two participants, is a painful process. We can only try to imagine the sheer soul-crushing disappointment experienced by Adrian: again his hope of some kind of semi-mythical loving normality fell apart leaving him bruised and broken. Of course it was tough for Resi as well, but for him the cut was much deeper.

On the surface Adrian could, for a time at least, appear confident and in control, often the life and soul of the party. But really he was a desperate drowning man, anxiously scanning the horizon for help that never came, fearing the next time the water closed over his head would be the last.

Not that people didn't try to help in their own ways, but it's difficult when you're an observer watching a person fall apart. Things happen in slow motion and the right course of action can appear opaque.

Take a closer look at *Brittle Heaven's* credits and you will spot the following,

"This album is dedicated to Resi."

Naturally for most people at the time it didn't mean anything significant but in reality it was the catalyst for many of the album's songs. As we know, Adrian loved the intensity of the early stages of a relationship but then suffered deeply from the stomach-churning slide that accompanies the end. It all then became his fuel, his inspiration. Resi gave him plenty.

It was during this period that Adrian's first love, Julie, made the difficult decision to cease contact.

"I decided around that time that I was going to cut myself off from Adrian. It was in 1990 and he was getting worse, having more and more episodes. I spoke to Win and said that although I don't mind, I don't know if it's particularly helpful you always calling me when there are problems. Win said that Adrian felt I was the only one who'd really stuck by him. But I explained that always calling me when he's having difficulties isn't great."

It must have been a tough call for Julie, but she'd moved on to a different stage in her life, with a new career and husband to think of.

"It was very difficult, my partner was amazing to be honest. He used to be so patient about it, even when Adrian turned up at our house and would pace up and down for ages. I'd just had enough by then and had visions of me having kids and one night opening the door and Adrian's there going crazy."

Julie comes across as a kind, patient and practical person and has nothing but good things to say about Adrian. They had a very deep relationship that meant a huge amount to both of them, but you can fully understand her taking the decision to focus on her new life. For Adrian, and his mother Win, she must have been a source of stability and understanding during times that were both frightening and uncertain. There's a feeling that he was forever looking in vain for the security of those days with Julie, projecting unrealistic imagined futures onto people who either didn't want, or were simply unable, to give him what he needed.

Regardless of events, Adrian was now in full preparation mode for his next album with all the implications that always had for him mentally and emotionally.

Despite Alexandria's fairly weak sales, Play it Again Sam were still prepared to underwrite another record and had allocated a modest £10,000 recording budget. As Adrian later said to me, it was, "not really enough."

During the period when he was working on what would become *Brittle Heaven,* there were a further two suicide attempts that took place while he was over in Holland. Both were witnessed by Marco and Sonja. The first involved him slashing his wrists at their home, the second took place down by the river in Haarlem. The sad fact is that these occurrences would soon be joined by an additional two known attempts, including an incident in Dublin, where the police were called, as well as another where Adrian, back in Wimbledon, threw himself in front of a car, later to be immortalised in song on "Last Train out of Shatterville."

He'd been working on his vocals and Bob recalled the situation being serious enough that Win travelled to Holland where Adrian had been admitted to hospital in Blumenthal.

Adrian had mentioned to me in late 1991 that he needed to carefully prepare for recording the vocals,

"The bass, drums, guitars & keyboards have all been done in Holland, I'm taking a four week break to get myself back to full strength to do the vocals, because the vocals have got to be really good."

A pattern was firmly in place that with the passing of time it's easier to discern. Bob had already reached an understanding as to how the flow of Adrian's life worked, but like many of us faced with something we can recognise but not fully understand, he struggled to find a solution. For a man who liked to learn and solve it must have been beyond frustrating.

Bob, "It was very difficult to help Adrian really. I think one of the things I did in the later years was I tried to get him to think about things other than music. I think that one of the problems was he was too obsessed with music. He was always thinking about lyrics and so on. It was one of the psychologists who said that Adrian should try to think of other things. I encouraged him to become interested in chess." (Adrian's father actually had quite a history when it came to chess. He and his brother John had both been exceptional players, Bob himself was junior UK champion in 1949 and 1952).

Bob had cracked part of the riddle by realising that music was not such a simplistic thing as 'therapy' for Adrian. But any attempt to get him to focus his mind on other things was always going to be up against his all consuming passion: music.

Bob, "It's really not good for a person that something you like the most in the world is also the worst thing for you."

Ultimately this was the reality with Adrian, his music, and his illness. Making music that was, on the surface at least, less intense and troubled wouldn't alter the basic facts.

Bob, "And of course the illness always seemed to coincide with doing an album when he was thinking most of all about music and the lyrics and so on."

For thinking we can probably substitute 'obsessing' but the sequence of events is exactly as Bob says and sadly wouldn't alter.

Ironically playing chess did become something Adrian enjoyed, this was after all the boy who loved games as a child and even dreamt-up and made his own. David Hawkins, one of Adrian's friends from the Crooked Billet pub, recalled playing with him in his piece for the *Book of (Happy) Memories,*

"One day Adrian asked me if I could play and I said yes, from then onwards barely a week would pass without us pitting our wits against each other while others around us drank their beer and smoked."

At first it was David who had the upper hand but before long that changed,

David, "As time passed I found that it was getting increasingly difficult to beat Adrian. That was the thing with him, once he put his mind to something he would usually get better and better at it."

You can make a case for that with Adrian's solo career, in terms of the focus and quality of his music, but *Brittle Heaven* did not follow that trend and turned out to be a disappointment not only for some fans but for Adrian himself. Not that it necessarily felt that way initially. As ever he was very excited about the record during recording, telling me,

"In terms of sound I think it's gone back more towards the Sound. The whole thing's the story of a relationship that goes well and then goes wrong, it's really good. A lot of the songs are very tense, they're great, there's a track called "Lowlands" which I think is going to really knock you for six!"

Adrian loved the new songs and cited "Lowlands" in particular, viewing it as better than even a classic like "Silent Air," saying,

"I wouldn't carry on if I didn't think I was improving."

Obviously some of this was the talk of an artist totally immersed in the draining creative process of creating something new, he was more ruefully matter of fact when talking to Jan in 1996,

"I tried to pace myself but *Brittle Heaven* was a hard one to do. It's maybe the album I'm least enamoured with in retrospect."

Part of the problem was the concept,

"Conceptually it was maybe a mistake, the stages of a relationship thing, it's not a particularly mind-blowing concept is it! It's one of those funny albums that leaves a false impression of being mediocre but still has some really strong songs on it."

Adrian remained a big fan of "Lowlands" as well as "Nowhere to Fall" but was less keen on the tracks where he tried to "rock-out."

"It didn't sell many copies but I did it you know..."

There was probably a shrug of the shoulders there for an experience that was difficult and a result that didn't measure up to the possibilities and vision in his head.

So how could a record with a good number of strong songs end up a relative disappointment?

Recorded at Bananas studio in Haarlem with the Citizens plus a female backing vocalist, *Brittle Heaven* feels like a classic case of trying to make a major label record on an indie-sized budget. Mind you today having £10,000 to spend on recording would be viewed as not too bad at all, back then however it meant restrictions.

Beyond that, it's 'Achilles heel' is something that was becoming common in the early '90s, 'CD bloat,' that desire to use up the extra space on a CD regardless of whether you should. Trim *Brittle Heaven* of three or four songs and it would tighten it up immeasurably, maybe drop the concept as well.

For someone like Adrian who valued the song placement crucial to a vinyl record, this one may have just become too long and winding.

Brittle Heaven ended up flattering to deceive, but in many ways is an emotionally broken record dressed up in clothes it can't afford to wear.

Flying out of the traps with the title track the signs are there immediately. Firstly the title itself, even the longed for heaven is here known to be 'brittle,' liable to shatter at any moment. The yearned for security, love and safety is just a mirage. Although the songs here were inspired by Adrian's relationship with Resi there's a growing sense that the female 'others' in Adrian's lyrics are in fact ciphers for his idealised emotional redemption. Whether anyone could possibly have fulfilled the need in him for peace in his head seems unlikely. Any relationship built under such circumstances would surely always crumble.

There's a sprightliness about *Brittle Heaven* (the track) and the following song "Flight 23" that makes them easy to like but maybe harder to love. Perhaps this is what led to Adrian preferring the album's slower songs.

Anthony Thistlethwaite returned to add sax and yes there's a bit of Springsteen/Waterboys bluster but it doesn't entirely convince, it's as if Adrian was trying to persuade himself that he was more 'up' than he really was.

It's all relative of course and both songs are still an enjoyable listen despite the oddly thin sounding production.

But then "Universe of You" shows us how it's really done. Delicate, heart-tugging, nuanced and with a real pull of emotional gravity. It's a love song with an undertow of pure desperation,

"The only time I'm really free is in the universe of you."

And then we have the other problem, highlighted by "Faithful" - the Citizens are not the Sound. That keyboard part opening the song makes you wonder what Max would have added to the mix. It's a stirring song, but the acoustic version I pestered Adrian to play me in the front room at 2 Hillview, as a taster for the new album I hadn't yet heard, was much rawer and much better.

"Prisoners of the Sun" is pretty but a little inconsequential, for someone of Adrian's songwriting skill it's a decent B-side.

The following one-two punch of "European Streets in the Rain" and the abject "Nowhere to Fall" is much more impressive. There's a drama to "European Streets" that works well paired with its even stronger counterpart. It's no surprise Adrian highlighted "Nowhere to Fall" because it is pretty devastating in its beauty and the honesty of lyrics such as,

"So low and lonely
When you said don't call
I hit the point where
There's nowhere to fall."

The band are significantly better at handling tracks like this than their up-tempo neighbours such as the following "All the Words," a decent enough song that became a single.

I wonder what could have been achieved if Adrian had gone for a sparse, more acoustic record that removed the disappointing attempt at studio sheen and focussed on the brutal emotional grit of the best songs here?

A song like "Lowlands" would have been a highlight of that record, perhaps with some real strings to tear your heart out.

"Truth that Lights the Way" meanwhile desperately needs Graham, Mike and Max to pull it back from the precipice of anonymity. Again, not a bad song in itself but it, and the following "Healing Kiss," with its slightly awkward bongo driven indie-dance groove, suffer when mixed in with the stronger tracks that *Brittle Heaven* offers.

The final stretch begins with one of the most lyrically disturbing songs on the album. "Box of Happy Memories" shares some inspiration with Steely Dan's "Reelin' in the Years" in the way it takes the idea of someone closing down a relationship and methodically collecting and locking the evidence away, frozen emotions preserved for posterity. Adrian is in agony here,

"There's a wreck walking round your town
Using the same name as me
He's a bombed out shell because well
There's nothing where his sanity used to be
Now his heart and mind's been consigned
To your box of happy memories
And there's not much room to breathe
And you know that fine detail
But you shut the lid down tight anyway
And you hope nobody's there

But can't you hear my suffocating cry
From your box of happy memories."

"Ashes" is a little too polite musically but works well enough as a
precursor to the grand album finale, "Tidal Wave Goodbye." Another of
Adrian's favourite's, it's epic qualities could have benefitted from a
more pared back arrangement and real strings but it's still a fitting end
to a difficult record and allows him to acknowledge,

"I know this love is drowning me
But I still come back for more
We had the special way
The real heart and soul
I threw it all away
It's the only way I know."

Dropping in a Joy Division reference along the way, Adrian seems to
have reached an understanding that the intensity of emotion he
experiences in a relationship, especially in the early stages, is simply too
much for him to cope with. Destruction and pain inevitably follow.

Brittle Heaven turned out to be a frustrating album, the period of its
making traumatic and troubling for Adrian. That the results weren't
what he hoped for is no reflection of his skill or the emotional
investment and sheer effort he put in. In plain sight within the album
lies a potentially better, more striking record that needed a more subtle
and sympathetic band to realise. Adrian would learn from the process
and seek to put things right in the future.

Upon its release in May 1992 *Brittle Heaven* received a respectful critical
response, but the days of guaranteed coverage in the UK along with full
page interviews was over.

David Cavanagh in *Sounds* acknowledged the Sound's failure to make
their commercial leap and gave us the obligatory Bunnymen mention.
Pithily describing Adrian as, "unplagued by glamour" but still blessed by,

"a young man's voice and aiming stoically for daytime radio," Cavanagh inadvertently gave us a rerun of Adrian's problems. 'Aiming for daytime radio' was a futile exercise that *Brittle Heaven* had no chance of achieving. Praising the "punchy" songs that he felt were, "immediate in an understated way," while perceptively highlighting a "strange dizzy optimism," which is an interesting way of describing the 'brittle' nature of Adrian's mental state at this moment.

Worryingly Cavanagh, who sadly himself died by suicide in 2018, says this,

"Those close to him speak of alarmingly debilitating depressions."

It's very sad to see reviews having to directly refer to the actuality of the artist's life, but by now it was hard to avoid it.

Over in Holland reaction was politely enthusiastic, *OOR* liked it but felt the songs were not quite at the level of *Alexandria* and used energy sapping words and phrases like, "solid" and "without genuine surprises."

The review ended on a tellingly relevant query,

"All well and good, but the question is who, except for the man's fans, is waiting for *Brittle Heaven*?"

Speaking to Adrian just before the album's release it seemed he had readied himself for a tough future,

"I know my next LP isn't going to be a hit, that's not the reason I'm making it. I'm making it because I think it's fucking better than the rest!"

In a 1992 interview with Dutch radio station KRO the interviewer describes Borland as, "swimming against the tide." Adrian responds by saying, "That's the best thing to do," but he must have been feeling both the pressure and exasperation of being back and still having to answer the same old questions.

A Dutch TV interview, from the period after *Alexandria,* digs into the reasons for the Sound's implosion. When pressed for an explanation, Adrian pauses for a moment, looks uncomfortable, and then fudges the answer by saying, "There were loads of reasons, too many." He says he "got depressed" but quickly moves on, maybe he just didn't fancy dwelling on it but there's a feeling of avoidance that may go deeper than simply being less than candid in an interview.

Asked whether we can look forward to the "brighter side of Adrian Borland", he looks surprised, laughs and says,

"This *was* my brighter side, it gets darker after this."

CHAPTER 18

Do me one favour tonight, play that Roxy song and have a glass of wine, there's nothing more to this and never will be

In a world newly transfixed with grunge, Adrian set out on tour promoting the glossy *Brittle Heaven*. His dates for 1992 were mainly confined to April and May and geographically to his heartland of Holland with a few stray Belgian and German shows thrown in. There were no UK shows that year.

On the positive side he still had a record deal with Play it Again Sam, who were keeping the faith despite *Brittle Heaven's* meagre sales.

When the touring ended Adrian went on holiday with a couple of friends. The two week jaunt to Crete probably couldn't have come at a better time.

David Hawkins describes the trip in affectionately evocative terms as part of his contribution to the *Book of (Happy) Memories,*

"In September 1992 Adrian, Peter Trower and I went on a two week holiday to Crete. Looking through my diary entries for those weeks the most striking feature is the number of references to Adrian talking with other people. On one occasion he was talking to a Cretan girl called Marianne and it transpired her brother was a huge fan of the Sound and so Adrian was invited to his birthday party. It obviously pays to be a 'rock star!' ".

It wasn't the only time Adrian was recognised by islanders during their stay but the last night's events held the fondest memory for David,

"On our last night before returning to London there had been a power cut and the owner of the Aquarius Bar, where we had spent too many hours and much too much cash, asked if we could find Adrian and get him to bring his guitar to the bar so he could play some songs in exchange for free drinks."

Adrian of course obliged and the clientele were treated to an acoustic gig including a version of Bowie's " 'Heroes' " with the two friends on backing vocals.

"It was a great way to end the holiday, the memories of which I shall treasure."

It's well to remember that for all the darkness in Adrian's life there were many nights like this, filled with friends and laughter. So much so that sometimes it's hard to reconcile such tales with the less palatable times, but that's the complex and sometimes contradictory nature of life isn't it?

Adrian on a boat while on holiday in Crete

Before the trip to Crete it will come as no surprise to learn Adrian had been moving on with new music. Demos were needed for Play it Again Sam and so he got in touch with Bart van Poppel. Adrian had originally met Bart in 1982 when he worked as an engineer for a PA company and was sent out on tour with the Sound. Becoming a fan on hearing the first soundcheck, he was there in the audience for later tours. In summer 1992 Bart received a call from Citizens' keyboard player Victor

Heeremans who explained that Adrian was doing some recording and was interested in using Bart"s home studio. He said yes and soon enough Adrian was in another living room recording demos.

Bart owned a TEAC eight-track recorder which was up in the attic, he details the recording process that developed in the sleeve-notes of the reissued *Amsterdam Tapes,*

"Vic had some programmed drums, bass and synthesisers which we put on two tracks, so we had six left to record guitars, vocals and some additional instruments."

The whole experience sounds pretty idyllic for one of Adrian's recording sessions, maybe he wasn't feeling the pressure so much,

Bart, "It was a fantastic week with a great atmosphere. Adrian stayed over and we recorded with the windows wide open, because it was a bloody hot summer!"

The German wine flowed freely and Adrian had a particular album that he was keen on blasting out: U2's *Achtung Baby.*

The record had been released the previous November and had been a huge commercial and critical success for the band. More importantly it rejuvenated them after they'd hit the creative cul-de-sac that *Rattle and Hum* turned out to be. Notwithstanding Adrian's ever present concerns over U2's alleged plagiarism (this time round he raised questions over the provenance of "Who's Going to Ride Your Wild Horses") the album was a textbook example of 'from the ground-up reinvention' in the Bowie tradition.

Adrian would go on to cover "One" as well as other U2 songs, his almost comedic grudges mixing with a clear love of, and fascination with, their music.

Another of his Crooked Billet friends, James Walton Ingham, who he would go on to work with, tells a story that illustrates the depth of Adrian's legendary Bono/U2 paranoia,

"One of the things that people used to tease him about was being paranoid and thinking that some of his music had ended up being used by someone else and he hadn't received the credit he deserved. I think he always felt that. He had a tape where he'd intercut the first song from one of his albums with the first song from *Achtung Baby,* then there was this second song from one of his albums, and then the second song from *Achtung Baby etc.* He'd splice them all together and just tell you, 'Listen to this, listen to this, it's the same thing!' "

I strongly suspect Adrian looked on in admiration at the extent of the *'Achtung Baby* effect' and would have loved to engineer something similar for his own career.

Unfortunately the songs recorded with Bart, while strong and a conscious move away from the *Brittle Heaven* era, led to Play it Again Sam deciding their relationship had reached its end.

Adrian had been dropped.

We can easily appreciate that this move hit Adrian hard. There was a degree of bravado around the Sound's departure from WEA, although it threatened their very existence, the Statik end-point seems to have been a mutual decision followed by the label's financial implosion. But here it was purely a case of Play it Again Sam hearing his new material and issuing an eventual "No thanks".

In the *Book of (Happy) Memories* Win recounts his crestfallen mood, she had just retired from her teaching job and remembers Adrian saying to her, "Mum, now they've dumped both of us."

The songs recorded with Bart ended up forgotten in his closet but were not lost. Released in 2006 as *The Amsterdam Tapes* and reissued in remastered and expanded two disc form in 2023. Taking the decision to replace the programmed elements with sensitively recorded real bass, drums and other assorted instruments Bart did us all a great favour, firstly in looking after those tapes and then taking the difficult move of 'finishing' the songs.

The good news is that it works: we are given a bona fide unreleased Borland record and what fan wouldn't want that? Obviously Adrian hadn't intended to release these tracks in this form so may not have liked some of the artistic decisions made. In common with other periods of his career selected songs would later be reworked in different form over the next couple of years. But notwithstanding any qualms you may have, *The Amsterdam Tapes* is a very enjoyable listen and stands as a more satisfying release than *Brittle Heaven* turned out to be.

Ironically Adrian had cited *Brittle Heaven* as being a move back towards the sound of the Sound; we know it didn't work out that way but that itch must have still been there. Not that he would ever betray himself by deliberately replicating the past, that wasn't his style, just like aping current trends was something he disdained. But one listen to the determined rush of "Darkest Heart" suggests he was craving that familiar musical release. Elsewhere tracks such as "Ordinary Angel" seemed to challenge U2 in the anthemic stakes, albeit recorded a world away in much reduced circumstances. The songs are varied, some modest and more acoustic in nature such as twinkly Velvets-style strum "Dying," while others are expansive rock songs like the six minute "Sea of Noise."

"Dying" features another revealing lyric, once again ruminating on another human connection that didn't deliver Adrian what he hoped for, hopes dashed once more,

"I don't mean to be unkind
It's just my defences coming up
And If I feel I've been left behind
Then I fear I've already lost"

While "Soul Explosion" talks of 15 years spent searching for an enlightenment that now, "just seems further away."

These are demos - so not everything is perfect but it's always worth hearing.

And then there's that first appearance of an underrated Borland classic, "White Room." We shall meet it again but for now get an early taste of its intimate shivering beauty.

With the right band these songs would have translated brilliantly to the stage. Adrian was certainly thinking in those terms. Oddly, or maybe less so, back in 1991 a rumour spread, not as easy in pre-internet days, that the Sound were reforming. I asked Adrian about it and he laughed,

"No they're not! It's my fault 'cos I started this rumour at an Iggy or Kraftwerk gig earlier this year, it's definitely not happening, for a start the person who probably won't do it is the drummer. But even Graham & Max have gone off the idea now."

It was probably the Kraftwerk Brixton Academy gig in July of that year. Adrian spoke of a London Astoria show to make up for the UK missing out on the final six months of the band. As delicious a thought as it may have been, it's hard not to wonder what would have happened. But as they say, 'you can never go back.'

Whatever form it took, Adrian was craving the band dynamic. Early in 1992 he told me he had got as far as looking at the financial implications of a trip to New York where he was thinking of joining up with Jack Rabid and his band Springhouse. Jack is the legendary creator of *The Big Takeover* magazine (and website) as well as being a huge Sound fan. When I mentioned the plan to him many years later he was amazed,

"He did???? I didn't know that. Woah, he should have told me. I would have flown him over on our dime to produce our second album! He could have played on it too. Probably would have been a very different record, a little more jagged edged I would imagine, with some really interesting guitar parts, he had a knack for spaces in music too."

Another fascinating 'what if' that didn't happen, overtaken by events and practicalities as many things are.

But he didn't give up on the band idea. Returning home to England and back, for now, to 2 Hillview, Adrian retained some of the Amsterdam songs and also began working on new material. He crossed paths with Mark Hunziker who had moved to the UK from Switzerland and had been working with various bands around the London scene. Hunziker was a fan of the Sound but beyond that was able to trade ideas with Adrian as an equal. Usefully he also had a home studio with a six-track recorder.

Interviewed for the Lovefield *Neon and Stone* release in 2021, Mark described the working process,

"Sometimes Adrian came to my place with a finished song, sometimes just a verse and I would write the chorus. Other days we'd just jam and see where we landed."

Of course Adrian wrote the lyrics.

"Musically we shared a lot of ground, but he had a side to him that leaned more into pop territory, my input was a bit heavier and more rock based."

Hunziker confirms he loved the early Sound albums and was interested in moving more in that direction. The work they were doing began to shift towards a more 'rock' feel and the natural step was to get a band together. So easy sounding and yet so very, very hard and that's before you try keeping it together.

Adrian got lucky in locating bass player Neil Rickarby, a veteran of under-appreciated (that word again) new wave dance band Way of the

West and, for a while, drummer Mark Wilkin (sadly Mark died in 2022 in a motorbike accident.)

It wasn't just a simple case of strength in numbers, for a talented musician like Adrian a band needed to be a partnership between musicians. Talking to Jan in 1996 he decried acts that were just a case of "follow the leader" with members adding little but falling in behind the main songwriter. Although declaring himself "not a fan" he praised the Who for their sometimes chaotic approach, "You can hear a 'fight' going on with the band members all trying to 'make their case.' "

Asked why he tried to form a new band, the reason for Lava/Lovefield, as they would be known in succession, was clear,

Lovefield: Neil Rickarby, Adrian Borland, Mark Hunziker, Mark Wilkin

"I missed being in the Sound, but it didn't work out. It's not so easy. When you're 17 or 18 people are more likely to go in wholeheartedly. It's harder to find that commitment when people are older. It's hard to develop, people have decided what kind of music they want to play."

He missed something vital to his approach: the sense of unity that was embodied in the call to arms of the Sound's "Acceleration Group,"

"You go into battle together, it's an 'us against the world' kind of thing that you don't get when you're 37! With the Sound on stage we were all thinking as one."

There were however immediate problems,

"We just couldn't find a decent drummer! We had this Spanish guy and it was the second rehearsal, we were playing a song called "Baby Moon" and he just said, 'I don't like melody.' What, you don't like the melody? 'No, I don't like melody.' "

Even then Adrian was open to compromise,

"I said I get that, give it a chance I'm not against creating grinding rock, great slabs of destruction, I'm all for that, don't give up on the band yet. I wanted the drummer to be part of it but he thought Nine Inch Nails were a bit too commercial!"

It couldn't work.

"That was the problem we'd gone too far into a direction but then we were back looking for members again as things fell apart with the original drummer and guitarist, which was more of a personal problem between those two members. Once you've written all this stuff you just want people to slot in conveniently on the other hand you want it to be a proper band. It was falling between two stools."

For Adrian it wasn't enough of a 'band' to justify him not simply doing things his way solo, the end was inevitable,

Adrian, "My enthusiasm waned and the bass player left, he was fed up auditioning all these drummers, we went a year without a drummer, it's too long!"

You can feel the frustration that comes with trying to get a band off the ground. Add in all the soul-destroying practicalities of writing, rehearsing and playing in an expensive city like London and the effort ends up too much for all.

The band played two gigs, one under the name Lava in September 1993 at the Union Tavern in London. I was there and noticed Chris Roberts in attendance, Adrian was obviously trying to crank up the process looking for music press interest.

The show itself was impressive for such an early stage in a band's gigging life. All new songs of course, aside from blazing versions of the Sound's "Kinetic" and "Where the Love Is" included as a very welcome encore.

Going for a drink with Adrian before the gig he was full of energy and enthusiasm as usual, asking me to help get them gigs in Bath and Bristol. It all came to nothing though.

Thankfully the tracks recorded during that period were not wasted. Firstly it's a great example of Adrian's ability to hold on to his stronger songs, waiting for the right moment to use them. More than anything this was about finding the best musical setting. The wonderful "Baby Moon" was a product of the Lovefield period. Adrian was proud of his 'quality control' and he knew it was a strong, memorable song that just needed to be put on the shelf until he moved on to an album with the specific musical texture that would suit it. I wonder whether in his dreams he saw it as a track with commercial possibilities?

Songs from the band's demo sessions circulated on cassette and CD-R amongst fans for years before finally receiving a welcome official release in 2019 and 2021 as the Lovefield and Neon and Stone albums. (When talking to Jan in 1996, Adrian confirmed that he intended the demos to get a release within the next couple of years).

Although the full band isn't featured, and these are of course demos, the two albums are still a treasure trove. This is a long way from *Brittle Heaven* but, although we're in pleasingly edgier territory, the Lovefield tracks still retain the melodic qualities heard back there; clearly a disappointment to that Spanish drummer.

Live, a song like "Coal" was a dynamic thrill and even here, in more rudimentary form, that excitement still comes across. The beautiful "Take This Candle" is a classic instance of Adrian offering succour and reassurance without the glib platitudes that tend to mar many artists attempts at putting an arm around a listener's shoulders.

"Eternal Something" provides a raw and worrying sequel to "Winning" that finds Adrian questioning the path he's taken and where all that tender hope ended up,

"Do you ever wonder where your life has gone?

And do you ever wonder where the strength comes from to carry on?"

Here all the hope has ended up in, "a bottomless pit" while the protagonist faces "lying eyes, slammed shut doors."

It's hard not to join the dots between the events of the previous few years in Adrian's life. But as ever he leaves out enough detail to keep his songs relatable to all.

Nestling in there; "Baby Moon," a track Adrian was certain would be better served at a later date, here it's still yearningly lovely but just a little bit more earthbound than he knew it should be.

Although the reasons set out above were key, there was another behind Lovefield's disintegration: Adrian was far from OK. Interestingly Mark Hunziker had gone into the project unaware of his mental health problems, so the situation must have come as a disturbing shock.

Towards the end of 1993 he made yet another attempt to end his life, throwing himself in front of a car on a street in Wimbledon, not far from where he could often be found having a drink with friends. The result was another period of time in Springfield Hospital.

A further blow followed in quick succession. Max had contracted AIDS towards the end of the Sound's existence, and ultimately succumbed to an AIDS related illness on the 26th of December. Since the split, away from music making he'd worked with Graham at the lighting company they'd joined and had formed his own band called Crave playing a few gigs on the London club circuit and, maybe unsurprisingly, in Holland.

The death hit Adrian hard and put a final stop to any thoughts of the Sound ever getting back together.

Friend James Walton Ingham had become close to Adrian just before that period and saw the effect Max's death had on him,

"I think there was a part of Adrian that would have loved to have got the band back together again, but of course that was now impossible. I think (Max's death) probably hurt him more than he let on."

More bad news was to come the following year when Adrian's friend and ex-manager Rob Acda also died tragically young, at the age of 33, again from an AIDS related illness.

The turmoil of this period must have been extremely hard for both Adrian and his parents to navigate. The pressure on Win and Bob shouldn't be overlooked: it never really relented from the mid '80s onward. Yes, there were calmer times interspersed with the bad, but the fear of what could come next can never have been far away from their thoughts.

For Adrian he picked himself up, as he had done many times before, and looked to his next project.

He certainly had the songs, the flow of new material rarely, if ever, stopped, it was two years since *Brittle Heaven* and there were still some strong songs from the Amsterdam demos that he wanted to include as part of a new record.

The album that would be called *Beautiful Ammunition* was really Adrian's first truly 'solo' release. There were guests, but no co-writes and the bulk of the work was down to Adrian.

One of those guests was friend James Walton Ingham who he'd met a couple of years previously,

James, "I was sitting outside the *Hand in Hand* pub on the green. It's lovely there next to Wimbledon Common. There's two pubs, the Crooked Billet and the Hand in Hand. I'd sit outside with my guitar and a group of friends with just people passing by. You'd always meet somebody different every night and obviously with a guitar you kind of attracted the attention sometimes of unwanted people."

James paints an important picture in terms of the world Adrian frequented when he was out and about in Wimbledon. His home from home was of course the Crooked Billet but he also could often be found in the Hand in Hand. Although in his last months the atmosphere changed, for many years this was a place he enjoyed seemingly endless laughs and conversation with some who knew his background and others who didn't. If you'd wanted to bump into Adrian Borland this was the place to go.

That balmy summer night in 1991, James ended up talking to Adrian, spurred on by the presence of a guitar, always a good ice-breaker. He remembers thinking Adrian looked like he wanted to grab that guitar, but he didn't. Instead they chatted, touching on music, with Adrian mentioning he had been in a band that James, "probably hadn't heard of." He hadn't. James describes the night vividly, you can easily imagine that relaxed summer evening in the heart of England. Adrian was on his own and obviously keen to chat.

Their next encounter was a few months later when the weather was cooler, James was inside this time and Adrian's mood was very different.

James, "This guy came in and he looked like he hadn't shaved. His hair was a bit of a mess and quite greasy, he looked quite clammy. Actually he seemed upset and was quite agitated, like he'd been drinking. But he wasn't drunk. He remembered me and I kind of remembered him. He came and sat down. I was taking pictures around the table, you know, 'click, click'. I just got a picture of him, I found it the other day when I was going through some boxes of photos."

Adrian didn't look happy in the photo and it soon transpired he was not in a good way, James now understands the pain he was likely in,

"At the time I was young, probably quite insensitive, and just in a good mood. But then it emerged he'd broken up with a girl and was very upset about it."

James manages to carefully describe a scene that, knowing what we know of Adrian, is all too recognisable,

James, "It was almost like you felt you were eavesdropping on something you shouldn't. He was just describing how they'd broken up and how upset he was. He was touching his hair and saying, 'Yeah, I know that she... I know she still loves me.

Of course she still loves me'. It was like he was talking to himself, but it was to everyone else as well. I don't remember being particularly supportive or anything."

James is unduly hard on himself. We've all faced similar situations no doubt and in response we won't always have been the supportive person we feel we are. Remember though, James didn't know Adrian well at that point. But he certainly identified the worrying see-sawing of moods that Adrian was subject to. The lost and lonely person he saw that night feels like a troubling memory.

Even in the apparently 'safe' environment of a local pub, amongst friends, Adrian's mood could be fragile and open to anxiety, an anxiety that some probably weren't observant enough to register,

James, "Sometimes we'd be sitting in the pub and he'd be fine, but then if it got a little busy or he felt uncomfortable, you'd see him clench his knuckles, you just felt this kind of discomfort. There were times when Adrian would have to just get up and leave when he felt threatened, I was never quite sure what the problem was."

As time passed James would get to know Adrian well and would recognise the cognitive dissonance surrounding this talented musician and the life he lived.

Adrian and James

Some regulars probably wondered who the sometimes loud person propping up the bar was and whether his tales of rock'n'roll notoriety were just the hot air of someone who'd had a few too many to drink. James tells of a revealing moment when Adrian's outside world collided with the cosy bubble of Wimbledon-style suburbia. A Dutch or German visitor, who looked like an alternative music fan, in terms of appearance, spotted Adrian and reacted in disbelief, 'Oh my god Adrian Borland! I can't believe I'm meeting you here!' "

Adrian and the shell-shocked fan ended up chatting well into the night, while the regulars wondered what the hell had just happened,

"At first people looked like they were wondering, how much did he pay this guy to do that? I think people started to think actually, you know what, maybe there's something to this. It was similar when I once saw him do a couple of local gigs and a few people from the pub came along. They were all sitting there joking and laughing saying, 'Sing us a song, you fat bastard!' "

During this period Adrian would occasionally play at a pub in Colliers Wood, the Red Lion, where the landlord put on acoustic music nights in the backroom, before the pub closed and became a Co-op supermarket. All a long way from the Paradiso. In fact Adrian's gigography gets sketchy from this point on, quite simply he played far fewer gigs and they were, in the main, much more low key.

James felt sorry and embarrassed to see the kind of reaction some people had, of course the mood changed when those present heard Adrian sing and play and understood he was the real deal. It can be hard for people to reconcile what they think they know with a hidden reality right under their nose.

Meanwhile Adrian was going through another cycle of love, rejection and disappointment as James explains,

"There was a woman that lived just up the road who I knew well, she was a very kind person and still is. She'd bump into Adrian and would have seen him in the pub with me. I remember she just got chatting to him and must have said, 'Why don't you come and have a coffee.' She invited him to her flat and was just chatting away, but I think he developed quite strong feelings. She was like a muse for a while, he wrote some lovely songs about her, including, "Simple Little Love" and the track, "Beautiful Ammunition."

Within Adrian that 'intensity switch' was flipped on again and the creativity flowed, but the vertiginous slide back down from those giddy heights would swiftly follow,

James, "I think maybe it transpired that he had more feelings for her and she wasn't reciprocating them. Or she may have given him a bit of a knockback or given him the brush-off, letting him down easy. He was very upset and went away and wrote, "Ordinary Angel."

Which explains lines like these,

"How could you make me feel like this? I tasted grace and got drunk on bliss."

"Beautiful Ammunition" itself was an unabashed love song, (Ammunition was also a play on the Latin 'amo' - I love) but with a troubling hint of the past,

"Opposite her in the sun, I can feel all life come."

When Adrian felt like that we know he would equally feel the chill in that person's absence, as the Sound's "Burning Part of Me" made clear,

"In her heat, I feel like the sun
But it makes me shiver when I feel the difference
It makes me shiver when she's gone."

An early version of "Ordinary Angel" appeared within *The Amsterdam Tapes*, by the time *Beautiful Ammunition* was recorded it had changed slightly and the title song had vanished.

The album was dedicated to, "BELA and the Ig." The same 'Bela' as mentioned in its phantom title track. Whether 'Bela' ever knew we shall never know, apparently it wasn't the actual name of the person in question, but it was pretty close...

Adrian recruited James and his partner in a folk trio, Vikki Stillwell, as well as Mark Hunziker, studio engineer Mark Kelsey and Neil Rickarby, a refugee from Lovefield.

Recording took place at the very basic, but friendly and ultra reasonably priced Survival Studios, located within a less than beautiful business park in Acton, since bulldozed to make way for the Crossrail project. Places like this are vital for bands trying to survive in the painfully expensive capital where decently priced rehearsal and recording facilities are as rare as hen's teeth.

As the U2 punning sleeve-note says, "Recorded and mixed in 99 hours at Survival Studios, Acton, baby."

Described in the credits as, "A Lovefield Project," possibly an indication that Lovefield as an entity hadn't quite been put out to pasture.

Adrian was back on a label set up by his dad, Bob explained how this came about when interviewed for *Walking in the Opposite Direction,*

"As far as Resolve was concerned it was purely to help Adrian as we were really very concerned about him because he was getting extremely depressed. He had a massive amount of songs he'd written, certainly over 40, and he just wanted to get them recorded."

It appears that after rejecting the 'Amsterdam songs' Play it Again Sam had vacillated as to whether there was a chance they would release anything else,

Bob, "He was still expecting Kenny, who was the owner of the label, to agree to release another album. But Kenny didn't give him a definite decision on it. He kept Adrian waiting and he was getting very, very frustrated and came back to England in this depressed state because of the uncertainty of the recording contract."

Bob's aim had been to reduce the stress by providing an outlet for Adrian's music,

"In order to relieve Adrian of his depression really, I decided that we would do what we did before with Raw Edge Records. It seemed appropriate to choose an alternative name, and Adrian suggested Resolve."

Resolve (a firm determination to do something) was an appropriate name for their label as it was certainly what Adrian needed if he was to continue as a recording artist.

Bob, "And so it was just a case of me paying for Adrian to go into a studio. He always preferred to record in a proper studio. He wasn't happy doing things at home really."

Where to start with *Beautiful Ammunition*? A sometimes superficially poppy record that in fact is as soul-searching a journey as Adrian ever led us on, full of the pain of rejection, with repeated attempts to rationalise his situation and find a way forward. And that's before we consider the religious themes that appear from time to time, not that Adrian was a stranger to religious language in his songs but here it was different, it felt like he was maybe getting some succour from a faith of his own.

Although still falling prey to a slightly excessive CD-style length, something the editing eye and ear of an external producer may have prevented, *Beautiful Ammunition* is nevertheless a stronger and more convincing record than its predecessor, *Brittle Heaven*.

And what a start it gets off to.

"Re-United States of Love" leads us into the place Adrian wanted us to visit this time round. A beautiful song, resting on a simple piano riff and featuring just a suggestion of backing vocals from Vikki, it's lovely. That opening lyric feels directed at the listener,

"It's so good to see you, we know it's been too long."

Followed by a Sound reference and a restatement of belief in something deeper,

"Take me straight to the heartland, I know it's deep within."

"Open Door" builds on the mood, touching on anthemic but with a beautifully intimate and subtle chorus, Adrian's whispered vocals warm and soothing. Lyrically there are "angels" and talk of "spirit" but also an acknowledgment that love has been either "untouchable" or "uncontrolled."

When I first heard *Beautiful Ammunition* I was struck by the surprising amount of religious language. Looking back it had been there since the earliest Sound songs (for example, "No Salvation") but the mood here felt different. Jan noticed the same thing and asked Adrian about it in his 1996 interview,

Jan, "Did the use of religious imagery on both *Beautiful Ammunition* and *Cinematic* indicate a change in your attitude and outlook since the days of Sound songs like "Possession" and "Judgment"?

Adrian, "Without becoming a fanatical born again Christian, I would say I've gradually revised my view of god. I still can't define god but I do think there's some sort of collective spiritual power."

He goes on to explain that, perhaps unsurprisingly, the track, "Stations of the Cross" was a religious song,

"The imagery is there. I still believe that it's up to individuals to take responsibility though. I don't believe in the Catholic idea of confession. "Rootless" was a very anti-fundamentalist song. It was bleak, I was saying we shouldn't all be defined by race, religion etc. We should all be trying to be human beyond the fundamentals of religion. Not so narrow-minded. I was trying to show the futility of a point of view. I want to be rootless!"

Adrian ultimately confirms that although he didn't firmly belong to one faith, Christianity was the closest to his beliefs and that his earlier thinking had been, "wrong."

To illustrate the point further, James Walton Ingham confirms that during a particularly difficult period, Adrian told him,

"My Christian faith tells me that it's going to be alright. Everything's going to be fine. You know there's a lot of hope in these songs as well. Like, "Shoreline," there's a lot of hope."

"Shoreline" is a hushed acoustic strum and contains the following lines,

"And if you listen to your heart

372

You could hear the finest song
One that's singing
Turn your life around
Get up off the ground
The ocean has forgiven you and you're free."

Again how much all of this was some sort of wish-fulfilment, Adrian reassuring himself, is unclear.

Certain statements made here by Adrian might come as a surprise to some, but he had obviously been on some form of journey in relation to what he believed spiritually. In terms of belief, eventually perhaps he and Bono grew closer together...

Rewinding through the album, you encounter a song that shows the risks involved in what Adrian sought to achieve on *Beautiful Ammunition*. "Rocket" flies close to cloying 'moon in June' love song territory and the slightly incongruous female vocal will prove the final stumbling block for some.

The mood changes on the knowingly titled, "Stranger in the Soul" an ashen versed look at Adrian's internal fight,

"He must have strayed to be part of me
To look through my eyes at the changing world
There's only one way to set him free
But I choose to live
With the stranger in the soul."

Adrian seemingly seeking to accommodate that other side of him, however unrealistic such a task would prove.

"Break May Fall" seems obviously about his new muse, but the plea went unanswered,

"We met by chance

I saw you shine
That ancient dance
Seems new each time."

The scenes are replayed in "Past Full of Shadows,"

"And all the times
You didn't read between the lines
You misread the signs
The action of a second
Can turn the day
And a seed of darkness
Can lead life to decay."

At the halfway point of a 16 track album sits the stunning "White Room." Rescued from *The Amsterdam Tapes,* it's a shimmering quiver of a song with a stately VU-like delicacy. One that would justify a place on any Borland best-of.

The late David Berman (another victim of suicide) and his final band, Purple Mountains have a track called "Snow is Falling in Manhattan." It's really a song about a song, envisaging the songwriter leaving the gift of the warmth and reassurance in the track, to you the listener,

"Songs build little rooms in time
And housed within the song's design
Is the ghost the host has left behind
To greet and sweep the guest inside
Stoke the fire and sing his lines."

Adrian does something very similar on "White Room," at the spine tingling moment he turns and speaks directly to each individual in his audience, partially quoting a line of Roxy's "More Than This" in the process,

"Do me one favour tonight

Play that Roxy song and have a glass of wine
There's nothing more than this and never will be."

It's Adrian's best route to speak to you, but for him the tone is as
worrying as ever,

"Can't you see how this splits me
Then you'll see how I crack
So don't fade away
Back into your white room."

He does it again with "Lonely Late Nighter" this time we're with him in
his room at 2 Hillview, as his spins records and drinks wine late into the
night. It's hard to think of anything more quintessentially Adrian,

"I've locked out the world
And the only sound in here
Is the click of the run-off groove
And something I forget to say to you."

Adrian alone in the darkness with only music to fall back on.

Time and again on *Beautiful Ammunition* the acoustic prettiness hides
some disturbing ruminations on life and the point Adrian had reached.

The shortest track "In Passing," dedicated to Max and Rob, is a 1:17
requiem for lost friends, as stark and honest as such a purpose requires.

Adrian, "There's a point where it sounds like I'm smiling and I had to
decide whether to keep that in, but that was the human emotion of
remembering the good times and affection."

At the height of Adrian's attempt to cheer himself comes, "Someone
Will Love You Today," complete with a lyric that may come as a shock to
some Sound fans and seems to value spontaneity over finesse.

That cut title track, maybe removed as Adrian felt a little bashful at the sentiments expressed after being politely rebuffed, still has Adrian looking for beauty in the world and seeking salvation, not in organised religion, but in a passing pair of eyes. With a heart that big pain can only follow, it's the risk you take. Also when you're literally using someone else as the 'ammunition' or 'fuel' for life, then it won't be a surprise that few people are willing to take on such a draining role.

There's little point in surveying the charts in the year *Beautiful Ammunition* was released. Adrian was now working so far off the grid that selling 500 copies of his new album would be deemed a success.

As Bob suggests, Adrian *needed* to make this record, songs were bursting out of him with no planned record in sight. He was in his element once a project was underway and he had the scope clear in his head.

James describes how it felt to see Adrian in full creative flight,

"He would come in and say, 'I wrote a great song today!' Those are the moments I really cherish where you'd see that look on his face and any depression or anxiety he may have had in the intervening months would just disappear. Then seeing him working in the studio, he just looked so happy."

Adrian, "That album was cathartic, I had all these songs lying around that I'd written on acoustic guitar, it was like spring-cleaning for me. A song lives when it's released. It's like 16 sketches really, a blueprint, it could have been much more produced and still could be if someone chose to cover any of it. There's room there."

It's a rich and rewarding record, not everything works fully, but taken as a whole *Beautiful Ammunition* is an important step in Adrian's difficult solo journey: where he went next would be a very different place.

CHAPTER 19

*No-one can see the film that you star in and they won't pay the price to
come in, to your cinematic life*

It must have been a relief for Adrian to have recorded and released
Beautiful Ammunition, but for the first time since the early days of the
Outsiders he probably didn't expect much attention from the UK music
press. In that respect he was correct.

There was still some media coverage in the expected places,

Dutch magazine *OOR* was cautiously positive, describing the album as,
"balanced and atmospheric but somewhat uniform, without either lows
or highs."

They rightly saw it as an improvement on *Brittle Heaven* but were
concerned by the "lacklustre production" which for them meant it
wasn't up to the level of *Alexandria.*

Longtime fan Jack Rabid reviewed the album for his magazine *The Big
Takeover* and had some similar concerns but was still broadly
appreciative,

"This third outing, his first since leaving Play it Again Sam, is much like
Alexandria and *Brittle Heaven* in that it often strays into a too-genteel,
almost adult contemporary feel (though it never is as ossified as most
VH1 fodder); Borland does have real soul to his guitar pop). His music as
a solo artist is still too light and airy compared to the true spark of the
three talents who backed him all those years in the Sound, and is too
glossy compared to what might work better with this material, a lo-fi,
more dirty, home demo approach, which would better bring out what
Borland excels at: natural-beauty songwriting and his familiar voice."

It's ironic that Jack recommends a home demo approach, when for
Adrian these recordings weren't far from demos. Still some fair points,

well made, that foreshadow what would change with Adrian's next record.

The UK was by now fully in the grip of Britpop-fever, labels were scouring the streets of Camden brandishing cheque books, on the hunt for anyone who looked the part and had even the most rudimentary musical ability. There was money to be made, for some.

They were strange times that Adrian will have viewed with a raised eyebrow and a knowing smile. Naturally his thoughts on Oasis et al were wittily scathing, and inadvertently revealed a possibly unexpected favourite record of his from 1995,

"I think Scott Walker's *Tilt* is brilliant, it's not easily listened to but it's superbly done. So what if it's not commercially successful, the music's there and that's what matters. It's forever. I'd rather be him than Noel Gallagher!"

It's instructive to hear Adrian talking of music being there "forever" and completely dismissing commercial factors. If ever you were in any doubt that was how he felt here he makes it clear, although perhaps he simply understood the commercial reality he was now facing,

"Oasis: if you're 15 I suppose it is quite exciting, pissed with the lads, jumping around the room, I'm not making judgments about that. But Noel Gallagher isn't a good songwriter, they make a good 'noise', but it's not the technical things in the songs. It's cynical, but that's the trouble with Oasis; they make you into a cynic. You don't get that with Sonic Youth, sitting there thinking, oh where did that riff come from? Because that's not what's hitting you on the head! Noel Gallagher is old enough to know what's going on and that's what's cynical about it."

Adrian conceded that there was "a pop renaissance" in full flow,

"I'm not really a big pop fan, never have been, I can admire what's happening more than it excites me. It's not my thing, I'm not involved in it, I'm detached from that."

While it was probably good that Adrian had understood 'his place' in the scheme of the modern music industry, whether he fully accepted it is possibly less clear. It's hard to accept you aren't still a contender in some form at least.

Money remained an eternal issue, here he was still favouring the old process of going into the studio and making a record, all something that came at a financial cost, James Walton Ingham recalls how Adrian felt about it,

"I know he enjoyed it, a bit like my father used to enjoy putting on a tie and going into the office. Adrian loved the whole process of going into the studio, booking the studio, choosing the studio, budgeting it. Whereas today he could do everything at home."

Perhaps it was partly the *structure* that working in this way gave him, the purpose it instilled. That way there was something between him and the internal struggle he sought to escape. In practical terms Bob and Win were picking up the tab and remained happy to do so.

James confirms Adrian was fully aware of the importance of his parents in his life, not just in practical terms,

"Losing his parents, I think that was another really big fear towards the end. It really troubled him: mum and dad, what would I do without them? He knew he was very lucky to have such understanding, such support and such security. You're never going to get that kind of love from anyone else."

But still, for the penultimate time, Adrian left the safety and familiarity of 2 Hillview and experimented with getting his own place.

James, "It was in '95 and he was living along the Ridgway in Wimbledon, above an Indian restaurant. It was a squalid place - it wasn't a good time. He couldn't really handle being away from the security of home and was drinking too much and not eating properly. He was living with another guy and they just butted heads the whole time."

The fractious atmosphere burst out one evening when Adrian and his flatmate went out for a drink,

"I remember they turned up outside the pub one night and this argument just erupted out of nowhere. Adrian was trying to defend himself, verbally. The landlord came out and pointed at him saying, 'You're banned.' That was horrible for Adrian. They banned the wrong guy, Adrian was just trying to stand his ground. It was a really bad period. He didn't feel safe if he wasn't living with his parents."

It wasn't the last time Adrian would be banned from a pub. The combination of factors, of which alcoholic over-indulgence was significant, left him feeling vulnerable and in due course he returned to 2 Hillview.

More songs had been amassed and Adrian was keen to make another record. Friend and White Rose Transmission bandmate Carlo van Putten confirms that Adrian did feel some embarrassment at having to rely on Win and Bob for funding.

Bob also realised this, "Well, that was typical of Adrian, really. I didn't worry too much about it though. We did recover some of the money. Not all of it, but most of it. I was quite happy to do that."

But first there was another essential Borland side-project to take care of.

Actually it's worth pausing for a moment to bear in mind that he was entering one of the most creatively prolific and rewarding periods of his short life. Despite the darkness and chaos that was forever threatening to overwhelm him, the years between 1995 and 1999 would see Adrian finally feeling more at ease and in control of his post-Sound musical world. The result would be several records that stand amongst his most striking achievements, each one paving the way for the next.

In short: this is not one of those rock'n'roll stories that begins with a bang and ends with an artistic whimper, as everything inevitably 'goes to shit'. For better or worse, he cared too much to ever let that happen.

Adrian had met Dutch singer Carlo van Putten after Carlo's band the Convent had recorded a cover of "Winning" for a CD series called *Undercover*. When the song was included on the Convent's second album Carlo sought out Adrian's address and a copy made its way to 2 Hillview.

The result was a surprise telephone call from Adrian answered by Carlo's wife. He recalled the moment in the sleeve-notes for *The Scales of Love and Hate,*

"My wife at the time told me an Englishman was on the phone, someone with an incredibly beautiful voice, to my surprise it was Adrian."

After telling Carlo how much he liked the Convent's album, describing it as "very Joy Division-ish," Adrian suggested a joint German tour. Financially the tour didn't work out leading to Adrian putting forward the idea of him going solo and being the opening act. For Carlo this was an uncomfortable idea and a compromise was reached with Adrian appearing as 'special guest' and at the finale joining the Convent for a version of "Winning".

Adrian actually remembered it slightly differently and recalls receiving a call from the band asking if he was OK with them recording a version of "Winning." Of course it could be he was a little bashful about making the approach to Carlo.

However the contact came to be, Carlo was living in Germany at the time and Adrian came to stay during that initial tour, the first of several visits over the next few years. It was from these trips, and their growing friendship, that both the acoustic recordings first released as *Last Days of the Rainmachine,* and later in expanded form as *The Scales of Love and Hate,* came, as well as the idea for the White Rose Transmission project.

Incredibly they were even able to record songs out in Carlo's garden, a space they dubbed 'The Echo Garden'. Many of the songs that would appear on the first two White Rose Transmission albums had their genesis either in The Echo Garden or indoors at Carlo's house, in addition there are a handful of tracks that remained unused as well as demos sent from Wimbledon as Adrian worked on ideas.

Listening now these recordings provide a fascinating view of both Adrian's work in progress as well as his state of mind. As has been suggested there's something special about hearing him playing and singing in such circumstances, secure amongst friends, you even get the occasional spoken intro from the man himself.

Two songs that didn't appear elsewhere are particularly stunning but also troubling.

"The Scales of Love and Hate", with at the end, its sly snatch of the melody of "Love Will Tear Us Apart", delves back to "Temperature Drop" with talk of "fire and frost."

"Dreams crashing down, the balance is lost, there's no neutral ground, it's either fire or frost."

And that was Adrian's life in a lyric, but by the end the fire was as painful as the frost was chilling.

Equally "Love is Such a Foreign Land", with background noise of birds chirping, indicated he was reaching a state of saddened acceptance but with conclusions, or questions, that didn't bear answering,

"You're not easy to forget
But you're no reason to get upset
I've met you a hundred times
And you never know the score
You've got one eye on the door
You keep me down
When I should be high
Love is such a foreign land to you
As the angels packed and left
They winked at me and said
Hey Adrian, why don't you give it up?
There's a thousand ways to live
There's a million ways to give
You've got to learn when you've taken enough."

The bitter pain of rejection hangs heavy, but then to hear Adrian mixing gallows humour and directly addressing himself with the ultimate question, is uncomfortable but strangely reassuring. Surely if he was joking about it, everything would be OK?

White Rose Transmission itself was intended as a collaboration of equals, with Carlo singing and Adrian, writing, producing and playing.

383

Meanwhile their chosen name referenced the non-violent anti-nazi resistance group that formed in Germany in 1942.

The band's debut self-titled release begins with the very Borland-like "Unkissable," transformed from the demo recording into something very different, Adrian's guitar returns to its Sound-era tension and Carlo takes lead vocals. As a statement of intent it hooks you instantly.

Adrian's presence is felt but Carlo is the frontman, I suspect Adrian enjoyed the experience much as he did his involvement in Cassell Webb's *Llano*.

Towards the end comes an undoubted highlight: the string assisted, sweeping beauty of "The Sea Never Dies", it's Borland at his most affecting and elegiac.

Adrian spoke of the album to Jan in 1996,

"It's very German, gothic-romantic, Teutonic. If it rocks, it's in a deliberately strange way, the lyrics are very flowery, they could have been written in the 17th century! Actually a bit of Bowie comes through in a few songs. We were just finding our feet with the first record, the next will be more extreme."

Adrian was planning ahead but had a new solo record to think about first.

The decision was made to return to Acton and the affordable and aptly named, Survival Studios.

With Bob picking up the tab Adrian set about recording a very different record to *Beautiful Ammunition*.

Featuring some of the same supporting cast as its predecessor, including engineer Mark Kelser, Neil Rickarby, James Walton Ingham, Pat Rowles and special guest, old friend and Lush bassist, Phil King.

Adrian had very specific aims in mind when he made *Cinematic*, as he explained to Jan the following year. The album's title came in part from 1995 being the 100th anniversary of what is generally considered the birth of movies, (the Lumière brothers being the alleged first to present moving pictures to an audience, in Paris in December 1895) but beyond that Adrian was thinking in terms of sound and impact as well as the issue of the specificity of some of his songs.

Adrian, "On one level it's the room you give the listener to use their imagination. On another, it's a purely musical thing. I cut another version of *Cinematic* where the vocals were really sibilant and the music was very edgy. Apart from the fact I hate sibilant vocals, I mean it's OK for some punk tracks, but I suddenly realised I had to recut the album because it was the exact opposite of what I wanted it to be, I wanted it to lie there in front of you and for you the listener to go in where you want to. I didn't want it to 'come out at you'. I wanted it to be like a 'gauzy screen' where you reach for the things you want to hear rather than them coming out and grabbing you round the neck. It's a technical point, but the sound of a record is important to me."

The conversation is very revealing in terms of the depth of thought and intent Adrian gave to how a record worked once out in the world. In this case he'd really thought of the 'cinematic' effect of a group of songs presented to the listener and how they would approach, interact and experience the music,

"In the cinema you're experiencing emotions you maybe never want to experience in real life but you can do it because it's one step removed from you. The difference between *Cinematic* and my other albums is (the existence of) that step away from the listener, which may be a good thing and people may prefer that to the emotional 'in your face take it or leave it' stuff of my other work. Which is what I wanted it to be."

There's a sense Adrian was a little wary of the raw and personal content of his songs resulting in a possible loss of subtlety. Or perhaps he felt this meant they 'dictated' to the listener how to react, so for him these songs were less obviously personal. For us we may question how true that actually was.

As usual Adrian's stress levels increased as the date approached for recording. Engineer Mark Kelser recalled the atmosphere during the sessions when interviewed for the *Cinematic* expanded remaster sleeve-notes. Note that Adrian was working the night shift with recording beginning at 7 each evening.

Mark, "It was a tough record to make because of his constant anxiety. He couldn't calm down, just sit back, listen to his music and go, 'Yeah I like that.' "

Mark didn't realise the extent of Adrian's mental health problems,

"I didn't know much about his struggles at that time, but over the three months of recording I became aware that he was in a really dark place."

Bob actually came to the studio to speak to Mark and to explain what was happening. Still through all this Adrian was focussed and determined; he had a clear idea of the type of record he wanted.

Fans who had found *Beautiful Ammunition* to be a step too far from

Adrian's post-punk roots would have been relieved by the production, sounds and textures on display right from the opening notes of "Dreamfuel." Synths, programmed drums and sparsely strummed guitar usher in a very different kind of song, unlike anything in Adrian's post-Sound career to date. It's certainly no Sound retread but embraces their atmospheric way through the darkness.

"Bright White Light" ups the anthemic factor to great effect with some welcome feedback guitar from Adrian and a big, bold chorus, but in truth Adrian had originally been thinking of the explosive illumination of Hiroshima.

Then two classics in a row: the stark and resonant "Why Can't I Be Me," complete with tastefully underplayed backing vocals from I V Webb, the song rises to crescendos then pauses and flips back to the eerie verses. Hearing Adrian, on the surface at least, singing from a female perspective is a welcome development. Indeed he'd later recount tales of people who had spoken to him of the song reflecting the struggles they faced in their respective relationships. It's tense and taught and sees him moving into new areas, in short: sublime.

As is the title track. A more sparse acoustic approach is entirely appropriate for the song's metaphor that sees a person's life in cinematic terms, but ultimately as a film no one really wants to see. Adrian lets loose with some plangent guitar and leaves you wondering just how far we are from how he saw his own existence.

"And no-one can see the film
That we've been in
From the cutting room floor
Then it's straight into the bin
With this cinematic life."

His grasp of dynamics is in full evidence here, tracks such as "Night Cascade" retain a lightness of touch despite slightly clunky programmed drums, while "Neon and Stone" uses a great mechanistic guitar riff to create a feeling of downcast monotony.

Apparently a song about homelessness, it's still hard not to see Adrian in lines like these,

"I hear the laughter from another life
The night is young for someone
But to me it's as old as October's leaves
God don't bring on the winter please
Can't you see my broken city heart."

The image called to mind? Adrian clad in his long overcoat, striding the cold, hard streets of London or whatever city he found himself in.

Adrian had felt he could tie the songs on *Cinematic* together using the theme of the 100 years that had elapsed since that day in Paris in 1895. It was a fairly loose theme so not really a 'concept album' as such but rather a loose connecting thread.

"Long Dark Train", takes its inspiration from Nazi Germany, where the image of a train carries the most sinister import, but then applies that to the 'train' the people of the UK had ended up aboard when they found themselves subject to a brutally right-wing government. As we've seen, Adrian had felt continued anger and frustration with the way the country had been torn apart under the long years of Tory rule. His feelings remained clear,

"This long dark train
For years it's rolled
We cry in vain
The doors stay closed
Driven for the few
By sleight of hand
It runs the length
Of this shattered land."

The second half of *Cinematic* continues the wide-ranging subject matter and includes musical settings that may have been more pleasing to that melody-averse Lovefield drummer. Not that melody is abandoned, but these are far darker, grittier songs.

"Antarctica" is initially as chilly as its title but still manages to slide into a more approachable and soothing chorus. Elsewhere "We are the Night" flirts with a kind of electro-darkwave groove, "Western Veil" probes Islam and beyond and "Dreamfuel 2" delivers Adrian's first, albeit brief, instrumental.

But still there's a very familiar Adrian pacing the corridors of "I Can't Stop the World," the same one that gave us "Total Recall" ten years before. Forever frozen in the chill of abandonment, struggling with the absence of the warmth of a symbolic 'sun',

"And if I could stop the world I would
Or if I could freeze the time where it stood
But there's nothing I can do to stay with you."

As we move towards the carefully placed closer first there's the grinding "Spanish Hotel." According to Adrian, a look at cocaine addiction but not, of course, from his own experience, although he'd had plenty of time to observe.

Guest on bass was old friend Phil King, at that point in shoegaze pioneers Lush, having journeyed through a range of bands since first encountering Adrian all those years ago.

Phil, "I remember bumping into Adrian in Charing Cross Road and him asking me to play on the album. Then he came round to my place in Marylebone and played it on my Portastudio, so that I could work out a bass line."

Lush had a significant profile at that point and Adrian maybe hoped for more,

Phil, "We were recording a Lush album at the time and he came up to the studio near Holloway Road. He asked if we needed a support group for the next tour, but I had no real sway. I felt bad as he had helped me out in the past."

It must have been difficult for Phil, wanting to help Adrian but not realistically being able to, the truth is that it wouldn't have been an appropriate match even if it had been possible, but naturally Adrian wanted to effectively promote a project he was excited about and proud of. It's the struggle for attention at the heart of the music business in microcosm.

We know Adrian picked his closing tracks carefully and "The March" is no exception.

"There's no time like now I said
But I should have said it to myself
It's never too late to see
The path you've taken
Has caused your life to be
Far from your heart
Lost in the cold
And we are such a curious blend
Of weakness and strength."

It's a lyric he probably couldn't have written even only a few years earlier. There's a lifetime in bruised experience within the lines of this elegant rumination on the paths we take, some we chose but most we don't. If he'd read F. Scott Fitzgerald I'm sure he would have nodded ruefully at the final lines from *The Great Gatsby*,

"So we beat on, boats against the current, borne back ceaselessly into the past."

Adrian knew he was lost in the vicious current of his life, unable to escape himself or his past.

390

Still, for now, he was reasonably happy. He'd more or less made the record he'd had in his head, allowing for the natural instinct of any artist to feel they've fallen short in their aims. *Cinematic* was an important album for Adrian; he was finally coming to terms with the legacy of the Sound, learning what he did well and seeing he could have a place in the world. The process was ongoing and would move to greater heights on the next album.

For fans, although it's still a CD length album, the variety on offer and the inventive-on-a-budget production maintains *Cinematic*'s focus to a greater degree than was true of its predecessor. And the sound more than hinted at what Adrian did best. Creatively the future looked bright.

There was even a boost when old contact Keith Cullen at Setanta Records (home of Into Paradise) picked the album up for Adrian's first US release since *Shock of Daylight*. They even went as far as issuing a promo 'catch-up' compilation, covering selections (compiled by Jack Rabid) from Adrian's career to date, *Cinematic Overview*.

Sadly in the end it didn't mark the commercial move forward Adrian must have hoped for. Keith confirms what happened,

"Some of Adrian's solo work I wasn't too keen on, but I thought *Cinematic* was great. He gave me a copy and I offered to put it out. Sadly Adrian was quite mixed-up. It's sad when you see someone you admire like that. There wasn't really a chance of us doing anything further."

Press coverage in the UK was confined to fanzines, over in Holland *OOR* were loyal as ever praising *Cinematic* and noting the more 'modern' sound, varied subject matter and "dark atmosphere". Concluding: "*Cinematic* works - the tension is back."

Encouragingly the album picked up a bit of press in the States. A review from Mitch Myers in *Alternative Press* summed things up succinctly,

"Here is the story of a young English punk from the '70s and his travails in the music biz over the next 20 years. Working in near anonymity with bands such as the Outsiders, the Sound and Second Layer, our hero remains resolute in his effort to bring honest, heartfelt and challenging records to a small group of dedicated followers. Ultimately, he settles on a solo career and sets his sights on spreading his message to the denizens of America. Cinematic in scope, sound and lyrical content, this album is everything you'd expect from a cultured cult artist such as Borland."

The Setanta arrangement petered out and Adrian was left energised creatively but still without the support he needed in terms of management and record label. It was a position that felt increasingly fraught. But Adrian being Adrian, plans for the next record were of course well underway as he explained to Jan in March 1996,

"Lyrically things will change and I'll be back to singing about myself again, but perhaps with more atmospheric backing, a more intriguing backcloth to my voice. Maybe more space to get away from what I'm saying if you want to."

The last comment feels odd, it's almost as if he was worried about his own intensity alienating potential listeners. It's extraordinary that not for one moment did he ever consider compromising, possibly trying his hand at following whatever was the latest 'thing' that week. With his songwriting ability conceivably he could have churned out something that may well have caught the ears of those who held the purse strings, but you can imagine how disgusted he would have felt at such a thought.

He'd come this far and had no intention of lowering himself now, no matter what practical, or other difficulties, he faced.

Above all else, he knew he was on an upward trajectory artistically and didn't want to waste time when he could be getting to the next level.

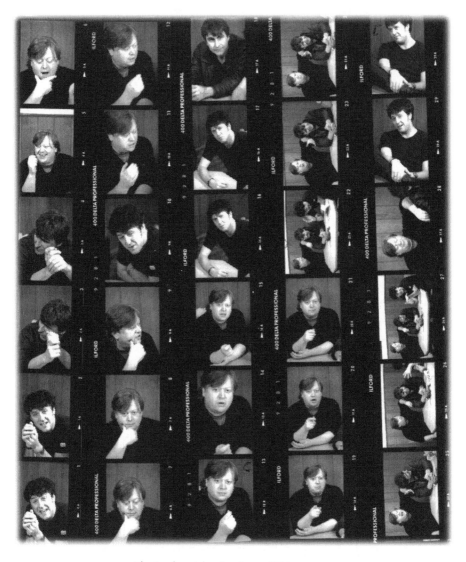

Photoshoot by Andreas Dittmer

CHAPTER 20

Back to nowhere at all

Something odd happened to Adrian in late 1995.

He was the subject of a song by ex-label mate and fellow cult hero Mark Burgess of the Chameleons. Adrian had always been coy about the Chameleons. I asked him about them back in 1992 and he flatly denied having ever heard their music. I had a suspicion he might just be lying, bearing in mind he'd been on the same label and was a voracious music fan himself.

He was acutely conscious of the fact that many Sound fans were also fervent Chameleons fans, but Adrian was very competitive, and I think the idea of close contemporaries working in a similar area to him musically was something he found awkward.

When Jan interviewed him in 1996 the subject came up, it was Adrian who raised it and Jan needed convincing the lyrical reference was intentional, such was the oddness that many listeners, including me, experienced at the time.

Adrian, "Did you hear about that song written about me by Mark Burgess? I've never met him, but he seems like a nice guy. It's a tribute in a way but the meaning I haven't deciphered yet. It must be more about the impression he gets of me from my music."

It was such a strange thing to hear Burgess name-check Adrian in a song, the track in question was "Adrian Be" from the *Paradyning* album released by Mark and multi-instrumentalist Yves Altana.

The key lyric was simple,

"I know how Borland feels."

Some confusion has arisen since, with people thinking it was a tribute released after Adrian's death but no, it was well before and, as Adrian confirmed, predated his friendship with Burgess. It's a beautiful, tender and heartfelt song of care, concern and understanding. Adrian was understandably surprised but ultimately very touched.

Adrian and Mark Burgess

The story behind the song is included in Mark's autobiography, the very enjoyable, *View From a Hill*. Mark had been aware of the Sound but surprisingly found the guitar sound off-putting. He'd received a phone call from Carlo van Putten during which Carlo had mentioned Adrian was having mental health problems, Burgess finished the call and in a moment of empathetic inspiration sang the line "I know how Borland feels" over the song he was currently writing. All a very natural and spontaneous process.

Adrian apparently commented to Carlo, "Yes that's very nice, best song on the album, but he does know I'm not dead doesn't he?"

In a way this was Mark doing exactly what Adrian had done for thousands of people: offering an arm around the shoulder to other humans regardless of whether he knew them or not. Simple but effective. In another sense it was a form of recognition from a peer, something of importance to Adrian.

Asked whether Adrian was forever looking for recognition, James Walton Ingham responded in the affirmative but as ever his more detailed response is more nuanced,

"It could be embarrassing because people would just think he needed that attention, the recognition. But it wasn't an ego thing. You need that fuel to keep yourself going or else you get lost. He was often floundering and lost and in a bad way. Sometimes I'd see him of an evening, and he would have had way too much to drink, wandering around just looking for somebody."

It's a painful image, one that makes you want to look away or pretend it's not happening.

But 1996 would see a development that would tentatively begin the process of ensuring Adrian's music reaching a wider audience around the world; namely the long overdue reissue of the Sound's back catalogue on CD, which up until then had only consisted of Statik's *Counting the Days* compilation and *Thunder Up.*

Funnily enough it was all the work of a key figure in the Sound's past their booking agent the late Mick Griffiths who, on a shoestring, had set up his own label, Renascent.

The label's mission statement?

"We started as a label because nobody else seemed interested in re-releasing our favourite albums on CD - the only solution was to do it ourselves! We only put out music we love."

The label went on to release CDs from the Comsat Angels, Woodentops and Wild Swans as well as a steady stream of Sound albums, including the incredible *Dutch Radio Recordings* (a series of live albums) and the blistering *BBC Recordings.*

Adrian had told Jan that he really wanted everything out on CD, so it must have been a relief to see it actually happening. Starting with the Statik albums made sense as, according to Adrian, WEA were demanding £3000 payment per territory that each album was to be released in.

Of course eventually that was sorted and the WEA albums finally made it to CD. What didn't happen was the album of Sound re-recordings Renascent and Adrian had planned. This would have featured reworked Sound classics recorded with the House of Love's then rhythm section. Adrian was looking forward to it, saying it would be fun to 'deconstruct' his own songs and that it could end up being more mellow and quiet than the originals. Whether it would have worked we shall never know as time moved on and the moment was lost.

Another very intriguing project that was also lost to time was the semi-mythical Velcro Puppy.

Adrian told Jan about 'them' back in March 1996,

"It's dance orientated with a deliberate trash aesthetic. There's some interesting things on it, hopefully it will emerge sometime. It has a pop leaning, a novelty value, maybe top 30. It's kind of in the techno field and has its own sense of what's right and wrong, it's not particularly musical! We have a track called "Rock'n'roll is the New Rock'n'roll." It's like the Glitter Band produced by the Orb, a techno Velvets or a trash Kraftwerk. None of these stupid phrases really describe what we are! Noisy guitars that loop over dance rhythms with weird noises and stupid words!"

The recording involved a mystery collaborator called Miriam and never appeared. Adrian's tape archive has been scoured but nothing found, maybe he was springing an early April Fool on Jan, or perhaps this could have been Adrian's chance at a chart hit. Certainly he wanted it to remain more or less anonymous, maybe with an eye on people listening 'without prejudice.'

"I'm not ashamed of it, it's just not relevant who's involved. Whether it comes out is a big question!"

He summed it up beautifully,

"Musically it screams, 'I am garbage, love me!'"

Carlo van Putten recalls taking a bus with Adrian while on a visit to London. They stopped off at a studio somewhere in south London where work had been taking place on the Velcro Puppy recordings, there he was treated to a preview of another track called, "Euro Year Zero." Carlo confirms it was definitely Velcro Puppy.

Adrian's great lost masterpiece? Probably not, but it sounds like a lot of fun and I'd love to hear it. More evidence of the restless nature of Adrian's musical appetite, clearly he'd seen others do inferior stuff in a similar-ish vein and rightly thought, "I can do much better than that," using his broad influences to create something with commercial appeal. Why couldn't he do that?

Instead he turned to something much more important to him: his next album.

It wouldn't be made for Resolve, Adrian had a new record deal with a label called Earth. On the surface that sounded good but look at the label's address and it may seem quite familiar, we're back on the Ridgway in good old Wimbledon SW19, this time at number 12. It's a beautician now, back then a hairdresser run by ex-Capital Radio DJ Phil Allen.

He later talked up the label as looking for new artists but the reality was it never released anything beyond Adrian's next album *5:00 AM* and its sole single, "Over the Under." However there was a budget for recording and it was more than had been available for *Cinematic*.

Adrian in the studio

In addition there was also an old friend assisting. The late great Tim Smith of the Cardiacs would produce and record the album in his 16 track studio located in a converted shed, as well as contributing drum programming, keyboards and harmonium.

On board again was bass player Pat Rowles, someone who would be playing a larger role in the years to come. Pat had been a Sound fan and saw them at the Marquee, going backstage to meet Adrian,

Pat, "We went into this tiny dressing room which was absolutely rammed with the band and fans, and I was right next to Adrian, so just for something to say, I said, 'Oh, great gig first time I've seen you.' This seemed to fascinate him. 'Was it really? It's the first time you've seen us!?' As if to say, 'How come you've never made the effort before?' "

That dressing room at the Marquee was squalid and covered in graffiti, there's actually a photo of the band back there included in the second Edsel CD box. You can get some idea of the 'facilities' available at that great venue.

Pat, "A couple of years after that, a mutual friend said, 'Adrian Borland's looking for a bass player to do some gigs'. So hell yeah, you know, I'm v there. I showed up at the house of the drummer who was going to be involved and we seemed to hit it off straight away. I had a copy of the CD of the songs, which was the *Beautiful Ammunition* album."

Pat got the call again after contributing to *Cinematic,* this time he'd be part of a smaller more focussed group of musicians recording in quick intense sessions, as Pat explains,

"There was no live recording as such, it wasn't the kind of situation where you set the band up in the studio to get a live drum track down, because the drums were all programmed by the producer, Tim Smith. So I came in when the drums and guide guitars and vocals were there. They were very quick, intense sessions. I was working outside London, so I'd have to get back to London, load up my gear, drive back out of London again to the studio."

They worked fast,

"We did all the bass parts in literally four or five hour sessions. So they're not quite as good or detailed as I might have liked them to be."

Pat admits to being a perfectionist, but he does highlight the difficulties and the pressure that comes with operating on a low budget. If you care about what you're doing, which all involved did, then it can be tough.

"It was very intense. Sometimes we were there until two in the morning and there's me knowing I've got to be up for work at six and still have to get home first!. But yes, they were memorable, Adrian was very appreciative at the time of all the effort that people were making for him."

Asked how Adrian was in the studio Pat confirms,

"It could vary a lot at that time. Overall he was relaxed and appreciative. He was always very receptive to ideas. For example the reason the song "Vampiric" sounds the way it does is because all he had was the chord change. I use harmonics quite a lot in my bass playing and I came up with that quite high bass line which has an open 12th harmonic between the two chord changes. He loved that."

Pat paints a picture of high intensity but very productive sessions, something that we can appreciate when we hear the fantastic results.

Talking about the album to *Limit* magazine the following year, Adrian was still very pleased with it,

"The last two albums were essentially demos. Even *Beautiful Ammunition* is very simply put together, only acoustic guitar, synthesiser and a few drum machines. Everything is very basic, which I like, but it's quite a different thing to record with a 16-track machine, even just from the point of view of atmosphere. With *Cinematic* I felt the same, but perhaps that album was somewhat overambitious. Perhaps the time was not yet ready for it. With *5:00 AM* I had 39 days to make it the way I wanted. Tim Smith of the Cardiacs was very good as a producer. He never tried to change the music, he just tried to maintain the individuality of the artist. I'm very happy with this album."

Another detail worth focussing on amongst the album credits is the following:

"Layout and artwork: Diana Overton."

Actually it's not a great cover, but Adrian hadn't been excelling in the artwork department for a while, the later reissue put that right thankfully. More importantly though, Adrian was in a new relationship and Diana was the person in question. Win confirms he'd met her at a party when still a teenager and that Diana had got in touch that year.

James Walton Ingham recalls the change,

"He had a new partner, I'd never known him to have a girlfriend but he'd hooked up with a girl that he'd been with as a teenager. For the first time ever, I thought it was going to be alright."

James had heard the news from Adrian's mum, Win,

"I called from my new home in Dorset to speak with Adrian in 1996 or so and his mother told me that he was doing very well and had a new 'ladyfriend'. I was astonished and delighted to hear this. I met up with them both in the Swan pub in Wimbledon when I was up for a family visit. Diana was very warm, attractive and personable. She gave Adrian a huge confidence boost and restored much of his long-lost self-esteem. They really seemed very comfortable together; no tension or disharmony. She'd bought him a very smart grey collarless jacket."

Hearing such news and seeing the evidence of Adrian's apparent new stability must have been a relief. James later received a visit down in Dorset,

"I also recall a visit they made to me in Dorset, Adrian having insisted on coming to see me. We walked along the winter beach and caught up with one another.

I cooked them a huge pasta meal and they watched the football in my front room before driving back to Diana's Surrey home. Her 'wheels' gave Adrian more freedom and he was able to get out of the 'goldfish bowl' of Wimbledon Village."

It was clear Diana had become a vital part of Adrian's life,

"Diana had designed his new album cover and paid for Adrian to have his hair tinted a bolder, grey/blond that really suited him. She had championed him and treated him well. She bought him a beautiful left-handed Gibson 335 guitar. He seemed so happy and calm that I made the huge mistake of thinking I didn't need to worry about him anymore. I'd always feared for him and that he would self-harm or drink himself into desperately poor health. This seemed unthinkable now he had love and a new home."

You can see a photo of Adrian proudly holding the Gibson within the *5:00 AM* booklet.

That James' optimism proved unfounded is no criticism of him, it's exactly what a good friend would have fervently, but with fingers crossed tightly, hoped for Adrian.

The cover itself clues us in to the reason for the title; *5:00 AM*, the time dawn reaches us around the equinox. Adrian's craved sun back again, another day beginning. Or maybe it wasn't so clear, talking to the *Limit* he provided clarification,

"The title describes the most terrible time of day for me; at 5:00 AM you simply feel bad, whether you haven't slept yet or even if you simply have to get up. For me this is a dividing point. End of the night, beginning of the day, something comes to an end, and something new begins. Many of the songs mention these things."

Adrian with his Gibson 335 guitar

It's no surprise to hear a person with a history of depression talk of dreading that time of day - it's a zone of time where you are alone with your wildest thoughts and the pressure of starting a new day weighs heavily.

Interestingly Adrian had a loose concept in mind,

"For a while I had the crazy idea to sort the titles according to their length and begin with the shortest one, so that the numerical data on the back cover read like the points in time during one night. Unfortunately it became impossible to maintain the title order, but I still found the idea useful, to describe the moments within one night. But

"Kissing in The Dark," for example, takes place on a bright summer day. The darkness is only a metaphor for kissing a stranger. Thus it's not a strict concept album, but it has very much the atmosphere of a journey through one night."

Critically the UK was largely silent but *OOR* gave a reasonably fair assessment of Adrian's position, after his "promising start" with the Sound,

"A series of interesting but not always equally successful solo albums only ensured further and further declining sales. Maybe he will succeed with this CD to regain part of the past glory. *5:00 AM* can compete in intensity with the best of the Sound. Borland has also succeeded in reproducing the echoes from his new wave past in a modern sounding production."

Describing the music as "dramatic" and possessing a "sparkling freshness" they concluded that, "*5:00 AM* comes right on time to restore the waning confidence in Adrian Borland."

That last comment must have stung but reflects a not uncommon perception of Adrian's career at this point in time.

Dutch newspaper, *De Volkskrant* followed a similar line,

"In the early eighties there were two young English bands in the Netherlands who seemed to make it: U2 and The Sound. They both grew into live favourites, but as U2 went on to achieve world fame, the Sound lagged behind. In 1998, U2 have just finished one of the most lavish and profitable tours in live music history while former Sound singer Adrian Borland can only claim to be world famous in Haarlem, where he regularly performs in small venues."

An accurate but painful juxtaposition of Adrian and his love/nemesis U2. The paper agreed Adrian had never stopped writing compelling pop songs, concluding,

"*5:00 AM* sounds almost immediately, pleasantly familiar, like a straight continuation of the music that Borland made in the heyday of the Sound. Emotional, dark and heavy on one hand, but very incisive in its best moments."

There's an illuminating comment from Adrian in response to a question posed in the *Limit* interview, where it's suggested *5:00 AM* has a similar kind of energy to that possessed by the Sound,

"Sometimes you try to dissociate yourself as hard as you can from your

407

past. But then you reach the point where you have to accept that it's a part of you. You can then try and see what new things can be created as a result. At times you must fight your own style, in order to be new, and at other times you have to surrender to your own style, in order to be good. I mean, I could start writing only songs about fishing or acoustic ballads about sailing, but who wants to listen to that!? I would only torture my brain and lose my public at the same time. There are a lot of people, particularly in Germany, who lost interest in me during the last record who will like this album a lot. Perhaps *5:00 AM* takes up where *Thunder Up* left off."

It's not unusual for artists striking out on their own, after time in a band with fans and a reputation, to struggle to acknowledge or even identify what made them successful at their art in the first place. Just look at all those best forgotten comeback albums littering musical history. Adrian worked through the various stages of coming to terms with the demise of the Sound and with each solo release took an important step. *5:00 AM* was the culmination of that process.

Let's be clear it's not the Sound and with hindsight would have benefited from a real drummer of the calibre of Mike Dudley, but never mind, you work with what you have and Adrian excelled himself here.

If the opening song "Stray Bullets" doesn't tingle your spine then you may be reading the wrong book. A glorious rush of sound hits you in the gut, Adrian singing of a life out of control,

"I was shot into the fray
I ricocheted from wall to wall."

We are in a familiar place, Adrian is singing of the joy of new love, he's high on the feeling,

"I was sunk by punches, thrown by lies
I came off worse
Loat all direction

Until I made the connection
In the whites of your eyes"

Once more Adrian has found a connection. But knowing what we know of him can we be anything but concerned by lines such as these,

"I was brought to life
I was hit
Gunned down by love
I never thought it would find me
I never thought it would find me in time."

For him love was always a high stakes, high risk, visceral thing. Maybe that's how it should always be, but with Adrian you always feel it went dangerously too far, meaning that its withdrawal was cataclysmic. Still for now it was energising him, and so by extension, his art.

And he seems to have known it. "Dangerous Stars" sees Adrian embracing a mechanical sound that feels closer to what the more commercial moments of *All Fall Down* may have led to. It's a big sound that belies its recording situation and budget limitations. Lyrically there's Adrian in the gutter looking at the perfect stars but from such a distant perspective knowing that, "you can't see the edges from here." In effect he's longing for something that will destroy him.

"When I stuck my hand in the heavens
All it came back with were cuts
From the dangerous stars
Those dangerous stars."

Coincidentally the lyric bears a close relation to a Bunnymen track: "Stars are Stars" from that debut Korova album, *Crocodiles* which included the line,

"I caught that falling star
It cut my hands to pieces."

409

For McCulloch he was catching a *falling* star, for Adrian it was about reaching *up* to the heavens.

That the next two songs are "Vampiric" and "Baby Moon," tells you just how strong *5:00 AM* is.

"Vampiric" rests on subtle, string-stroked verses but bursts into a burning chorus. The question is: who is the vampire in the relationship in question?

Finally, "Baby Moon", as Adrian told the *Limit* it's time had eventually come,

"Some of the songs I had as far back as 1993, for example,"Baby Moon". I waited for the chance to record it in the right way. It's been like that with a few songs, where you wait for a decent budget. You can't waste your best material on a lo-fi production."

Adrian cared and was right to hold on, *5:00 AM*'s version smokes the Lovefield take, allowing this skyscraping song to unfurl in the way it was meant to: a classic Borland anthem right until the lovely circling riff fades.

Then "City Speed" hits and the territory shifts completely, a frantic intro with trumpet darting in and out, there's a confidence on display that shows just how happy Adrian was with this material. He went into detail in the *Limit,*

"The song is dedicated to Carlo van Putten of the Convent, because we did the things that I sing about together. Every time at the end of the working day, we got into the car and drove to Bremen. It's about such trips, where you see the high-rise buildings emerging slowly, if you drive off the motorway and the city is there in front of you."

Adrian always believed in the multi-layered song and resisted fixed meanings,

"Much of that is within this song, but a song is never only about one thing. In "City Speed" there are thousands of journeys in hundreds of different cities. It also means London, the people on the streets there, or in New York. Actually each city is symbolised. You rush through somewhere and maybe stay one moment, where you want. Then perhaps afterwards you move on to the next journey."

It's a vivid picture of the strange impermanence of all our lives, intense experiences that end too quickly or sometimes not quickly enough.

The darkness really descends with the almost Cure-like textures of "Kissing in the Dark's" opening verse, but again we shoot into the light via the chorus. Resting on a sinister synth pattern, it's a long way from all of Adrian's solo work to that date bar maybe *Cinematic* and yes does have echoes of the spaces explored on *Thunder Up*. Many Sound fans will have felt as if they were home again.

But look carefully at that lyric,

"Kissing in the dark
It's all we've known
A few inches taller
But don't say we've grown
Kissing in the dark
It's all we've done
In the cul-de-sac
Where our feelings run."

Adrian and Diana were "A few inches taller" than when they'd first known each other as teenagers and the "cul-de-sac"? Hillview. Win believed Adrian had only 'met' Diana back then but maybe Adrian didn't tell his mum the full story.

Then an unexpected twist as Tim Smith's harmonium takes "I'm Your Freedom" towards more unfamiliar zones. Adrian trying to reassure a partner that he brings possibility not control,

"I'm your freedom not your keeper
I'm desire not denial."

"The Spinning Room" takes us back to the more prevalent *5:00 AM*
sound, with its mechanistic rhythms and hypnotic synths.

Remember Adrian often said to understand him listen to his lyrics. He
also made a point of saying these new songs would be more about him
than the sometimes wide-ranging themes of *Cinematic,*

So what to make of this?

"I don't remember how I got
So close to you
That I can't pull away now
I gravitated to the core
Now I can't find
The way to where I was before
I float here with the debris
A kind of wreckage too
Turning like a satellite
That's locked into an orbit around you."

More intensity created by a connection with an unspecified other, but
how will such a feeling play out in the longer term?

Then a switch to a more conventional driving rock song, "Redemption's
Knees." Adrian's guitar to the fore and a subtle, sinuous bass line from
Pat, it leads us effectively towards the final three songs.

"Between Buildings" sees Adrian conjuring up another machine-driven
framework for an examination of the choices we make in life and the
roads we chose not to explore.

"Every course that we didn't take
Is a life we'll never know

So many turns I've refused
To leave this life behind
Was I scared of what I'd lose?
Or afraid of what I'd find?"

The clanking rhythm and ascending synth line mirror the claustrophobic feeling of being trapped in a life that makes no sense, it's a song that sees him taking the bleak texture of tracks like "Night Versus Day" and updating it for the '90s.

As ever we can see Adrian's hand at work in the sequencing of *5:00 AM*, after the experimentation of "Between Buildings" comes the single, "Over the Under."

And what a single: anthemic but not pompous, stirring but avoiding cliche. It's what Adrian did so well and remains one of the jewels in his solo catalogue. Listen to his voice and remember the stress he would suffer when preparing for the vocal sessions, here he sounds impassioned but never over-plays hand. Musically it's a more straightforward track but still has plenty of nice sonic touches lurking just below the surface.

A song of bittersweet hope from a person who has more that tasted despair,

"Wasted years
I turn my back on wasted years
And the shadows that they throw
I'm out of here
I want to live
At least I'm going to try
And I'm over the under now."

But it couldn't be the finale of *5:00 AM* because Adrian had another song in mind, the beautiful, "Before the Day Begins."

Spectral verse leads to elegiac chorus, the lyrical resignation is disquieting however,

"What were you waiting for?
What twist of fate?
Whatever you were waiting for
Never came
What were you dreaming of?
What kind of special love?
Each time drawn in like a moth
To the flame."

Could it be any more personal? And yet still something the listener can potentially identify as an ache they can feel or at least recall. There at the close an acknowledgment that some escape while others never make it,

"Lying there with your open eyes
And your dying innocence
When you drowned in the sea of life
Did your own one make no sense?
Before the day begins
Do you thank your stars
Or count your sins
Or think of all the finer things
That finally came?"

It's a hushed and stunning end to one of Adrian's best records, whether with or without the Sound. Nevertheless it's lyrical tone was a slightly jarring mix of excitement at new love layered with resignation over past disappointment and its seeming inevitability.

Artistically he was moving fast from album to album and the thought was now; where next?

First he needed to make sure as many people as possible heard his new music, and there lay a problem.

While promoting *5:00 AM* Adrian was operating in drastically reduced circumstances. UK press interest was minimal, so it was probably hard to turn down a live on air interview for a local radio station, Thames FM. The recording is uncomfortable to listen to. Adrian's slot is their regular 'local music segment,' he's polite but it all feels horribly awkward for an artist of his skill and previous stature. At one point the DJ refers to Adrian having sent him a translation of a German review of the album, Adrian is quick to say someone else sent it, not him. You can feel him bristling at the thought he was down to photocopying reviews and sending them out himself to promote his own record.

But there was good news: a short Dutch, Belgian and German tour had been put together so Adrian got a band together, christening them, appropriately, the Stray Bullets. The tour wound up with a rare London gig at a decent venue, the Borderline.

Pat remembers the time with mixed emotions,

"The gigs were great, but the longer it went on, the more it seemed that there was a division between Adrian and the rest of us, which, with hindsight, could have been partly due to his illness. At the end we did all have a falling out. He felt that we hadn't properly appreciated the opportunity to come on tour with the 'great Adrian Boland'."

It was a clash between Adrian's view of life and its realities and the demands on a group of people with outside lives and responsibilities. These were no longer people in their early twenties, they had jobs and families,

Pat, "We didn't think he appreciated that some of us had other lives outside of being great songwriters and musicians and had day jobs to go back to having given up holiday time, pay, etc. to come on the tour. Obviously, we did it because we wanted to and knew we were going to enjoy it. But at the same time you do expect a certain amount of appreciation and by the end we felt that he thought it was one way traffic, that we were all getting loads out of it and perhaps not putting enough back in."

Adrian and Pat on stage together

Listening to Pat talk of the everyday practical challenge of organising Adrian is pretty amusing,

"Getting Adrian up wasn't so easy. He would just lie there, and by midday you would almost literally have to drag him out of bed. "

'Adrian, we've got to go. We've got to set off for the next town, the next gig.' So we'd get him up and showered, then he'd dress in the van as we set off."

Pat did get a taste of Adrian's greater popularity on the continent and came to a familiar conclusion as to part of the reason why,

"I think his image was a problem, perhaps in Europe people are less image conscious. Maybe all they want to know is how good the songs are? How good is the music, not what does the guy look like?"

Asked what awareness he had of Adrian's illness, Pat's answer is interesting and probably reflects what many felt,

"With Adrian it was more subtle and I just thought he was being a difficult artist a lot of the time, you know, a lot of creative people can be idiosyncratic, difficult, single-minded and hard to deal with. And so that's what I put a lot of it down to."

Noticing the signs of mental illness isn't always an easy thing to do.

Pat paints a picture of Adrian that we know well, humorous, entertaining and often the life and soul of the party. But within that superficially normal description there was a deep need for attention,

"He'd come back to my flat and immediately he would grab my left-handed acoustic guitar. You and your friends might have had an idea that you were just going to sit around and shoot the breeze, but no, Adrian was the centre of attention. He would sit there playing the guitar and almost take over the room through force of personality and the fact he was such an entertaining performer."

Asked if Adrian lived for the attention and recognition, Pat confirmed,

"He certainly thrived on it. He was definitely at his best when he had an audience, whether that was in a venue for him to perform his songs or just a room the size of this with three or four people. He did love attention for sure."

Again, I don't think this was a simple case of having an ego to feed, we all have that to varying degrees, no this was something different. The difficulty when you need attention like Adrian clearly did, is what then happens when it isn't available or moves elsewhere. For him it was another case of going from the heat of the sun to the chill of darkness.

There was quite a party mood in the UK at the time Adrian was out of the country on tour. On the 1st of May, after what felt like an eternity, Adrian's hated Tories had finally been driven out in a landslide election victory for Tony Blair's 'new' Labour. Imagine, for Adrian there had been a conservative government for most of his adult life, now the era of 'Cool Britannia' was about to begin and, for a while at least, things looked positive.

Someone who witnessed Adrian's happiness at Labour's victory was Mark Burgess. Sharing a bill at a gig in Bremen the two finally met, leading to a barnstorming encore of Bowie's "Rebel Rebel," captured in shaky quality on YouTube. Mark describes Adrian as, "a bear of a guy, with a quick wit and a great sense of humour."

But after spending the next few days with him and Carlo, he realised this was a complex character. Adrian needed to be collected from the airport after going to Holland for an acoustic gig and had suffered a panic attack. Later Mark and Adrian fell into conversation about Joy Division and Ian Curtis. Unsurprisingly Adrian mentioned he understood and respected Ian's decision to end his life.

Mark, "He told me that he often thought about suicide, having attempted it himself. As we spoke I sensed the deep seriousness of this conversation. This was more than self-pity or ego talking."

Burgess later watched Adrian and Carlos' band the Convent perform a version of Joy Division's "Shadowplay," ominously concluding,

"I remember thinking that this guy was a tragedy waiting to happen."

Adrian playing with the Convent

Finally, away from music, over the summer of 1997 Adrian took a fairly momentous step; he moved into Diana's rented house in Gilders Road, Chessington where she lived with Sammy, her young son from a previous relationship, who Adrian seems to have got on well with (accordingly to Pat he wrote him a song called, appropriately, "Sammy's Song"). There was even a 'house-warming' party.

Chessington is about six miles from 2 Hillview. It's a fairly anonymous suburban town most famous for its theme park, Chessington World of Adventures, oh, and Adrian's old friend and Cardiac founder, the late Tim Smith came from there.

I suspect those who knew Adrian well were very pleased to see the possible beginnings of some form of stability, however that must have been tinged with a nagging thought: is this really a place where Adrian could feel at home? Try as you might, it's hard to see him pushing a trolley around the local Aldi, living the suburban life much like his parents.

Then the more frightening thought: Adrian was placing all his hope on this relationship, what would the fallout be if things didn't work out? It's tough enough for anyone when a relationship fails but for a person like Adrian, with a deeply idealised vision of how transformative such a bond could be, combined with a mental illness that threatened to pull him apart, the ramifications were worrying to contemplate.

Add to that another ever-present need: to make a new record.

Asked by the *Limit* whether he had any "concrete plans," Adrian replied in what to some may sound a humorous tone, but for those who knew him the choice of words described a disturbing reality,

"I must get back into the studio soon, because it's terrible to walk around with 40 songs in my mind, sooner or later my head explodes if I don't record them."

The warning signs were all there in plain sight, but what could anyone do?

CHAPTER 21

When that train pulls out in the cold morning light, just be on it

At this point it feels as though a portentous voice should be announcing that, "The storm clouds were gathering…" However the sad truth was they had always been uncomfortably close and were instead now beginning to dramatically darken. But this metaphorical storm wouldn't simply result in the welcome tension release of summer thunder.

To add to the mix of behavioural triggers, Adrian had been thrown into a state of worry by correspondence he had been receiving relating to Sound financial issues. Today Mike Dudley feels this unwelcome development had more effect on Adrian than he would have let on. Ironically it brought Mike back into Adrian's life, if only via correspondence, as his input was needed in responding to the other party.

Bob Borland saw the consequences,

"I think that was quite a nasty episode. Adrian became quite disturbed by it and he went downhill after that."

One of the letters half-jokingly suggested Adrian should consider leaving the 'music business' and getting a 'normal' job. The disputed amounts involved weren't large but Adrian's resources were minimal, as Pat Rowles confirms,

"I think that was pretty much always the case. I don't think he ever had much of an income. He relied to a great extent on his parents."

So any issues with money had the power to hit him hard, as we shall see once the recording of his next solo record, to be called *Harmony and Destruction*, got underway.

However this wasn't the only piece of the past resurfacing in Adrian's life, he had also been thinking about his son. Maybe it was reaching his fortieth year or the effect of spending time with Diana's son, Sammy, but something changed Adrian's attitude towards his unknown offspring in Germany.

Bob confirms that when Adrian first heard he allegedly had a child he didn't engage with the mother Elke,

"In about 1982 we received a card from a girl called Elke. Saying she had had Adrian's child and it's a boy. We said, wait, 'What's this, Adrian?' He said, 'Nothing to do with me.' He wouldn't admit he was the father and didn't respond to her."

That changed in 1997.

Bob, "In 1997, he finally admitted that he was the father and he decided to try to visit his son."

Adrian visited the German town in question but Elke had moved, her neighbour confirmed that the child resembled Adrian. The experience must have been difficult for him but clearly his lack of previous contact had also been hard for Elke, who when located didn't wish him to be involved in her or her son's life, going as far as now casting doubt on the parenthood question.

Bob confirms Adrian was distressed at not being able to have access to his son but there was little that could be done and the matter was taken no further leaving a painful sense of regret over unexplored possibilities. For Adrian the only way to deal with that was to immerse himself in his music.

With new songs coming thick and fast the good news was that he was now able to record basic demos at home, as Bob confirms,

"Adrian was living with Diana in Chessington. I bought him a MIDI recording system to use there and he started getting quite good at using it. It was a good way for him to record initial versions of some of the

songs."

During this period Adrian was in regular contact with Carlo van Putten and the two of them were planning White Rose Transmission's second album. In a dream pairing for fans the involvement of the Chameleons' Mark Burgess was sought and secured.

Writing in his autobiography, *View From a Hill*, Mark touches on both White Rose Transmission and his burgeoning friendship with Adrian,

Mark, "I was invited to take part in a recording session by Carlo and Adrian Borland who were collaborating on what would be their second album for their project White Rose Transmission. I'd been a huge fan of their first album and was extremely pleased when Adrian asked if I'd play bass on the planned sequel. After rehearsing the material I'd been given, I spent a couple of weeks at the studio working on the album."

With their similar musical backgrounds Mark confirms he and Adrian got on well together, not something that's always guaranteed. Mark was massively impressed with his songwriting abilities. Adrian had written a song for Mark to sing, "Digging for Water," but had been shy in actually asking him to sing it, so got Carlo to broach the subject. Mark loved the song and was amazed to find Adrian had composed it during a flight to Bremen - typical Adrian. He was more than happy to sing it.

Mark tells several anecdotes about Adrian that are both funny and bittersweet in equal measure.

One that is purely amusing is the tale of the night a group of friends including Mark and Adrian attended a Red Sky Coven gig. Adrian was visibly unimpressed, as Mark says he, "spent the whole evening watching cynically from the bar." Later Adrian apparently described the night as, "Fucking shit, New Model Army were shit and he's (Justin Sullivan) just as shit on his own."

But then a hilarious volte-face: bumping into Justin Sullivan after the gig

Adrian gushed effusively saying, "Great gig! Totally enjoyed it!"

Maybe he was just being polite, but more likely this was the vulnerable Adrian who found it difficult sharing the spotlight with other artists.

On a more sombre note Mark describes a conversation he and his then partner had with Adrian about Ian Curtis. In Mark's words, "he emphasised how much the man, his lyrics and the drama of Curtis' suicide had meant to him and he got very emotional."

Adrian broke off the conversation in order to compose himself. It's a touching but also disturbing glimpse of what was going on under his affable surface.

But there's another story that Mark tells, that also shows us how Adrian wanted one version of his future to look.

While recording Mark confirms Adrian and his girlfriend Diana had numerous arguments over the phone. Mark's description of Diana as, "long suffering" is on one level light-hearted but on another, knowing what we do, a cause for concern.

Apparently back home Diana had formed the view that Adrian was living the rock'n'roll life, out partying and womanising. The irony was that he was planning to ask her to marry him.

I'll let that sink in: Adrian was actually on the verge of an act that many who knew him never expected to happen. He went as far as buying an engagement ring, Mark driving him into town to purchase it. Exactly what happened on his return to England we don't know, aside from the certainty that the vision of his future Adrian had dared dream of was a leap too far, for one or both of them, and would never happen.

The recording of what became *700 Miles of Desert* went well and plans were made for a joint German tour, on the surface the mood seemed positive.

It feels like we're hurtling towards an immovable event, time is passing quickly and there's not much of it left. As a result White Rose Transmission's second album was destined not to appear until after Adrian's death.

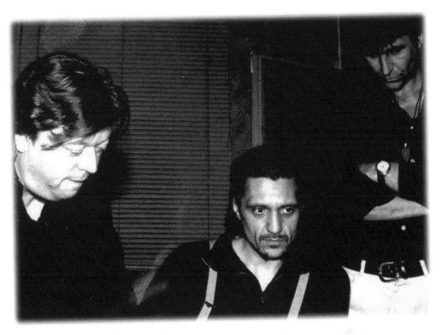

Adrian, Rolf Kirschbaum and Mark Burgess in the studio, working on
700 Miles of Desert

If you've never heard it, you really should make time, because this is a hidden gem deep within Adrian's 'body of work.' His generosity of spirit is on full display within this collaboration with people he viewed as equals, although not an obviously commercial record it's still a very approachable one, full of hooks and detail if you look carefully enough.

Remember his desire to make music with a cinematic quality? Well as soon as the opening track, "Summer Road," takes its languid steps towards the heat haze on the horizon, you will see what he meant.

And then there's Adrian's voice joining us, deeper in the mix that we're used to, but welcome just the same. Not that Carlo hasn't already proved he can handle being main vocalist, the arrangement where Adrian supplies 12 of the 14 songs, produces and plays various instruments, works even more impressively than last time round.

I'm sure he welcomed taking on the different role and the pleasure of seeing his songs interpreted so effectively.

Carlo, "Adrian and I always had an open way of communicating with each other. We really just said what we thought and felt about our music and songs. He always made me feel good and that I mattered as a singer. Also, his gesture to let me sing on our WRT project: I remember a fan was upset and wrote an email asking why he doesn't sing on the songs. Adrian replied, do you already have all my albums? No? Buy those first. Carlo sings here."

After the seven minutes of "Summer Road" have unwound there's another beauty waiting; "Hallucinating You." Adrian is out there in the unrelenting heat stumbling through a desert of the soul. Even when he sees salvation, is it a mirage?

"Was it a trick of light
By the blood red moon?
Was it lack of sleep
Dreams come too soon?
When I turned to speak
You passed right through me
Was I hallucinating you?
Was it alcohol
Or a failing mind
Too many loveless days
Too close behind?
Were you conjured by the fumes
Of too many smoked filled rooms?

Was I hallucinating you?"

Adrian feared the return of those "loveless days" more than nearly anything else, but here he was, questioning the stability of the ground he was standing on.

The 'journey through a desert' metaphor is a sadly apt one for Adrian. It's interesting that he handed Mark Burgess a song where the search for relief seems, on the surface at least, to have been successful,

"I was digging for water
I was digging for faith
I was digging for water
I found an ocean today."

But then Adrian himself takes the vocal spot for the stark and worrying, "Walking in the Opposite Direction." A pointed rejection of the 'world as it is,' a place Adrian struggled to exist in, this time he wasn't optimistically looking for a 'different wheel' but turning his back on it all,

"My spirit's free
You won't get me
Into the shell your life is locked in
Your value system's broken down
I see it blocks the road it stopped in
And every day the things you crave
Make a play for my affection
I tell you straight
I won't be swayed
I'm walking in the opposite direction
They scream at me from flashing screens
They hassle me from city walls
But these are other people's dreams
They don't resemble mine at all."

There's a sense Adrian may have been addressing another person rather than the simple mass of population, maybe a person close to him. Perhaps it's no surprise to find him singing this one himself.

The album closes with the stirring, epic "Dead Guitars."

"As my eyes burn with frustration
And my heart is growing tired
In my head are all the contradictions
In my hands a mess of splinters
Chrome and wire
Dead guitars
Well I played her like a song
But now the song is gone
And I sang every one of her praises
And she left me with all these empty phrases
On dead guitars."

Here's Adrian ruefully considering what he's left with, having turned a love into song only to find the love has gone, but he still has the songs to sing.

We can always read too much into these things, it's very tempting, but in the circumstances it's difficult not too.

Back in England Adrian and Diana had moved. They were now living way out 'in the sticks' in the tiny village of Ivinghoe Aston in Bedfordshire. Adrian was 33 miles to the northwest of London, the furthest from the capital he'd ever lived aside from when he was staying outside the UK.

The relationship was under pressure and there was to be no engagement. At a point early in the recording of the next album Adrian moved back to 2 Hillview and they were no longer a couple.

During the making of *Walking in the Opposite Direction* Bob was asked what happened,

Bob, "I can't really tell you that. I don't know exactly what it was that caused things not to work in this case. I think Diana found Adrian to be sort of, 'cramping her style' in some ways. So she felt that it was all too demanding. In Diana's case, it may be that she simply found it difficult to cope with Adrian when he was ill."

It's important to see things from Diana's perspective. Having a young child she had to consider Sammy's welfare. If Adrian was in the house and having a psychotic episode it would be frightening enough for her but even more so when worrying about her child. What would you do? It's a sobering question to carefully bear in mind before passing an unwise judgement.

Win describes events, "Adrian moved back in with us and his belongings were sent back bit by bit. It was awful."

Today Carlo is quick to confirm that he believes Diana loved Adrian very much, but sometimes that's not enough to guarantee a relationship has a future and with the two of them there were multiple instances of breaking up and getting back together, until the final split.

Carlo, "Adrian was really in love with Diana. But she was afraid because she had to look after her child. She knew in the past he had tried to kill himself in other people's houses and she was scared about those situations. He couldn't deal with an ordinary life, he needed to go deep into things. One day he could write a song like "Over the Under" and the next, "Walking in the Opposite Direction." It's the way someone with manic depression is, the extremes of emotion."

Over in Germany Carlo heard of the break-up from Adrian in a phone call and relayed the news to Mark Burgess. In his autobiography Mark notes his physical reaction, it's sobering,

"Carlo told me Adrian had split up with his girlfriend and I remember feeling an immediate lurch in the pit of my stomach."

Mark could see the apparent stability that Adrian's relationship had brought to his life. Although of course we can't be fully aware of the internal dynamics of people's lives together or how sustainable a connection is in the long run.

Is it too simplistic to suggest that a safe, secure, loving relationship could have solved many of Adrian's problems?

Probably.

But Adrian had to have hope in something and that was what he believed in, or at least wanted to. He imbued the *idea* of a relationship with such a spiritual intensity, that when disappointment followed disappointment it was no surprise and no one's fault. The theme begins appearing in his songs from 1983 onwards, the same time as his emotional breakup with Julie. That theme being the search for something that, it became clear, was a chimerical concept.

But as Adrian sang, "What holds your hope together, make sure it's strong enough."

For Adrian sadly it proved not to be strong enough.

By this point in the late '90s the internet was rapidly becoming an integral part of more and more people's lives. As we all know the music industry would be transformed within a few short years, with all the pros and cons we now can see.

I suspect Adrian would have found it useful in many ways. Certainly he could have experienced the positive feeling that linking with fans he never knew he had, all around the globe, would have left him with.

He was already testing the waters and taking tentative steps, on 18th March 1999 he posted the following "missive" online,

"I'm going to be, or have been, so busy with music this year I thought I'd let anybody who's interested in on it. Firstly I've just finished producing and writing (most of) the next White Rose Transmission CD *700 Miles of Desert*. Everybody involved worked hard but enjoyed themselves immensely and the end result is better than any of us expected. It's hard to be objective but I'll just say the final mastered slice of silver has rarely left my CD player. Carlo felt the same. I think it's quite an addictive record, perhaps it should carry a government health warning. It's 64 minutes of music but it doesn't feel like it and has a wonderful flow and atmosphere. Despite the fact that I don't sing on it, it's probably one of my favourite records I've been involved with (maybe because I don't sing!). Anyway it's a journey I can recommend to anyone interested in moody guitar music with atmospheric beats and classical touches.

In April I begin working with Wally Brill (who produced *Heads and Hearts*) on my 6th solo album. Six is my lucky number so maybe I'll find a wider audience with this one. This is going to be another epic. I might call it *Destiny Stopped Screaming* as I'll either finally get the music in my head on tape or I'll feel like quitting altogether, so it will fit either way! Other possible titles are *Body of Work 19*, *Get Me a Witness*, *In the Field*, *Land Meets Ocean* or *Harmony and Destruction*. Please email Red Sun with your choice! So I can ignore it anyway.

I'm really looking forward to recording this. Pat Rowles (bass) has invested time and money into this because he felt so strongly about getting these songs out this century. Expect a more experimental approach but within a song context (still no jazz allowed). We'll be working with Pro-Tools so the only limits are money and imagination.

After that the White Rose CD will come out and we expect to tour Germany and Holland in late June. While I should be gigging in October for my solo CD, I'll also be recording a 12 song acoustic record with Wally Brill, using percussion, trumpet, violin, viola and atmospheric electric guitar. Songs for this are already written, believe it or not, although the exact choice may change if I write a few significant songs in the summer. Expect *Throat, Wire and Wood* to be released early next year.

All the Sound records should be available, three new tracks for *All Fall Down* which were deemed too dark by WEA in 1982! Ha! And also coming shortly, *Propaganda*, an unreleased Sound album from 1997, pre-*Jeopardy*, raw aggressive material.

After that lot I will need a decent new year's party. Any offers? To those that still care, thanks, see you soon. You'll be hearing from me!

Adrian Borland

PS: Sane, as we speak."

I've reproduced the message in full because it gives a fascinating insight into Adrian's mind at a point six weeks' away from leaving this life. Complete with all his self-deprecating wit and boundless enthusiasm. The ideas were coming thick and fast, almost too fast.

When he spoke to Jan back in 1996 he expressed the desire to work more with loops and samples moving beyond the guitar. His wish? Not to end up a "pub circuit singer." There was so much more to do.

The excitement around the new album was palpable, and Pat Rowles was going to be involved again despite parting on slightly awkward terms back in 1997.

Pat, "It was about two years after the tour for *5:00 AM*, late 1998 and Adrian got in touch with me, I hadn't heard from him for quite some time. He said he had a whole bunch of new songs and was going to be in a studio in Clapham doing some recording. It was a studio that I knew and he said, 'Do you want to come in and play some bass for me?' "

Adrian obviously rated Pat and wanted him involved, also he wasn't really one to harbour bad feeling, certainly not when it stood in the way of making a great record,

Pat, "I thought, okay, we didn't part on the best of terms, but life's too short. I'd had some time to think about the way things happened and what the hell, it's going to be fun. So I met up with him. We just put it all behind us and I heard the new songs and played some bass for him."

Adrian was no longer linked to Phil Allen and the ill-fated Earth Records so money was once more an issue,

Pat, "I heard the rest of the songs he was planning for the album and realised he just didn't have the money for the studio time."

Pat took a leap of faith and offered his own cash to finance the recording,

Pat, "I said how much do you need? I had a little bit of money put by that I wasn't doing anything with. When he said it was only a few thousand, I thought, OK, I'll almost certainly make that back. I don't want to be blasé and say 'it's only money,' and it might sound pompous, but I figured the world needed a new Adrian Boland album more than I needed to make sure I had this money."

It speaks volumes about Pat that he was prepared to make this offer and it also says a lot about Adrian and the songs he had waiting to bring to the world.

Coincidentally at the same time Renascent were focussing on the pre-Jeopardy recordings that would be released as *Propaganda*. Working on restoring and mixing the ancient tapes was none other than *Heads and Hearts* producer Wally Brill.

Adrian had contacted Wally,

Wally, "We hadn't spoken in a long time. It was surprising but he called me up and said, 'Look, I want to make a new record. It's a solo record. I want it to be different. I'd like you to produce it.' "

Wally was flattered.

"I was very much of a fan still, so the opportunity was terrific. I had an interest in a studio in London at the time called the Premises, and so we decided to meet up there. I was in San Francisco when he called me so I went over to London."

For Adrian the arrangement worked well, at least at first. The Premises is an impressive studio complex in Hackney. Certainly it was a step up from what Adrian had been used to but came with an increased price tag, still the plan was coming together,

Pat, "I knew that a drummer friend of mine (John Miracle) from the States was going to be over at the same time and loved Adrian's music, so would love to play on the album. It all just seemed to fall into place. So in the meantime, I met up with Adrian and we started doing full track demos of the new songs, and I met Wally Brill with Adrian. Next thing I knew the studio was booked."

Pat was good on his word and paid in advance,

Pat, "I paid half the money upfront and we started the recording process.

As Pat confirms Adrian had a very clear idea of how he wanted the songs to sound, he knew they were strong and wanted to make sure they got it right. Pat was taking a break from work and had the time to travel up to stay with Adrian and Diana in Bedfordshire, where they would record further demos.

Carlo van Putten confirms today that Adrian was very conscious that this record needed to be even better than the already great *5:00 AM,*

"Adrian was determined to make a great record and even as we were recording *700 Miles of Desert* he was planning *Harmony and Destruction* in his head."

The stakes were high, Adrian was also fully aware of the debt of gratitude he owed Pat.

Pat, "He was very appreciative. We went to a party one evening during the recording process and sat down together and he said, 'You know, I really appreciate you doing this for me, I'm not sure how I can thank you enough.' I said, and it sounds a bit of a cliche, but, 'Just make a great album, that's what we're here to do.' "

You can sense how much was resting on what would become *Harmony and Destruction,* clearly Pat could feel that.

Pat, "I said I think these are some of the best songs you've ever written, they deserve to be heard so let's make it worthwhile. it just seemed like the right thing to, there's not a hell of a lot you get a chance to do in this life that really amounts to much and here was a great songwriter, somebody who I think as the longer time goes by will be more recognised, who was just stuck in a place where he couldn't bring his songs to fruition. There needed to be another Adrian Boland album and here we were with the chance to ensure that."

You get a real sense of people putting a lot on the line for this record, in particular Adrian. Remember there was no more stressful time for him than when making a new album, in particular when it came to recording the vocals.

Bob and Win were worried about their son, but that wasn't new for them, they understood that the way he worked wasn't conducive to maintaining his mental health,

Bob, "Well, I was worried, but you couldn't change him. That was Adrian. If he wanted to make an album, he wanted to make an album. Of course I think he probably didn't sleep well because he was spending a lot of his time thinking about the music, you see. Also he was probably drinking more than he should. Of course it would have been very good if Adrian had simply recorded an album by doing it in stages, just recording one or two songs at a time, and building up an album like we did originally with the Outsiders. But he didn't work that way, he wanted to go into a studio and record everything as quickly as possible."

I've no doubt Adrian needed the intensity that resulted from working like he did, but the same intensity had to go somewhere. The result was huge disruption to a state of mind already destabilised by multiple external relationship and financial factors and, crucially, the effect of withdrawing from his medication.

Carlo recalls having to get serious with his friend about the importance of consistently taking his medication, but Adrian felt it hampered his ability to put everything into the music, especially when the need came to sing. So here he was: not sleeping well, skipping his medication and drinking too much alcohol.

Pat, "I have very vivid memories of us, playing songs such as the album's closing track, "Living on the Edge of God," being in that room with Adrian, watching him play, he sounded like a man singing for his life."

It's true, Adrian literally was "singing for his life."

Pat describes the mood well, "It was as if that was what he was put on this planet to do and this was his chance to do it. There he was in a room with a drummer and a bass player who were on his side, supporting him, backing him, and he could be who he really was. It's the best way I can put it."

Wally was excited by the way the sessions were going,

"Adrian was doing his guide vocals, to show the band where they needed to be, they were never intended to be kept. They were simply him pointing out where things were. In some of them he's actually counting bars. You'll hear him go, "One, two, three." But for the most part, his vocals were indicative of what was going to be a great recording. He was playing his guitar at the same time. Again, it sounded great. It sounded like a fantastic three-piece band, just really great, really powerful. It was pretty thrilling."

Pat's job was more or less done,

Pat, "We got the backing tracks, the rhythm tracks, bass, guitar and the drums down in about five days. The time had come for me to return to my real life, my day job. I had a couple of weeks in which to go on a nice holiday somewhere and then start a new IT job. So I said goodbye to everyone, went to Crete with my girlfriend thinking I'd had a fantastic time and that when I came back they'd be pretty much finished. I'll be able to go to the studio, show off my suntan and hear an almost finished album. I was so excited to find out how it was going to turn out."

But this is where things get difficult. Adrian was living back at 2 Hillview and Win and Bob were seeing evidence of his distressed state, including apparent issues relating to Wally.

Bob, "He was getting increasingly agitated and I particularly remember a part of that was apparently being caused by Wally Brill."

We need to be careful as naturally there can be tension between a producer and an artist and in Adrian's mind a degree of paranoia was operating, which was not uncommon, but Bob reports that his son was feeling undermined by Wally,

"Adrian was always complaining about the fact that Wally kept on mocking his songs, referring to "Living on the Edge of God" as "Living on the Edge of *Dog*" or something, and Wally kept on repeating this sort of thing. It was making Adrian quite ill and I was finding him more and more difficult really."

Worryingly Bob confirms,

"After a while, Adrian started to drink during the recordings, which he never did before and then he also stopped taking his medicine. It got to a state where I felt I had to go off on holiday. It was about a week before he committed suicide."

Wally was also seeing concerning behaviour from Adrian,

"He decided he was going to stop taking his meds. I told him he shouldn't do that. I basically said to him, I don't think you're going to have a problem recording the vocals. I think you should go home, rest up, take a week, do whatever you need to do, take a couple of weeks, take whatever you need, rest up, feel good, come back. But don't stop your meds. If you've got a serious mood disorder."

Adrian's general behaviour was talking a worrying turn,

Wally, "He became erratic and he would run out of the studio and go to a really rough pub down the street called the Lion. It was a very rough, right-wing, nationalistic place and here goes Adrian, just being Adrian. He'd go in there and we were worried that he might get into trouble. But he'd go and he'd hammer down the alcohol and come back to the studio half an hour later, having 'power-drunk'. So he comes in and would be talking really, really fast about unrelated things. He'd just say stuff that was unrelated to anything that was going on. I remember one situation where he was in the reception area of the studio and he started shouting out to people trying to start conversations, but really erratically, people he didn't know, just some stranger walking by."

It's quite painful to hear these stories.

Wally and Adrian agreed to take a short breather,

Wally, "So that's the point at which we suggested that he take a break and go home. Keep taking the meds, get back to his level, and we'd pick up later. He may have taken two or three days off over a weekend or something and then we were going to start again. But this was when the tragedy struck."

So *Harmony and Destruction* wasn't finished.

But at this point let's use artistic license to press pause and hold back the inevitable end for just a bit longer, mess with the timeline and instead listen to what Adrian poured his heart and soul, and everything else, into. To do that we need to release pause and select fast forward until a few years have passed.

Adrian performing in De Roemer, Haarlem, one of his last gigs

Wally and Pat had a dilemma: should they attempt to 'finish' Adrian's record?

Adrian had only completed the 'guide vocals' so that was an immediate problem. Ultimately they went ahead and mixed the record, with Pat then finishing it off. The process left both with some regrets.

Wally, "The music was released and I thought it probably should be, but with the disclaimer that this was a work in progress not a completed record. We decided to do the mixes and see what it was like. That was a process that I began. Pat was with me. He had very strong ideas about what this record should sound like. I guess my disagreement with Pat was that if Adrian had wanted him to produce the record, he would have asked him to produce the record."

Pat had doubts about completing the album but in 2001 decided to press ahead,

"There were a lot of quite good guide and backing vocals from the demos to augment the excellent recordings from the Premises sessions."

They ended up using a studio in Clapham and worked with engineer Pete Barraclough. Pete had been guitarist in the fantastic Lucy Show, a band who had shared some similar qualities to the Sound (their *Undone* album is a neglected classic) so a great choice for the task in hand.

Understandably Pat and Wally found the process emotional,

Pat, "The moment Wally started playback of the first song that we were going to mix, he broke down in tears. He'd spent more time working on the album with Adrian than I had and was probably closer to the whole thing. He was really, really upset, as was I, just to suddenly hear that music again. We hugged each other and I remember him saying, 'This is going to be much harder than I thought.' "

Pat later finished the job without Wally who was surprised when the record was finally released,

Wally, "Nobody contacted me back. I finally just bought a copy and I had very strong opinions about it, although they've changed over time. When I first listened to it, I was livid, I was really angry. You mellow with age a little bit."

It's not a huge surprise for such strong emotions to result from the 'finishing' of *Harmony and Destruction* considering the events surrounding it.

Wally's concerns are valid: how could the record ever be what Adrian intended, without him involved? However Pat did what he could in good faith and has allowed us access to one of the best albums of Adrian's career.

As the opening notes of the glorious "Solar" ring out, any debate or disappointment falls away.

When Bowie released *Blackstar* we had three vital days to absorb its genius before he left us. With *Harmony and Destruction* (clearly subtitled: *The Unfinished Journey*, the album was mastered by the late Marcus Bell of the Opposition and released in 2002 by Red Sun Records, a label originally set up by Carlo van Putten but by then owned by Rients Bootsma) we never had that chance. It has always existed in the shadow of Adrian's death with all the weight that unavoidably places on its songs.

We're back with Adrian telling us, as Win highlighted, of needing the sun, "I don't work in the winter" he jokes. The vocals are clearly guide vocals, but this is Adrian Borland. He never did anything in a half-hearted way and so for all the looser feel and imperfections his voice rises about that and gives us even more raw emotion than a polished studio take would have captured. Musically the song oscillates between sinister and exultant, archetypal Adrian. Any doubts vanish and you realise he'd been creating a classic album.

"Angel Sulk" is a great big clanging and grungy guitar churn, here there's an "electronic eye" swapped for a "TV eye," just as you think you have the song pegged it takes a left turn into a shoegaze inflected guitar coda.

By now you've probably already fully accepted that *Harmony and Destruction* had to be released.

The stark and tense "Forever from Here" actually contains a lyric of escape. You can picture Adrian taking a rare walk out in the country and feeling a momentary sense of freedom and gratitude to the person he loves,

"As I lay on the grass
The speed of life began to slow
As the day it drifted past
The sky acquired a luminous glow
Everything that bothered me
Was left so far behind
All my tangled mess of thoughts
Unravelled in my mind
And you can see forever from here
You can see forever
And there's you by my side
We survived those scenes
And with you I feel alright
Won't forget how much that means."

Adrian's spontaneous interjections, *"Come on now!"* just add to the urgency.

There's a complete change for the witty, laconic "Scrapyard." Adrian surveys the city - it looks grim and his mood matches, but this song swings deliciously,

Infectious, self-deprecating and deeply touching all at once, classic Borland, don't miss the hilarious foul-mouthed ad-lib towards the end,

444

"Who's that you ask
But it's yourself in the glass
My how it's changed you
In this scrapyard
You flick your ash
Talk a mountain of trash
And sleep through a car crash
In this scrapyard
Are you sick or well?
It's getting harder to tell
You get immune
To the smell of this scrapyard
So stay clean tonight
Because the cemeteries never close
And any junkie of a fool knows
The city is a scrapyard."

We're back in 'cinematic' territory for the dark and brooding, "Startime." The lyric again troubling after all we've seen,

"Tugging inside me
Insuperable twin
Drags me to places
The sun's never been
Says I must taste everything
By chance or design
He's always demanding
Startime, startime."

The voice inside Adrian calling for attention and validation.

In another world "Summer Wheels" would have been a beautiful single. Stirring, comforting, it's what Adrian did so well. It's hard to listen without breaking inside just a little at the simple Blue Nile-style poetic economy of lyrics like these,

"Days slow to a crawl
All fireworks in the rain
Bear in mind
That the worst is behind you
And feel alive again."

And if you weren't already a mess of emotions there's the fade out,
Adrian whooping and calling out, bringing the song home. If the truly
finished version had omitted that then it would have been a lesser
experience.

Can we say 'brooding' again so soon? Maybe not, but the verses of
"Destiny Stopped Screaming" brood powerfully. A tough song to hear.
The only relief is that soaring chorus. When you take time to listen to
the lyric it's hard not to feel Adrian had reached some sort of
acceptance and from that had taken a decision,

"When the bells are rung for me
And I am done with breathing
Fold my arms in front of me
And whisper
Destiny stopped screaming."

"Get Me a Witness" lifts you up and out of it, subtle and dynamic, also a
reminder of the benefit of having 'real' drums on *Harmony and
Destruction*.

The chorus of "In the Field" strays into *Brittle Heaven's* occasional
folksiness and jars ever so slightly, maybe Adrian would have worked on
that, but it's no disgrace even when you wish Max had been on hand to
add keyboards.

"Heart Goes Down Like the Sun's" acoustic strum leads us into the final
quarter and the sinuously undulating "Land Meets Ocean," with its
further evidence of his mood of resignation,

446

"When I worked out that you weren't coming

And the flood I'd willed would never be."

But things get even darker with "Song Damn Song." Here Adrian provides a summary of what he'd been telling us all along. Writing these songs cost him dearly, performing them even more. On every level he was suffering, but what else could he do?

He even mocks himself and his, "sad little masterpiece," the whole song gets to the root of what he thought was the problem. And who are we to say otherwise?

"What drives these confessions
What kind of reward?
The need to be noticed, condemned or adored
Revealing your feelings and innermost thoughts
In a song damn song
Purity comes with its own complications
Trawling for truths a high risk occupation
You can end up a wreck on prescribed medication
Song damn song
You pour it all out
But it's burning like acid
Scarring the hearts of the ones who once trusted you
Was better off left in that box in your attic
Song damn song
The dark stuff will take on a life of its own
Turn like a monster and tear up your home life
And you'll be to blame for the seed that's been sown
In a song damn song
Your sad little masterpiece hurts you to strum it
It ruins your life
When the world got to hum it
You're forced to repeat it until you become it

Song damn song."

It's rare that an artist skewers every detail of his reason for being with such unflinching and brutal honesty. But then that's the subject of the song itself. Here he was with little to show in terms of recognition, forced to medicate and still out there on stage pouring it all out. It's the full articulation of what Adrian tried to explain to me in his dad's car on the way to our interview that day back in 1991. At the time I didn't fully grasp what he was saying, but now...

"A high risk occupation" indeed.

There's no refuge on the explicit "Last Train out Shatterville," a song that references past suicide attempts but treads a line between escape and finality. There are at least two readings of the lyric, one of hope and escape the other a conversation between Adrian and the darkness within him, culminating in that last act.

Softly strummed guitar and resonant bass from Pat frame a lyric so desolate it hurts every time,

"But I saw you on the street last dawn
As you slid from kerb to bonnet
When that train pulls out
In the cold morning light
Just be on it."

Harmony and Destruction has a harrowing high to hit before it goes, as well as a sly surprise.

"Living on the Edge of God" stopped me in my tracks the first time I heard it. Adrian sounds hoarse and desperate, as if now all bets are off and he's passed through some barrier of experience that leaves no way back,

"Oh a crazy voice

That cracks the machine
It's turned down in you
It's so loud in me
I'm like a broken radio
I've been just drifting in and out of sense."
Here he was acknowledging there was something in him that was
somehow defective and that very defect was destroying him. There's
still the wit and the poetry but he sounds broken. I'm not sure he was
"singing for his life" anymore, he'd gone beyond that. Art and life:
inseparable.

A wild, almost out of control end to an extraordinary and troubled
record. It sounds like they were conjuring spirits in that room, spirits
that Adrian couldn't put back in the box.

The music pulls back for a moment to reveal Adrian's acoustic guitar
and his lighter croon, but it's momentary, he cries out, thrashes at his
guitar and we're beyond transcendence, wondering whether we have a
right to hear this kind of honesty of emotion?

Then some hidden relief, although it's still close to the bone.

There's a secret track, not listed on the cover, "Death of a Star." A song
about our reaction to the death of a public figure, it's a wonderful
garage rock drive through the strange relationship between fans and
their idols. No doubt Adrian questioning what his own reactions would
be to losing the Iggy's and the Lou's of his world. It's a genius move and
gives us an easier but still poignant way out from a difficult, draining
album,

"Do you sit in the dark
Play that song and watch that film
Shrug and say, 'Life goes on'
Or do you wonder how it will
How do you feel

When a star dies?"
Adrian was a star and now we know how it feels.
We can't pause any longer: it's time to face reality.

CHAPTER 22

Try to find my place, sometimes I get so near, I journey aimless days, but always end up here...

Things got desperate over the weekend of the 24th April 1999.

Adrian left the Premises and headed home to 2 Hillview. Bob wasn't there, he'd taken a flight to Torremolinos to get a break from the pressure, leaving Win alone with Adrian.

On Sunday there was an unexpected development, as Bob explains,

"On Sunday 25th April there was trouble in the studio because they wanted to be paid a measly fee in the amount of £2,000, I think otherwise Adrian wasn't going to be welcome the next day."

It seems shocking now to think of this additional factor coming into play, picture Adrian potentially being prevented from completing his work after everything he'd been through.

It's important to note that Wally Brill disputes this account,

Wally, "I know that on the Friday I certainly expected we were going to be going in on Monday and resuming work. It's not consistent with what I remember. Adrian may have called Carlo, but I don't think there was any barrier to him working on in the next week or two."

Carlo confirms that Adrian called to try to see whether there was any way of raising the money urgently. Bear in mind the difficulty in arranging the transfer of money across borders in the pre-internet era.

Pat's memory is understandably a little hazy but he describes what he believes happened,

"I remember Adrian had an agreement he would do the recordings with only half of the money being paid initially, and then they broke that agreement and demanded the whole lot straightaway before he would continue. That of course upset Adrian. I seem to recall him making some desperate attempts to get additional finance. For example, I think from Carlos' friend Christian, I don't know what happened about it."

Carlo will never forget the call he received and Adrian's strange serenity,

Carlo, "I had him on the phone the night before he committed suicide. He sounded like an angel. I said, 'Hello Adrian, how's life?' He said, 'Carlo everything's great to be honest'. I asked how things were with Diana? Well he said, 'We just had a great conversation this weekend and we decided not to go on with the relationship. She can't deal with me as a person.' He told me the whole story."

Above all he remembers that Adrian sounded disconcertingly calm,

Carlo, "Adrian said, 'I need to go back into the studio tomorrow but I need some money.' According to Adrian the studio had allegedly said, 'You aren't recording tomorrow if that money isn't in our account.' "

Whatever happened it seems likely there was a monetary issue of some sort. After Adrian's death the remaining fees were waived.

Later that night Adrian went out and met up with some friends.

Bob, "Win told me that Adrian had been with Peter Williams and possibly some other people in a pub called the Cavern in Raynes Park, and that Pete told Win Adrian had been behaving oddly."

Win decided to report her son to the police as a missing person, which may seem drastic but she was probably unsure of what to do and was clearly very concerned.

Bob, "She'd reported him as missing, and later that night, or possibly early in the morning, Adrian had rung from this Indian restaurant to tell her that's where he was. I think she must have rung the Kennington police station or something and I forget the exact sequence, but at some point Adrian was in Kennington police station and Win was trying to persuade them to get a doctor in to examine him and they refused to do so."

The events of the night take on an almost farcical form,

Bob, "They arranged for him to get to Wimbledon police station and Win tried once more to persuade the duty officer to call a doctor and again he refused. She tried several times and eventually he arranged for Adrian to be sent home at about 3:30 in the morning. Adrian came home and went to bed after a discussion with Win. He then got up fairly early, probably about 6:00 and of course went to Wimbledon railway station. And then, you know what happened."

Bob believed Adrian also had one last telephone conversation with Diana early that morning before he left 2 Hillview for the final time.

Speaking to Win after Adrian's death she remembered him that weekend saying, 'There's always the railway...' "

Adrian had taken the final decision - he needed to leave.

Carlo, "I think he knew what he was going to do. When he asked for the money he said he really felt shit about it. I said it's no problem but I think everything came together at that point. His voice was beautiful, but the decision had been made. I think he was happy about doing it. I asked again, 'Is everything alright Adrian?' And he said to me, 'Thank you for everything.' I said otherwise I'll book you a ticket and you can come over. He said, 'No, I need to get back in the studio tomorrow.' I said that's not important, you need a break. He repeated that he was OK. We had an agreement that neither of us would do it (commit suicide) and I said to him, 'You know I'm always one step behind you don't you?' And he said, 'Yes, but I've got to go.' It took me years to work through it in my mind."

Adrian made his way to Wimbledon station, walking along a peaceful Hilliview and catching an early bus. He entered the main station concourse and negotiated the steps down to the various platforms. Arriving just before 6:30 AM, he was seen by a witness, and on CCTV, sitting on a bench with his head in his hands, then standing up and walking briskly towards the tracks as a train approached. The same witness confirmed he was purposeful and clearly didn't intend to stop.

The driver could do nothing, he saw Adrian jump, "in one movement," in front of his train. There was no chance of survival.

The various family, friends, acquaintances and band members started to receive the terrible news; by a horrible quirk some were actually on the London rail network at the time and heard the announcements that there'd been 'an incident.'

Those who were due to work with him that day were obviously shocked and traumatised by what had happened,

Wally, "My partner at the studio, Viv, came to the door just as I'm walking in and said, 'I've got to talk to you.' I went into the office with him and he said he'd just heard that Adrian had committed suicide. It was absolutely devastating. I couldn't process the information."

Pat had just returned from his post-recording holiday in Crete,

Pat, "On my return, a good friend met me at the airport and gave us a lift home. He broke the news to me that Adrian had taken his own life during the time I was out of the country. It was devastating, one of the worst moments of my life. I just had no inkling at all, it was totally out of the blue and so unexpected."

Bob received confirmation at the hotel in Spain and returned to Wimbledon as quickly as possible. For him and Win, the worst had finally happened.

Adrian's funeral took place and, as described by Pat, showed how many people loved him,

Pat, "There must have been two or three hundred people there. People came from far and wide. Mark Burgess of the Chameleons was there, all family and friends, people from throughout Adrian's history and career and from his childhood."

The experience for Win and Bob must have been beyond shattering. How do you even begin to recover from something like that? In the following few years Win in particular struggled to come to terms with what happened and died relatively young.

Adrian Janes kept in touch, seeing the aftermath and its ramifications for Win,

"I occasionally saw or spoke to Win after Adrian's death. It was something she never got over and on these occasions much of what she had to say were deeply sad reflections on his last few days. It was obvious that his suicide was a continuing torment to her and I'm sure this strain was a major reason for her own death a few years later."

Speaking in the *Book of (Happy) Memories* Win was movingly clear about the effect on her and Bob,

"Bob and I always thought he would never grow old, but we hoped he would accept his illness and take the necessary steps. Unfortunately it didn't turn out that way. His suicide came as a real shock to us. I wish we could have had more time together."

Life felt dull without him but Win confirms that she wondered whether she ever really knew Adrian, as she says, "he had such a complex personality, we feel privileged to have known him."

Years before at Springfield Hospital one of the doctors had apparently told Win and Bob that one day Adrian would succeed in taking his own life. It feels almost callous for someone to say such a thing, but it was ultimately true. Could better treatment and a more sympathetic, tailored medication regime have saved Adrian? Possibly but we can never be sure.

The 7th November 2016 edition of the *New York Times* ran a feature looking at some of the facts behind the act of suicide,

"A common yet highly inaccurate belief is that people who survive a suicide attempt are unlikely to try again. In fact, just the opposite is true. Within the first three months to a year following a suicide attempt, people are at highest risk of a second attempt, and this time perhaps succeeding. A recent analysis of studies that examined successful suicides among those who made prior attempts, found that one person in 25 had a fatal repeat attempt within five years."

Adrian's multi-step path to the end certainly supports that analysis.

Obviously I always knew we'd reach this point in Adrian's story, but that doesn't make it any easier to deal with. There's a part of you that wants to run down those steps and onto that platform, just like in the films, to grab him and pull him away from the brink, give him a hug and tell him a million reasons why he should stay, not go. But that's not how real life works is it?

At times it feels as if the characters in Adrian's life are bystanders to his unfolding tragedy. But maybe that applies to most, if not all, lives. The legitimate control and direction we can exercise on another's existence is always limited by a multitude of sometimes competing factors. A simple overwhelming feeling of powerlessness being high on the list. In many ways I suspect Adrian had always felt alone, even when his life was full of people and activity. But when it wasn't, then that's when the fear really grew.

On that cool early April morning he was as alone as he'd ever been but moved with clarity and purpose. The decision had been made. The option had always been there on the shelf ever since that night back in 1980 when Julie had the sense Adrian was processing the suicide of Ian Curtis and noting the availability of that final route out of this life, should it all become too much. Those earlier efforts may or may not have been fully committed, worked-out, suicide attempts, but this time there would be little chance of failure.

That the decision was so terrible for him and all concerned, from family and friends to the driver of the train and his family, is indisputable.

The way we live our lives is a strange mix of the logical and illogical. Influenced by random chance and cruel reality, Adrian never really accepted a 'normal,' allegedly mature existence. Why? Perhaps a mix of fear, disinterest, immaturity and sheer obstinacy. In many ways an entirely sane response to a crazy world that would probably have broken him anyway if he'd decided, or been able, to conform.

His life was soon on a course that, while it wasn't set in stone, nevertheless had a tragic inevitability to it. A mix of existential torment and frustrated ambitions combined with a deep and profound mental illness meant the likely end would take a lot to alter or avoid. Even if the second of those triggers had been resolved the outcome would very possibly have been similar.

Some say his illness "killed him" but I'm not sure that's correct. A life that didn't look the way he wished it looked killed Adrian, partly because his illness made it difficult for him to deal with the reality of his situation. It was a complex web of interrelated factors coming together to deadly effect. Over and over again Adrian was met by a life that felt cruel and unfair. There's only so much of that you can take.

And yet he achieved so much, from his music, to being a person who gave energy and love to others even if at the same time being able to infuriate and frustrate. We are all complicated beings and Adrian certainly demonstrated that complexity to a dramatically high degree, but behind the laughter and enthusiasm he was feeling it all too much and gradually his internal narrative mapped out a solution that was as logical as it was chilling.

Despite all of that, every last bit of joy and pain was fed into those songs. That complexity manifesting itself in a narrative of hope, balanced with a bittersweet understanding of the sadness within everyone's life. Maybe it was a malfunction in Adrian's brain that meant he was incapable of giving us anything less than the real deal. If so, what a glorious malfunction it was. The cost was absolute, but he knew the songs would last, left there for those who need them.

And that's the reason we're still here, listening and loving the music, feeling that tingle down the spine and forever wanting to truly know: who was Adrian Borland?

Adrian's room door

EPILOGUE

Chemical Brothers fever dream...

17th March 2023

I had a dream that Chemical Brothers sampled Adrian Borland's vocals from a Second Layer track, but the thing is, it wasn't a dream.

Back in Jan's 1996 interview he raises the subject of layering guitars with dance beats and incredibly Chemical Brothers are mentioned. Who could possibly have guessed that 27 years later things would have come some kind of strange full circle.

There's Adrian at the heart of a pulsing dance track, singing,

"We have no reason to live
We have no reason at all
We have no reason to live
When will they kill us all?"

Of all his lyrics there's an irony they picked these lines.

1.7 million YouTube views and counting.

It's funny to think that Adrian had been planning a project where he eschewed guitars and worked with loops, samples and electronics.

But all of that is nothing compared to the 6.3 million views for the Sound's "I Can't Escape Myself," (with the song also featuring in TV and films, including Sky's *Young Pope*) while "Winning" stands at a modest 1.4 million, with many other tracks in the hundreds of thousands.

Perhaps we shouldn't be that surprised after all we've learned of Adrian and his music, there are countless stories of people of all ages discovering his work many years after the fact.

Since his death we've had an excellent documentary, *Walking in the Opposite Direction*, as well as numerous reissues from the Sound alongside Jean-Paul van Mierlo's carefully remastered and expanded issues of Adrian's solo work on CD and vinyl.

Looking at those viewing figures, what would Adrian be thinking?

Well, it would probably have momentarily blown his mind. But then he'd likely laugh, nod his head and say, "Quite right! About time, but wait until they hear what I'm working on next…"

THE AUTHOR

Simon Heavisides was born in Sunderland in the northeast of England and grew up on the outskirts of Bristol. It was in his teenage bedroom that he first heard the Sound after taking a chance on *Shock of Daylight*. During a period of boredom in 1991 he decided to start a fanzine, *Blood Rush,* the first interviewee? I'm sure you can guess. A lifetime of writing about music, and in the distant past making it, followed, all leading up to the welcome opportunity to tell the story of Adrian Borland and his complex life.

DISCOGRAPHY

Adrian Borland

- Alexandria (1989), PIAS (Adrian Borland + The Citizens)
- Beneath the Big Wheel (1989), PIAS (Adrian Borland + The Citizens), 7" single
- Light the Sky (1989), PIAS (Adrian Borland + The Citizens), 7" single
- Brittle Heaven (1992), PIAS (Adrian Borland + The Citizens)
- All the Words (1992), PIAS (Adrian Borland + The Citizens), CD single
- Beautiful Ammunition (1994), Resolve
- Cinematic (1995), Resolve
- Over the Under (1997), Earth, CD single
- 5:00 AM (1997), Earth
- The Last Days of the Rain Machine (2000), Red Sun (posthumous)
- Harmony & Destruction (2002), Red Sun (posthumous)
- The Amsterdam Tapes (2006), Pop One (posthumous)
- Beautiful Ammunition (2017), SOD/SHLV (remastered, incl. 4 previously unreleased tracks)
- Lovefield (2019), SOD/SHLV (10 previously unreleased tracks)
- Cinematic (2020), SOD/SHLV (remastered, incl. 4 previously unreleased tracks)
- Lovefield - Neon and Stone (2021), SOD/SHLV (12 previously unreleased tracks)
- 2 Meter Sessions (2022) SOD/SHLV
- 5:00AM (2022), SOD/SHLV (remastered, incl. 2 previously unreleased tracks)
- The Scales Of Love And Hate (2022), SOD/SHLV (new mixes and masters from The Last Days of the Rain Machine, incl 4 previously unreleased tracks)
- The Amsterdam Tapes (2023), SOD/SHLV (remastered, incl. 4 previously unreleased tracks)
- Alexandria (2024), SOD/SHLV (remastered)

The Sound

- Physical World EP (1979), Tortch, 7" EP (reissued 2021, Reminder)
- Jeopardy (1980), Korova (reissued 2001, Renascent)
- Heyday (1980), Korova, 7" single
- Live Instinct (1981), WEA Records BV, 12" live-EP
- From the Lions Mouth (1981), Korova (reissued 2001, Renascent)
- Sense of Purpose (1981), Korova 7"/12" single
- Hot House (1982), Korova, 7" Single
- All Fall Down (1982), WEA Records (reissued 2001, Renascent)
- Party of the Mind (1982), WEA Records, 7" single
- Mining for Heart (1983), (part of flexi disc Vinyl Magazine #23)
- Counting the Days (1984), Statik, 7" single
- Golden Soldiers (1984), Victoria, 7" single
- Shock of Daylight (1984), Statik, EP
- Heads and Hearts (1985), Statik (reissued 1996 with Shock of Daylight, Renascent)
- Temperature Drop (1985), Statik, 7" EP
- Under You (1985), Statik, 7" EP
- In the Hothouse (1985), Statik (reissued 1996, Renascent)
- Counting the Days (1986), Statik, 7" single
- Thunder Up (1987), PIAS
- Hand of Love (1987), PIAS, 7" single
- Iron Years (1987), PIAS 7"/12" single
- Propaganda (1999), Renascent (reissued 2015, Demon Records)
- The BBC Recordings (2004), Renascent
- The Dutch Radio Recordings, vol 1–5 (2006), Renascent, 5 separate CDs
- Will And Testament/Starlight (2021), SOD/SHLV (incl. 4 previously unreleased tracks)

The Sound compilations

- Vital Years (1993), Gift of Life
- Cinematic Overview (promotional-only) (1995), Setanta

- Jeopardy, From The Lion's Mouth, All Fall Down ...Plus (2014) Edsel Records, 4 CD
- Shock Of Daylight, Heads And Hearts, In The Hot House, Thunder Up, Propaganda (2015), Edsel Records, 5 CD
- Counting the Days (2022), Demon Records
- New Way Of Life, (2023), Demon Records
- The Statik Years, (2023), Edsel Records, 5 CD

The Crazies

- A Simple Vision (2021), Optic Nerve Recordings

The Outsiders

- Calling on Youth (1977), Raw Edge
- One to Infinity (1977), Raw Edge, 7" EP
- Close Up (1978), Raw Edge
- Count for Something (2021) Cherry Red, Albums, Demos, Live, Unreleased 1976-1978)

Witch Trials

- The Witch Trials (1981), Subterranean Records

Second Layer

- Flesh as Property EP (1979), Tortch, 7" EP
- State of Emergency EP (1980), Tortch, 7" EP
- World of Rubber (1981), Cherry Red
- Second Layer (1987), LD Records
- Courts of War (2023), 1972 (Compilation)

Honolulu Mountain Daffodils

- Guitars of the Oceanic Undergrowth (1987), Hybrid Records
- Tequila Dementia (1988), Zinger Records
- Also Sprächt Scott Thurston (1988), Mission Discs 12" single
- Aloha Sayonara (1991) Mission Discs
- Psychic Hit-List Victims (1991), Area International, 12" EP

- Guitars of the Oceanic Undergrowth/Tequila Dementia (1992), Mission Discs

White Rose Transmission

- White Rose Transmission (1995), Strange Music
- 700 Miles of Desert (1999), Fuego

THE GIGS

Syndrome 1974 -1976

1974
?? 1974 - Urangi Club - Southfields (Second on bill with Vulture and Threnody)

1975
05-04-1975 - St. Matthew's Church Hall - SW20 (Supported by Nekrosis)
17-06-1975 - Raynes Park High School (Supporting 70% Proof and Blooze)
05-07-1975 - House concert at Hillview
05-09-1975 - Brycbox, New Malden
24-10-1975 - Elmfield, Tiffin Boys School
08-11-1975 - Banstead Church Hall
18-12-1975 - Bond Memorial Hall (Supporting Renegade)

1976
08-03-1976 - School Hall, Tiffin Boys School (Supported by teachers' band)
16-07-1976 - Small Hall, Surbiton Assembly Rooms
05-11-1976 - Small Hall, Surbiton Assembly Rooms

The Outsiders 1976 -1979

1976
21-12-1976 - Roxy Club, Covent Garden (Supporting Generation X)

1977
27-01-1977 - Roxy Club, Covent Garden (Supporting The Vibrators)
28-01-1977 - Canbury Park, Kingston Polytechnic (Supporting The Vibrators)
08-02-1977 - Winning Post, Twickenham (Supporting Saboteur)

18-02-1977 - Small Hall, Surbiton Assembly Rooms

24-02-1977 - Roxy Club, Covent Garden (Supporting The Jam)

19-04-1977 - Nashville Rooms, West Kensington (Supporting The Jam)

27-04-1977 - Hope and Anchor, Islington (Supporting The Fanatics)

02-06-1977 - Marquee, London (Supporting Doctors of Madness)

18-06-1977 - Small Hall, Surbiton Assembly Rooms (Supported by Ryde)

08-07-1977 - Wimbledon Village Hall (Supported by Greg Hill)

16-08-1977 - Vortex, London (Bottom of bill below Adverts, Steel Pulse and Masterswitch)

18-08-1977 - Roxy Club, Covent Garden, (Supporting London))

21-08-1977 - Marquee, London (Supporting Eddie and the Hot Rods)

05-09-1977 - Vortex, London (Second on bill with Siouxsie and the Banshees, Suspects and Verdicts)

14-09-1977 - Speakeasy, London (First gig secured by Jock Macdonald as manager)

23-09-1977 - Vortex café

29-09-1977 - Roxy Club, Covent Garden (Supporting Radiators From Space) (NB) This was the gig where Iggy Pop joined onstage to sing 'Raw Power'

20-10-1977* - Acklam Hall, London. Stiff/Chiswick 'talent contest'

21-10-1977* - Rainbow, Finsbury Park (upstairs) (With Suspects, The Meat and Youthenasia)

22-10-1977* - Man in the Moon, Chelsea (Supported by The Goats)

27-10-1977* - Roxy Club, Covent Garden (Headliners; supported by Martin and the Brownshirts and Nipple Erect Erectors)

29-10-1977* - Man in the Moon, Chelsea (NB) * are those where Bruce Douglas briefly joined the band as a second guitarist, at the suggestion of Jock Macdonald (who briefly managed the band)

05-11-1977 - Man in the Moon, Chelsea (Supported by Youthenasia and The Goats)

11-11-1977 - Royal College of Art (Supporting Bazooka Joe)

12-11-1977 - Fulham Greyhound (Supported by Youthenasia)

15-11-1977 - 100 Club, London (Supporting The Count Bishops)

16-11--1977 - Leicester Polytechic (One of five bands, including Youthenasia)
17-11-1977 - Roxy Club, Covent Garden (Supported by Automatics and The Goats)
19-11-1977 - Man in the Moon, Chelsea (Supporting The Goats)
03-12-1977 - Passfield Hall, London School of Economics
09-12- 1977 - Royal College of Art (Supporting Verden Allen's 7")

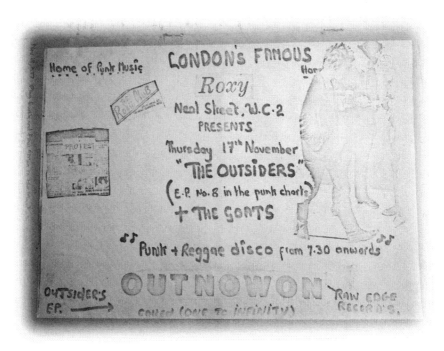

1978
13-01-1978 - City University (Supporting Verden Allen's 7")
08-02-1978 - Three Tuns Bar, LSE (Supporting The Visitors)
07-04-1978 - Kaleidoscope Club, Kingston
05-05-1978 - Kaleidoscope Club, Kingston
20-05-1978 - Squat party, probably Kingston area
02-06-1978 - Kaleidoscope Club, Kingston (Supporting Here and Now)
13-07-1978 - Ebbesham Hall, Epsom
18-11-1978 - Passfield Hall, LSE. (NB) Graham Bailey's live debut; also

first time Bi Marsh guested towards end of the set,
30-11-1978 - Livingstone House, North-East London Polytechnitechnic

1979
02-02-1979 - Kingston College of Further Education
03-02-1979 - Tolworth Recreation Centre (birthday party)
05-02-1979 - Corn Dolly, Oxford
14-02-1979 - The Stapleton, Finsbury Park
12-03-1979 - 101 Club, Clapham
24-03-1979 - The Stapleton, Finsbury Park
26-03-1979 - Music Machine, Camden (Supporting UK Subs)
29-03-1979 - Kings College School, Wimbledon
30-03-1979 - AJ's, Lincoln (Supporting UK Subs)
02-04-1979 - Grove Tavern, Kingston
06-04-1979 - Cardiff University
20-04-1979 - Wallington Public Hall

The Sound 1979-1987

1979
26-12-1979 - London - Fulham Greyhound (UK)

1980
03-01-1980 - London - Clapham 101 Club (UK)
14-01-1980 - London - Fulham Greyhound (UK)
26-01-1980 - Stratford Upon Avon - Green Dragon (UK)
21-08-1980 - Richmond - The Castle (+ Tenpole Tudor) (UK)
04-09-1980 - Birmingham - Golden Eagle (UK)
11-09-1980 - Glenrothes - Rothes Armes (UK)
12-09-1980 - Kinghorn - Cunzie Park (UK)
13-09-1980 - Kinghorn - Cunzie Park (UK)
14-09-1980 - Edinburgh - Harveys (UK)
15-09-1980 - Grangemouth - International (UK)
18-09-1980 - Kirkaldy - Dutch Mill (UK)

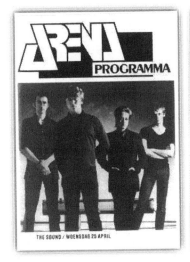 

19-09-1980 - Falkirk - Magpie (UK)

20-09-1980 - Edinburgh - Eric Browns (UK)

21-09-1980 - Cowdenbeath - Commercial (UK)

24-09-1980 - London - Moonlight Club (UK)

26-09-1980 - London - Old Queens Head (UK)

28-09-1980 - Brighton - Jenkinsons (+ Echo & The Bunnymen) (UK)

29-09-1980 - Bournemouth - Stateside Centre (+ Echo & The Bunnymen) (UK)

30-09-1980 - Bristol - The Berkeley (+ Echo & The Bunnymen) (UK)

01-10-1980 - Exeter - University (+ Echo & The Bunnymen) (UK)

02-10-1980 - Port Talbot - Troubadour (+ Echo & The Bunnymen) (UK)

03-10-1980 - Birmingham - Cedar Ballroom (+ Echo & The Bunnymen) (UK)

04-10-1980 - Manchester - University (+ Echo & The Bunnymen) (UK)

05-10-1980 - Leeds - F.Club (+ Echo & The Bunnymen) (UK)

06-10-1980 - Derby - Romeo & Juliets (+ Echo & The Bunnymen) (UK)

07-10-1980 - Colchester - Essex University (+ Echo & The Bunnymen) (UK)

08-10-1980 - Norwich - Uea (+ Echo & The Bunnymen) (UK)

09-10-1980 - Sheffield - Limit (+ Echo & The Bunnymen) (UK)

10-10-1980 - Scarborough - Penthouse (+ Echo & The Bunnymen) (UK)

11-10-1980 - Stirling - University (+ Echo & The Bunnymen) (UK)

12-10-1980 - Edinburgh - Valentinos (+ Echo & The Bunnymen) (UK)

14-10-1980 - Coventry - Poly (+ Echo & The Bunnymen) (UK)

15-10-1980 - St.Albans - City Hall (+ Echo & The Bunnymen) (UK)

17-10-1980 - Liverpool - University (+ Echo & The Bunnymen) (UK)

21-10-1980 - London - Richmond's Castle (UK)

24-10-1980 - London - Moonlight Club (+ Tuxedo Moon & Device) (UK)

28-10-1980 - London - Rock Garden (UK)

31-10-1980 - London - 101 Club (UK)

21-11-1980 - London - Half Moon Herne Hill (UK)

1981

01-01-1981 - London - ICA (UK)

09-01-1981 - London - Moonlight Club (+ The Denizens) (UK)

14-01-1981 - London - The Venue (UK)

16-01-1981 - Lampeter - University (UK)

20-01-1981 - Oxford - 100 Club (+ The Venigmas) (UK)

30-01-1981 - London - University (+ Associates/Repetition/23Skidoo) (UK)

13-02-1981 - London - University (UK)

26-02-1981 - Paris - Pavillion Baltard (Fr)

27-02-1981 - London - Venue (+ The Berlin Blondes) (UK)

05-03-1981 - Groningen - Vera (Nl)

06-03-1981 - Eindhoven - Effenaar (Nl)

07-03-1981 - Rotterdam - Exit Club (Nl)

08-03-1981 - Amsterdam - Paradiso (Nl)

14-03-1981 - London - Moonlight Club (+ The Lines) (UK)

15-03-1981 - Lille - Palais Saint-Sauveur (Fr)

16-03-1981 - Rouen - Studio 44 (Fr)

02-04-1981 - London - The Venue (+ Medium Medium & Felt) (UK)

18-04-1981 - Retford - Porterhouse (UK)

19-04-1981 - Caister - Silver Sands (+ Robyn Hitchcock & Flesh Habit) (UK)

01-05-1981 - Manchester - Rafters (UK)

08-05-1981 - London - Kingston Polytechnic (UK)

09-05-1981 - London - School Of Economics (+ Black State) (UK)

16-05-1981 - Coventry - Warwick University (UK)

28-05-1981 - London - African Centre (UK)

30-05-1981 - Warwick - University (UK)

15-06-1981 - London - Heaven (+ Out On/ Blue Six/ Eyeless In Gaza) (UK)

16-06-1981 - Cambridge - Jesus College (UK)

20-06-1981 - Glastonbury - Fayre (UK)

15-08-1981 - Nijmegen - Openlucht Theater (NI)

16-08-1981 - Rotterdam - New Pop Festival (NI)

21-08-1981 - Wageningen - De Junushof (NI)

22-08-1981 - Amsterdam - Paradiso (NI)

23-08-1981 - Groningen - Sterrenbos Festival (NI)

05-09-1981 - Stafford - New Bingley Hall Futurama 3 (UK)

18-09-1981 - Edinburgh - Niteclub (+ Comsat Angels) (UK)

19-09-1981 - Aberdeen - Victoria Hotel (+ Comsat Angels) (UK)

20-09-1981 - Kirklevington - Country Club (+ Comsat Angels) (UK)

22-09-1981 - Manchester - Polytechnic (+ Comsat Angels) (UK)

23-09-1981 - York - T.A Centre (+ Comsat Angels) (UK)

24-09-1981 - Leeds - Warehouse (+ Comsat Angels) (UK)

26-09-1981 - Birmingham - Cedar Ballroom (+ Comsat Angels) (UK)

27-09-1981 - Bath - Tiffanies (+ Comsat Angels) (UK)

16-10-1981 - Leuven - Flanders Festival (Be)

26-10-1981 - Cheltenham - Eve's (UK)

27-10-1981 - Canterbury - Kent University (UK)

28-10-1981 - Brighton - Polytechnic (UK)

29-10-1981 - Coventry - General Wolfe (UK)

30-10-1981 - London - University (+ Everest The Hard Way & Eyeless In Gaza) (UK)

31-10-1981 - Norwich - East Anglia University (UK)

01-11-1981 - Sheffield - Limit Club (UK)

05-11-1981 - Chesham - Elviga Hall (UK)

18-11-1981 - Apeldoorn - Gigant (Nl)

19-11-1981 - Groningen - Huize Maas (Nl)

20-11-1981 - Den Haag - Paard Van Troje (Nl)

21-11-1981 - Hiversum- Tagrijn (Nl)

22-11-1981 - Amsterdam - Paradiso (Nl)

26-11-1981 - Madrid - Rock-Ola (Sp)

27-11-1981 - Madrid - Rock-Ola (Sp)

30-11-1981 - Milan - 2001 (It)

1982

21-01-1982 - London - The Venue (+ King Trigger & Cosmetics) (UK)

29-01-1982 - Delft - Staminee (Nl)

30-01-1982 - Arnhem - Stokvishal (Nl)

31-01-1982 - Sittard - Don Kiesjot (Nl)

01-02-1982 - Enschede - Technische Hoge School (Nl)

02-02-1982 - Amsterdam - Paradiso (Nl)

19-02-1982 - Herenthout - Lux (Be)

20-02-1982 - Lommel - Zendpiraat (Be)

21-02-1982 - Rochefort - Salle Des Roches (Be)

22-02-1982 - Bornem - Volksbelang (Be)

24-02-1982 - Brussels - Ancienne Belgique (Be)

25-02-1982 - Kuurne - On The Beach (Be)

26-02-1982 - Zedelgem - Groene Meerschen (Be)

08-03-1982 - Loughborough - Art College (UK)

31-03-1982 - Oslo - Club 7 (No)

01-04-1982 - Stockholm - Kamera Paltzet (Sw)

02-04-1982 - Götheborg - Student Kaaren (Sw)

03-04-1982 - Copenhagen - Music Cafe (Dk)

04-04-1982 - Hamburg - Onkel Poe's (Ge)

08-04-1982 - Amsterdam - Paradiso (Nl)

09-04-1982 - Utrecht - Irenehal (Nl)

12-04-1982 - London - Hammersmith Palais (+ China Crisis & Thompson Twins) (UK)

18-04-1982 - Dusseldorf - Philipshalle (Ge)

19-04-1982 - Aachen - Eurogress (Ge)

20-04-1982 - Bochum - Zeche (Ge)

21-04-1982 - Köln - Sartory (Ge)

22-04-1982 - Neu-Isenburg - Hugenotenhalle (Ge)

23-04-1982 - Mannheim - Kulturhaus (Ge)

24-04-1982 - Appenweier - Schwarzwalthalle (Ge)

25-04-1982 - Munich - Alabama Halle (Ge)

27-04-1982 - Darmstadt - Lopo's Werkstadt (Ge)

28-04-1982 - Wurzburg - Musichall (Ge)

29-04-1982 - Kaiserslautern - Flash (Ge)

30-04-1982 - Luxembourg - Polyvalent 7000 (Lux)

02-05-1982 - Münster - Münsterlandhalle (Ge)

03-05-1982 - Bremen - Aladin (Ge)

04-05-1982 - Hannover - Rotation (Ge)

05-05-1982 - Berlin - Metropol (Ge)

06-05-1982 - Kiel - Ball Pompos (Ge)

08-05-1982 - Hamburg - Stadtpark (Ge)

23-05-1982 - Bath - Tiffanies (Ge)

11-06-1982 - London - Zigzag Club (+ The Alarm) (UK)

13-07-1982 - Zutphen - Tent (Nl)

17-07-1982 - Apeldoorn - Gigant (Nl)

18-07-1982 - Groningen - Vera (Nl)

19-07-1982 - Utrecht - Nv Huis (Nl)

22-07-1982 - Amsterdam - Paradiso (Nl)

23-07-1982 - Den Haag - Openlucht Theater (Nl)

24-07-1982 - Arnhem - Stokvishal (Nl)

05-08-1982 - Lokeren - Lokerse Feesten (Be)

06-08-1982 - Brussels - Mallemunt (Be)

07-08-1982 - Zonhoven - Alcatraz Festival (Be)

08-08-1982 - Venlo - Julian Park (Nl)

13-08-1982 - Blankenberghe - Blankenpop Festival (Be)

14-08-1982 - Adinkerke - Seaside Festival (Be)

17-10-1982 - London - Lyceum (UK)

07-11-1982 - Leicester - Poly (UK)

09-11-1982 - London - The Venue (UK)

10-11-1982 - Leeds - Warehouse (UK)

11-11-1982 - Sheffield - Limit Club (UK)

12-11-1982 - Birmingham - Poly (UK)

13-11-1982 - Bristol - Poly (UK)

02-12-1982 - Coventry - General Wolfe (UK)

03-12-1982 - London - Camberwell Art (UK)

10-12-1982 - Madrid - Rock-Ola (Sp)

11-12-1982 - Madrid - Rock-Ola (Sp)

1983

20-01-1983 - Utrecht - Tivoli (Nl)

21-01-1983 - Rotterdam - Arena (Nl)

22-01-1983 - Amsterdam - Paradiso (Nl)

23-01-1983 - Groningen - Oosterpoort (Nl)

24-01-1983 - Arnhem - Stokvishal (Nl)

25-01-1983 - Maastricht - Staargebouw (Nl)

26-01-1983 - Leuven - Lido (Be)

27-01-1983 - Ghent - Vooruit (Be)

28-01-1983 - Zedelgem - Groene Meersen (Be)

29-01-1983 - Brussel - Plan K (Be)

30-01-1983 - Antwerpen - Hof Ter Lo (Be)

31-01-1983 - Bocholt - Marian (Ge)

05-02-1983 - London - Kingston Poly (UK)

11-02-1983 - Lyon - West Side (Fr)

12-02-1983 - Lyon - West Side (Fr)

14-02-1983 - Bologna -Teatro Disco Puntacapo (It)

15-02-1983 - Milan - Teatro Orfeo (It)

16-02-1983 - Nove Vicenza - Palestra (It)

17-02-1983 - Firenze - Manila (It)

18-02-1983 - Brescia - Teatro Ctm (It)

19-02-1983 - Geneva - Le Cab (Ch)

20-02-1983 - Zürich - Rote Fabrik (Ch)

08-03-1983 - Copenhagen - Saltageret (Dk)

09-03-1983 - Götheborg - Rockbox (Sw)

11-03-1983 - Oslo - Chateau 9 (No)

12-03-1983 - Stockholm - Electrick Garden (Sw)

24-03-1983 - New York - Danceteria (US)

25-03-1983 - Philadelphia - East Side Club (US)

26-03-1983 - Washington - 9.30 (US)

1984

28-01-1984 - Vaals - 'T Spuugh (Nl)

29-01-1984 - Haarlem - 'T Patronaat (NI)

28-03-1984 - London - Marquee (UK)

04-04-1984 - London - Marquee (UK)

11-04-1984 - London - Marquee (UK)

16-04-1984 - Utrecht - Vrije Vloer (NI)

17-04-1984 - Enschede - T.H Complex (NI)

18-04-1984 - Eindhoven - Effenaar (NI)

19-04-1984 - Groningen - Vera (NI)

20-04-1984 - Amsterdam - Paradiso (NI)

21-04-1984 - Leiden - Lvc (NI)

22-04-1984 - Etten-Leur - Pop Festival (NI)

23-04-1984 - Den Haag - Paard Van Troje (NI)

24-04-1984 - Nijmegen - Lindenberg (NI)

25-04-1984 - Rotterdam - Arena (NI)

27-04-1984 - Götheborg - Mudd Club (Sw)

29-04-1984 - Stockholm - Kolingsborg (Sw)

30-04-1984 - Oslo - Studio 26 (No)

02-05-1984 - Copenhagen - Musikcafe (Dk)

03-05-1984 - Hamburg - Fabrik (Ge)

04-05-1984 - Berlin - Loft (Ge)

05-05-1984 - Münster - Odeon (Ge)

06-05-1984 - Detmold -Hunky Dory (Ge)

07-05-1984 - Bochum - Zeche (Ge)

08-05-1984 - Cologne - Luxor (Ge)

09-05-1984 - Halle - Halle3 (Ge)

10-05-1984 - Bocholt -Dochdu (Ge)

21-05-1984 - London - Marquee (UK)

22-05-1984 - London - Marquee (UK)

23-05-1984 - Rouen - Exo 7 (Fr)

24-05-1984 - Paris - Theatre Du Forum (Fr)

25-05-1984 - Geneva - Bouffon (Ch)

26-05-1984 - Lyon - West Side Club (Fr)

28-05-1984 - Turin - Studio 2 (It)

29-05-1984 - Florence - Manila (It)

31-05-1984 - Bari - Disco Country Club (It)

01-06-1984 - Catania - Teatro Sud (It)

02-06-1984 - Catanzaro - Stadio Comunale (It)

04-06-1984 - Pescara - Discoteca Le Naiada (It)

05-06-1984 - Rome - Teatro Palladium (It)

06-06-1984 - Imola - La Rocca (It)

07-06-1984 - Rimini - Aleph (It)

08-06-1984 - Fiorenzuola D'arda - Disco My Way (It)

09-06-1984 - Munich - Alabamahalle (Ge)

01-07-1984 - Den Haag - Parkpop (Nl)

08-07-1984 - Madrid - Rock-Ola (Sp)

09-07-1984 - Madrid - Rock-Ola (Sp)

12-07-1984 - Lisbon - Rock Rendezvous (Pt)

13-07-1984 - Lisbon - Rock Rendezvous (Pt)

26-07-1984 - Surbiton - Assembly Rooms (+ Cardiacs/Departure & Purple Gang) (UK)

03-08-1984 - Vaals - 'T Spuugh (Nl)

04-08-1984 - Sneek - Sneekpop (Nl)

21-09-1984 - Rotterdam - Pandoras Music Box (Nl)

23-09-1984 - Deinze - Futurama (Be)

09-11-1984 - London - ULU (UK)

30-11-1984 - New York - Ritz (US)

01-12-1984 - Washington - 9.30 (US)

05-12-1984 - San Francisco - Oasis (US)

07-12-1984 - Los Angeles - Club Lingerie (US)

1985

15-03-1985 - Birmingham - Polytechnic (UK)

17-03-1985 - Leeds - Bierkeller (UK)

20-03-1985 - London - Marquee (UK)

21-03-1985 - London - Marquee (UK)

28-03-1985 - Frankfurt - Batschkapp (Ge)

30-03-1985 - Zurich - Rote Fabrik (Ch)

31-03-1985 - Munich - Mirage (Ge)

01-04-1985 - Stuttgart - Maxim (Ge)

02-04-1985 - Hagen - Lass Das (Ge)

03-04-1985 - Bochum - Zeche (Ge)

04-04-1985 - Bielefeld - Pc 69 (Ge)

06-04-1985 - Hamburg - Markthalle (Ge)

07-04-1985 - Schijndel - Popfestival (Nl)

08-04-1985 - Hilversum - De Tagrijn (Nl)

09-04-1985 - Utrecht - De Vrije Vloer (Nl)

10-04-1985 - Sittard - Donkiesjot (Nl)

11-04-1985 - Rotterdam - Arena (Nl)

12-04-1985 - Tilburg - Noorderlicht (Nl)

13-04-1985 - Amsterdam - Paradiso (Nl)

ROCK WEEK AT THE ICA

Sat 27 Dec THIS HEAT / MASS / LEMON KITTENS
Sun 28 Dec ESSENTIAL LOGIC / ALTERED IMAGES / OUT ON BLUE SIX
Tue 30 Dec CABARET VOLTAIRE / SPEC RECORDS / IL Y A VOLKSWAGENS
Wed 31 Dec DOLL BY DOLL / THE SOFT BOYS / AFGHAN REBELS / THE FLATBACKERS
Thur 1 Jan THE PASSAGE / CRISPY AMBULANCE / BITING TONGUES
Fri 2 Jan THE SOUND / THE CRAVATS / THE JUMP CLUB
Sat 3 Jan BASEMENT 5 / REDBEAT / DISLOCATION DANCE
Sun 4 Jan JOSEF K / ORANGE JUICE / BLUE ORCHIDS
Doors open 7.30. Box Office 01-930 3647
Tickets £2.00 (ICA Day Membership 40p)
Sponsored by Capital Radio

INSTITUTE OF CONTEMPORARY ARTS
THE MALL SW1

14-04-1985 - Wilhelmshaven - Pumpwerk (Ge)

28-04-1985 - Turin - Teatro (It)

03-05-1985 - Rouen - Exosept (Fr)

04-05-1985 - Leuven - Mei'85 Festival (Be)

05-05-1985 - Amersfoort - Flint (Nl)

07-05-1985 - Bordeaux - Performance (Fr)

08-05-1985 - Toulouse - Le Pied (Fr)

09-05-1985 - Lyon - West Side (Fr)

10-05-1985 - Lyon - West Side (Fr)

14-05-1985 - Bologna - Tivoli (It)

16-05-1985 - Naples - Teatro Tenda (It)

18-05-1985 - Taranto - Tursport (It)

20-05-1985 - Milan - Odissea 2 (It)

21-05-1985 - Rimini - Viserba Dirimini (It)

31-05-1985 - Barcelona - Zeleste (Sp)

01-06-1985 - Barcelona - Zeleste (Sp)

02-06-1985 - Barcelona - Zeleste (Sp)

14-06-1985 - Paris - Eldorado (Fr)

15-06-1985 - Grootebroek - Veilinghal (Nl)

08-07-1985 - London - Hammersmith Palais (UK)

10-08-1985 - De Panne - Seaside Festival (Be)

27-08-1985 - London - Marquee (UK)

28-08-1985 - London - Marquee (UK)

22-12-1985 - London - Clarendon (UK)

19-12-1985 - Oldenburg - Echoes (Ge)

1986

04-03-1986 - Madrid - Universal (Sp)

06-03-1986 - Barcelona - Studio 54 (Sp)

07-03-1986 - Valencia - Pacha (Sp)

09-03-1986 - San Sebastian - Polideportivo De Anoeta (Sp)

29-03-1986 - Cartagena - Disco Patan (Sp)

04-04-1986 - London - Clarendon (UK)

19-07-1986 - Ciney - Festival (Be)

20-07-1986 - Oudenburg - Polderrock Festival (Be)

18-10-1986 - Madrid - Leganes Festival (Sp)

1987

20-05-1987 - Utrecht - Tivoli (Nl)

21-05-1987 - Groningen - Vera (Nl)

22-05-1987 - Amsterdam - Paradiso (Nl)

23-05-1987 - Den Haag - Paard Van Troje (Nl)

24-05-1987 - Brussels - La Gaite (Be)

26-05-1987 - London - Marquee (UK)

27-05-1987 - London - Marquee (UK)

28-06-1987 - Den Haag - Parkpop (Nl)

01-08-1987 - Nieuw Schoonbeek - Het Tuinfeest (Nl)

08-08-1987 - Sneek - Sneekwave (Nl)

09-08-1987 - Venlo - Summerpark Feest (Nl)

04-09-1987 - Lausanne - Hot Point Festival (Ch)

07-11-1987 - Vitoria - The End (Sp)

25-11-1987 - Utrecht - Tivoli (Nl)

27-11-1987 - Tilburg - Noorderlicht (Nl)

28-11-1987 - Leiden - LVC (Nl)

29-11-1987 - Noord Scharwoude - De Koog (Nl)

30-11-1987 - Deventer - Burgerweeshuis (Nl)

01-12-1987 - Nijmegen - Doornroosje (Nl)

02-12-1987 - Rotterdam - Lantaren (Nl)

03-12-1987 - Haarlem - Patronaat (Nl)

04-12-1987 - Amsterdam - Paradiso (Nl)

05-12-1987 - Zoetermeer - Boerderij (Nl)

Adrian Borland (Solo, Citizens and Stray Bullets) 1988-1998

1988

11-03-1988 - London - Mean Fiddler (UK)

07-05-1988 - Amsterdam - Melkweg (Nl)

13-09-1988 - Paris - New Morning (Fr)

22-09-1988 - Leiden - Cafe De WW (Nl)

1989

02-09-1989 - Haarlem - Patronaat (Nl)

23-11-1989 - Purmerend - Try Out Gig (Nl)

15-12-1989 - Haarlem - Patronaat (Nl)

1990

09-01-1990 - Hilversum - 2 Meter Sessie Radio (Vara) (Nl)

12-01-1990 - Tilburg - Noorderlicht (Nl)

13-01-1990 - Noord Scharwoude - De Koog (Nl)

14-01-1990 - Rotterdam - Nighttown (Nl)

16-01-1990 - Hilversum - Poppodium (Nl)

18-01-1990 - Groningen - Vera (Nl)

19-01-1990 - Utrecht - Tivoli (Nl)

20-01-1990 - Leiden - Lvc (Nl)

21-01-1990 - Amsterdam - Paradiso (Nl)

26-01-1990 - Hildersheim - Vier Linden (De)

27-01-1990 - Hamburg - Grosse Freiheit (De)

28-01-1990 - Bocholt - Doch Du (De)

29-01-1990 - Köln - Luxor (De)

10-02-1990 - Fulham / London - Kingshead (UK)

12-02-1990 - London - Dingwalls (UK)

19-02-1990 - Paris - New Morning (Fr)

21-02-1990 - Bologna - Centro Nivili - Salo Pol. (It)

23-02-1990 - Lausanne - La Dolce Vita (Ch)

24-02-1990 - Geneve - L'usine (Ch)

28-02-1990 - Oslo - The Voice (Sw)

02-03-1990 - Upsalla - University (Sw)

03-03-1990 - Stockholm - Electric Garden (Sw)

04-03-1990 - Götheborg - Unknown (Sw)

06-03-1990 - Lund - Highschool (Sw)

18-03-1990 - London - Bbc Radio (UK)

20-03-1990 - Brussel - Ancien Belgique (Be)

05-05-1990 - Haarlem - Festival (Nl)

18-05-1990 - Amersfoort - De Kelder (Nl)

09-06-1990 - Velsen - Beeckestijn Pop (Nl)

17-06-1990 - Deurne - Festival (Nl)

13-07-1990 - Lummen - Zwemdockrock Fest (Be)

1991

29-03-1991 - London - Mean Fiddler (UK)

30-03-1991 - Luik - April (Be)

26-04-1991 - Brussel - Ancien Belgique (Be)

13-09-1991 - Uden - Nieuwe Pul (Nl)

14-09-1991 - Apeldoorn - Gigant (Nl)

19-09-1991 - Leiden - Lvc (Nl)

21-09-1991 - Rotterdam - Rotown (Nl)

27-09-1991 - Hilversum - Tagrijn (Nl)

1992

10-04-1992 - Hilversum - Tagrijn (Nl)
11-04-1992 - Rotterdam - Rotown (Nl)
12-04-1992 - Hilversum - Kro Radio (Nl)
16-04-1992 - Amsterdam - Melkweg (Nl)
17-04-1992 - Zoetermeer - Boerderij (Nl)
18-04-1992 - Noord Scharwoude - De Koog (Nl)
19-04-1992 - Brummen - De Bliksum (Nl)
23-04-1992 - Leiden - LVC (Nl)
24-04-1992 - Zaandam - Drieluik (Nl)
25-04-1992 - Haarlem - Patronaat (Nl)
02-05-1992 - Uden - De Nieuwe Pul (Nl)
08-05-1992 - Bocholt - Doch Du (Ge)
09-05-1992 - Kortrijk - De Kreun (Be)
14-05-1992 - Brussel - Vaart Kapoen (Be)
15-05-1992 - Breda - Para (Nl)
16-05-1992 - Deventer - Burgerweeshuis (Nl)
22-08-1992 - Vaals - Spuugh (Nl)
23-08-1992 - Köln, Popkom (Ge)

1993

22-01-1993 - Velsen - Akoestival (Nl)

1994

26-05-1994 - Hamburg - Zillo Club (Ge)
27-05-1994 - Berlin - Knaack Club (Ge)
16-07-1994 - London - The Red Lion (UK)
27-08-1994 - Kuz - Osterholz Scharmbeck (Ge)
09-10-1994 - Hamburg - Zillo Club (Ge)

1995

29-04-1995 - London – The Red Lion (UK)

1996

10-02-1996 - London – The Red Lion (UK)

18-04-1996 - Deventer - De Elegast (Nl)

xx-xx-xx - Zeven - Dampfdepot (Ge)

1997

08-05-1997 - Deventer – De Elegast (Nl)

09-05-1997 - Arlon - Park de Exposition (Fr)

11-05-1997 - Brugge - Cactus Club (Be)

14-05-1997 - Bremen - Modernes (De)

15-05-1997 - Amsterdam - Winston Hotel (Nl)

18-05-1997 - Haarlem - Cafe De Roemer (Nl)

13-06-1997 - London - Borderline (UK)

1998

10-10-1998 - London - (Half Way Crazy Club) The Red Lion (UK)

The Red Lion

62 Colliers Wood High Street, SW19

Adrian Borland

Saturday Oct 10th

8.15pm to 11.45pm

Admission: £3.50 before 9.15
£4.00 after 9.15
Concessions: £2.50
Nearest tube: Colliers Wood
Buses: 57 155 N155

PERFORMERS

ADRIAN BORLAND first came to prominence in the 1980's as the front man of critically acclaimed band 'The Sound'. Since then he has developed a successful solo career establishing a reputation throughout Europe as one of Britain's best song writers. Already renowned for his passionate and intense live performances he will be playing a rare solo set on the 10th. Adrian's dynamic songs, powerful vocals and inspired guitar playing are guaranteed to impress any audience.

****

PHOTO CREDITS

Adrian Janes: 53, 65, 67, 68, 73, 78, 82, 89, 469

Asgard: 116, 137

Andreas Dittmer: vi, 382, 386, 393, 394, 396

Bi Marshall: 471 (2)

Borland Family (archive): x, 20, 22, 24, 27, 31, 35, 49, 50, 58, 94, 97, 98, 182, 260, 366, 499

Carlo van Putten: 419, 427

David Hawkins: 351, 352, 353

Diana Overton: 405, 421, 422, 460

Internet: 55, 121, 122, 194, 249, 475, 482, 483, 484 (1), 492, 493, 494, 495, 496

Fotoburo Koster: 303 (1)

Jean-Paul van Mierlo: ix, 36, 226, 266, 284, 299, 302, 303 (2), 327, 334, 458, 471 (1), 486

James Walton Ingham: 490

Joe Dilworth: frontcover, 328, 497

Maria Jo Neef: 220, 224, 242, 246, 281

Mark Hunziker: 359

Pat Rowles: 402, 416, 450, 489

Paul Evans: iii, 134

Polydor: 218

Rick Hussey: 17, 140, 180, 184, 202, 204, 229, 245, 479

Roy Tee: xiv, 104, 108, 118, 124, 126, 129, 143, 146, 155, 160, 167, 191, 215, 234, 239, 271, 273, 280, 285, 294, 349, backcover

Simon Heavisides: 461

SOD (archive): 29, 40, 48, 158, 308, 450, 473, 477, 480, 484 (2)

Sonja van der Veen: 371, 407, 441

Stefan Küppers: 296, 300, 310

Steve Budd: 173

Unknown: 100, 106, 138, 149, 195, 196, 217, 291, 306, 316, 350, 400, 452

Bob Borland with the portrait he painted of his son Adrian

Made in the USA
Columbia, SC
13 February 2024

31103761R20272